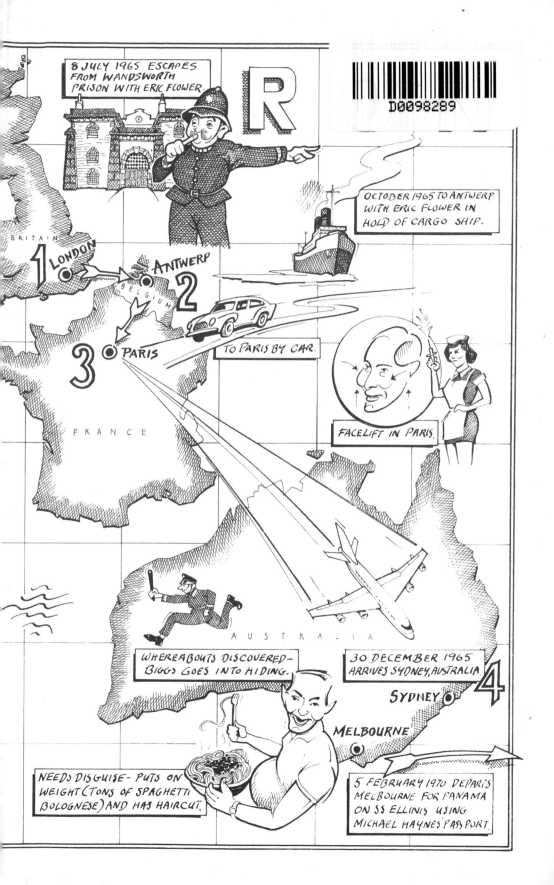

# ODD MAN OUT

## MY LIFE ON THE LOOSE
## AND THE TRUTH ABOUT
## THE GREAT TRAIN ROBBERY

**RONALD BIGGS**

BLOOMSBURY

First published in Great Britain 1994
Bloomsbury Publishing Limited, 2 Soho Square, London W1V 5DE

PICTURE SOURCES

Agencia JB/Vidal da Trindade: page 10 *bottom right*
Ronald Biggs' private collection: front jacket, pages 2 *top*, 8 *top*, 9 *bottom*, 10 *top*,
11, 12 *top*, 13, 14, 15, 16 *top*, back jacket
Charmian Brent: pages 1, 7
CBS Records, Brazil: page 12 *bottom*
Hulton Deutsch Collection Limited: pages 2 *bottom*, 3, 6, 9 *top*
Jean-Jacques Limbourg: front jacket *inset*, pages 8 *bottom right*, 16 *bottom*, back
jacket flap
Christopher Pickard: pages 8 *bottom left*, 10 *bottom left*
Press Association: pages 4, 5

Endpaper map by Andrew Farmer

A CIP catalogue record for this book
is available from the British Library

ISBN 0 7475 1683 9


10 9 8 7 6 5 4 3 2 1

Typeset by Hewer Text Composition Services, Edinburgh
Printed by Clays Limited, St Ives plc

This book is for my loved ones
past and present, my family,
my friends and my fans

## ACKNOWLEDGEMENTS

I would like to express my sincere thanks to my friend Christopher Pickard, who did not let me rest until he had steered me through the manuscript. Thanks also to his father, John Pickard, who provided valuable assistance checking, searching and snooping for background material in Britain.

Thanks to Christopher's attractive PA, Ana Claudia Fidalgo, who unstintingly and uncomplainingly sat polishing her nails while Chris and I did all the donkey work. At least she managed to keep Chris relatively sane.

Thanks also to Rosa for her endless cups of tea, and to Apple Mac for producing a computer that even I could understand.

To everyone at Bloomsbury, whom I hope one day to meet in person, sorry my fax machine refuses to have anything to do with yours. I think the trouble must be at your end!

Special thanks to everyone who helped, encouraged and supported me in this project, including all of you who wish to remain anonymous for whatever reason. And thanks again to Paul Seabourne without whom most of what follows would not have been possible.

# CONTENTS

Preface: 1963 and All That 1
1 The Great Train Robbery 8
2 Thursday 8 August 1963 23
*Map of the Great Train Robbery* 24
3 Aftermath and Capture 33
4 The Trial 44
5 Escape – The Making of a Legend 66
6 On the Run: London – Bognor – Antwerp –
Paris – Sydney 79
7 Australian Days 96
8 The Pacifics: Melbourne – Rio 121
9 Mr Haynes Settles in Rio 131
10 Caught – Slipper Drops His Catch 150
11 Celebrity Status – Life in the Spotlight 169
12 Kidnapped 192
13 Barbados and Back 210
14 A Star Is Born: Mike Biggs 237
15 An Englishman Abroad – Old Friends
Come Calling 249
16 Thirty Years On – Summing Up 264
Appendix 1: Key Dates 275
Appendix 2: Ron's Frequent Flyer Miles 279

# Preface
# 1963 and All That

What is it that fascinates us about Ronald Biggs and makes him a household name in so many countries around the world?

Is it the man or the myth that makes Ron, Ronnie, Biggsy, call him what you will, a latter-day Robin Hood, the man who is best remembered from a gang of sixteen who held up a mail train in August 1963?

One thing is for sure, the name of Ronald Biggs stirs the full range of emotions from respect and admiration to outright loathing. Yes, there are still many who believe, thirty years on, that hanging is too good for the likes of Biggs.

Ronald Arthur Biggs was born in London in the borough of Lambeth on 8 August 1929. The youngest of a family of five, he had a sister and three brothers, one of whom, Terence, died at an early age. His family was working class but he does not consider them to have been poor as he was not left wanting for anything.

In 1940, as war raged across Europe and the bombs fell on London, Biggs was separated from his family and evacuated to the relative safety of Devon and later to Cornwall. He returned to London at the end of 1942 and was sent to Santley Street School. In May 1943 his mother died. She was fifty-three.

Around this time Biggs discovered that if he was good at one thing it was taking objects of whatever size or value without having to pay for them. This led in February 1945 to his first appearance in court, for stealing pencils from Littlewoods. He was just fifteen.

That same year, in June and November, he made two further

court appearances for petty pilfering, but appeared to be back on the right track by 1947 when he volunteered for the Royal Air Force. It was during his short time in the RAF, although he had volunteered for eight years as a regular and four years in the reserves, that Biggs learned how to cook: his father, who had been a cook at one time, had already instilled in him an interest in cooking which he has never forgotten.

The RAF proved to have its temptations for a man with Biggs' talents, although his first run-in with his superiors was for going AWOL and not for any of his more light-fingered activities.

But his luck soon ran out and after breaking into a chemist he found himself up before the London Sessions in February 1949, an appearance which resulted in a six-month prison sentence and a dishonourable discharge from the RAF. He was nineteen and apparently destined for a life of crime.

Released from Lewes Prison for Young Prisoners in June 1949 he was up before the North London magistrates the following month for taking a car without the owner's permission. He was sent to Wormwood Scrubs and then on to Lewes, where his path crossed for the first time with Bruce Reynolds, who would turn out to be the driving force behind the Great Train Robbery.

Biggs was now firmly off the tracks, and a life of crime, court appearances and imprisonment was to follow over the next fourteen years.

As years go, 1993 was a pretty ordinary and indifferent period. Hardly one that will stand out in the years to come. The same cannot be said for 1963, a remarkable year by any standards and one that is now seen as a watershed in modern history as people tried to throw off the shackles of a 1930s mentality and enjoy the swinging sixties.

1963 is best remembered as the year when John F. Kennedy was assassinated, but it was also the year when Martin Luther King had a dream and the popular Pope John XXIII died to be replaced by the less charismatic Paul VI. 1963 was the year when the US, USSR and Great Britain signed a nuclear test ban treaty; Sir Winston Churchill was given honorary US citizenship by President Kennedy; the Soviet Union put the first women into space; the Pan Am building in New York opened its doors for the first time, while on the west coast Alcatraz closed its doors to prisoners for the very last time. Concorde had been developed to full mock-up size and the BAC-1-11 made its maiden flight. Mary Quant was becoming a household name.

Jim Clark won the Formula 1 racing championship but his great rival, Graham Hill, won the Monaco Grand Prix. Manchester United beat Leicester City in the FA Cup Final, Everton won the league and, at Wembley Stadium, the main soccer international of the year took place in May and pitted England against the 1962 World Champions, Brazil. A one-all draw, it was probably the first time that the thirty-three-year-old Biggs had come across the Brazilians.

1963 saw the start of Beatlemania as well as being the year their great rivals-to-be, the Rolling Stones, released their first single. It also saw the death of Edith Piaf but the birth of George Michael.

More sinister things were going on behind the scenes, things that were directly to affect the fate of Ronald Biggs when it came to his next day in court.

The British authorities, in the shape and form of the Conservative Party, who had held office since Churchill's return to Downing Street in 1951, were starting to lose their grip on power and all the trappings that go with it. So were the civil servants and other sundry hangers-on who had served them comfortably over a twelve-year period.

A disastrous by-election in Orpington resulted in Prime Minister Harold Macmillan sacking seven Cabinet Ministers on 13 July 1962. It reassured nobody. In the autumn of the same year, an Admiralty clerk in the office of the Civil Lord was arrested for spying. The Soviet spy, William John Vassall, was convicted and sent to prison, as were, in a parallel case, two journalists for the allegations they had made in articles regarding the Civil Lord, Tam Galbraith, and Vassall. The case did not endear the government to Fleet Street reporters.

In 1963, the press had a chance to get their revenge after rumours started to circulate that John Profumo, who had been Macmillan's Minister of War since 1960, was having an affair with a nineteen-year-old nightclub hostess, Christine Keeler. To make matters worse Keeler was also seeing the Soviet naval attaché, Eugene Ivanov.

The government might have got away with Profumo's indiscretion if some of Keeler's other lovers had been a little more discreet. Unfortunately, one of them, Johnny Edgecombe, tried to shoot his way into the house of Dr Stephen Ward, a society osteopath who had introduced Profumo to Keeler and who had invited Keeler and her friend, Mandy Rice-Davies, to share his house.

The shooting put Keeler's name back on the front pages and resulted in an anonymous call to George Wigg, the Labour Shadow Spokesman on Defence, who had clashed with Profumo in the Commons over the Vassall affair. The caller told Wigg to forget Vassall and concentrate on Profumo.

While the press kept their distance, thanks to threats from Profumo's lawyers, Wigg used his parliamentary privilege to raise the matter in the Commons during a debate. Profumo was not in the House but issued a statement the following day which denied his involvement or any 'impropriety' with Keeler, although admitting that he had been introduced to her and Ivanov by Ward at Cliveden, the home of Lord Astor.

Sensing that he was about to be made the fall guy for the entire Profumo affair, Ward wrote to George Wigg, MI5 and the Home Secretary, outlining the true course of events.

On holiday in Venice, Profumo admitted to his wife, the actress Valerie Hobson, that the rumours were true and that he had lied to the Commons. The house of cards came tumbling down and in June, less than two months before the Great Train Robbery, Profumo resigned, leaving an already unpopular government with even more egg on its face. A show trial of sorts was set up to prove Ward was Keeler's pimp and distract attention away from the government. Rather than go to prison, Ward thwarted the government's plans and took an overdose of pills. He was buried in London on 10 August 1963.

Thirty years later it can be seen that the Great Train Robbery, which took place on 8 August 1963, was one of the final straws that broke the camel's and the government's back. After the Profumo débâcle it once again brought into question the very fabric of law and order in Britain and made a mockery of the government and its institutions. Much to the delight of the general public, a cheeky London gang had audaciously made off with millions of pounds of the government's money – and from one of its own trains. The government had to face the fact that a gang of train robbers were shown more respect and affection by the general public than they were.

We may never know what went on in the corridors of power during this time, but pressure was put on Scotland Yard to solve the robbery quickly and bring to justice the people who appeared to have mocked the government. Even, as it turned out, if they were innocent.

Thanks to the discovery of Leatherslade Farm, where the gang had hidden before and after the robbery, and a few tip-offs, it was not long before the Yard tracked down many of the gang. But it was still long enough for Prime Minister Macmillan to have resigned on the grounds of ill health so that Sir Alec Douglas-Home could take his place and give the Conservatives a fighting chance of hanging on to power at the next election.

Four members of the Great Train Robbery gang known to the police, including its leader, Bruce Reynolds, were still at large, while the trial of those captured only added to the government's embarrassment. The trial culminated on 15 April 1964 with the sentencing of members of the gang, including Biggs, to thirty years' imprisonment, a far longer term than was being given out at the time to murderers and spies. While the powers-that-be may have thought that this would act as a salutary lesson to society as a whole, it backfired and made even bigger popular heroes of the gang.

Charlie Wilson's escape from Winson Green Prison on 12 August 1964 was another nail in the government's coffin. On 15 October 1964 Labour won the general election, albeit by a small majority, and Harold Wilson became Prime Minister.

Conventional ways and days had been swept aside for more unconventional times.

Events of the last thirty years have made us all the more cynical and suspicious. At the time, the death of Marilyn Monroe on 5 August 1962 was seen as a straightforward suicide and John F. Kennedy's assassination in Dallas on 22 November 1963 the work of a lone assassin. Today we wonder if Marilyn was not murdered by people directly linked to the President of the United States and question if the death of that President was not a *coup d'état* orchestrated by the various interested parties who wanted to see the escalation of the war in Vietnam.

Just as we may never discover what really happened to Marilyn Monroe or to John F. Kennedy, we may never know the true extent of the government's involvement in the Great Train Robbery and the trial that followed. Certainly the gang don't know – they were not political animals. But who in the government at the time of the robbery was so outraged and humiliated by Ronald Biggs' flight to freedom that he and others gave their okay and support to having him kidnapped in Rio nearly twenty years later?

Whoever they are or were, they would be the first to call foul if a foreign power tried to kidnap one of our nationals from the streets of London. They, and the Thatcher government at the time of Biggs' kidnapping in 1981, remained remarkably quiet when the same thing happened to Biggs in Brazil. Although it is known who was involved, nobody has ever been charged or even publicly reprimanded for the Biggs kidnapping.

As you read Ronald Biggs' own story that follows, never forget that there is a very thin line between a hero and a villain; it all depends on which side of the fence you are at the time and what your race, creed, colour or social background may be. Biggs was no saint, but then neither was Robin Hood or Butch Cassidy.

Ronald Biggs is a remarkable man. A survivor who has beaten odds that were stacked against him. At the time of the Wild West or in wartime he would have been deemed a hero because of his daring escapes and escapades; in peacetime he is still a villain. But let us not forget, Ronald Biggs is not a modern-day folk hero because of what he did in the early hours of the morning of 8 August 1963, but for the manner in which he – your basic man in the street – has kept himself one step ahead of the posse which has chased him around the world since his daring escape from Wandsworth Prison in July 1965.

Those who know him, know a considerate, kind and generous man. A family man, a loving father, a man who has accepted the rough with the smooth, knowing all along that he was destined to be the odd man out.

The final irony for Ronald Biggs must surely be that if he had held up a train in his adopted country of Brazil and had been sentenced to a thirty-year stretch, the British government and the media would have been outraged and demanded his immediate release and return. They do as much today for convicted drug smugglers.

Biggs is not looking for a pardon, as the papers often claim, only a little understanding. Something that the last thirty years have shown only comes from governments when there is a financial or political interest at stake. Did it take thirty years for Britain to 'forgive' Germany and Japan for the war?

If there is a government in the world that can honestly put its collective hand to its heart and say that it has committed lesser crimes than Ronald Biggs over the last thirty years, then it should cast the first stone. Until the British public wake up to this fact and demand that the time has come for the British authorities to stop their thirty-year persecution of Ronald Biggs then he, as a solitary individual, must remain the odd man out.

Read on, but as you do, remember that however remarkable the story of Ronald Biggs appears, what you are reading is fact and not fiction. The man exists, he is not a myth.

Christopher Pickard
Rio de Janeiro, Brazil
September 1993

# 1. The Great Train Robbery

It was just after 3 a.m. on Thursday 8 August 1963 when the walkie-talkie came to life. It was Bruce Reynolds: the train had passed through Leighton Buzzard and was now less than a mile away. After a wait of nearly one and a half hours by the side of the main line between Glasgow and London the moment had come – a moment that would come to be known as the Great Train Robbery.

Sixteen of us were scattered about the embankment that night, four of whom were never caught.

A good few stories have been told since about the robbery and what happened that night. Stories that have included everything from a German SS connection to a Mr Big linked to the government of the day. I have even read in the Brazilian press that I shot the driver in the head at point-blank range.

The facts, as always, are somewhat different.

The train robbery was the work of two different London gangs who came together for the 'Big One'. I was a member of neither gang, yet after everything I have read and heard since it is often difficult to believe that it was my friendship with one man, Bruce Reynolds, and the work that I had done as a legitimate builder for a retired train driver, that brought me to be lying on a grass embankment in Buckinghamshire that August night. I was the odd man out.

My journey to the embankment can probably be traced back to 1949 and my first spell in Lewes Prison at the age of nineteen as a YP (Young Prisoner). It was during this first time in Lewes – I went there twice – that I met a young ex-Post Office sorter by the name of Albert Kitson.

Kit, as we called him, was serving an eighteen-month sentence for taking part in a robbery of the Post Office where he had been working. He had made a wax impression of the key to the safe where the cash was held and passed it on to an old pro.

Kit and I used to walk together during exercise periods and more than once he made reference to 'large sums of money' that were transported by British Rail.

'If a group of really game lads got together,' he said, 'they could pull off the tickle of a lifetime.'

The following year I met Bruce Reynolds in Wormwood Scrubs Prison. I was back inside again with a two-month sentence for 'driving away a car without the owner's consent'. From the start it was clear that Bruce was a cut above the other cons. We became good friends over time and discovered a mutual interest in music, literature and breaking the law. I told him what Kit had told me about the large sums of cash being transported by rail. It was a piece of information he was never to forget.

Our paths crossed several times during the ensuing years – in and out of prison – but we never got up to any villainy together prior to the train robbery itself.

It was after a rather longer stretch, four years for burglary, that I concluded it was time to have a go at honest employment and I found work as a carpenter. I had learned the basics of the trade in prison and the work really interested me. When I came out of jail on that occasion I went to live with a pretty tough lady in Merstham, Surrey. Her name was Ivy and she was a very good friend of Bruce's. She was quite fearless and wouldn't shy away from a punch-up if she found herself facing one. But Ivy was a good sort and if you were a friend of Bruce's then you were a friend of Ivy's. She had little, if any, time for Old Bill and could always be depended upon to sell a bit of bent gear or to take care of the odd box of gelignite.

Bruce would visit us from time to time, usually arriving in a ritzy sports car of some kind and always impeccably dressed. He was moving up in the world of villainy and was beginning to build a reputation as the 'Prince of Thieves'.

In the late fifties a train was held up on the London-to-Brighton line – about a mile from where I was living at the time. The signals had been tampered with and the train had stopped at a quiet spot close to a bridge which spanned the road from Merstham to Redhill. The thieves got away with precious little, but it was believed to be 'the work of professionals', according to a police report at the time.

In early 1958 I changed jobs, leaving a muddy building site in Redhill for the cleaner work of erecting partitions in offices, mostly in and around central London. The job entailed travelling to London by train and it was on one of these journeys that I first saw Charmian Powell, the future Mrs Biggs, then sweet seventeen. We were mutually attracted and in less time than it takes to say 'rabbit' we were making mad, passionate love in hotels, empty train carriages and on the floor of the classrooms of the school where Charmian's father was headmaster. It didn't take Ivy long to discover my 'little piece on the side' and I was promptly given colourful marching orders.

In a romantic moment Charmian and I decided to elope, but like most young lovers we were hard up. Then, with a little persuasion from me, Charm dipped her hand into the cash-box where she was working and filched £200 (now about £3000). Off we went, à la Bonnie and Clyde minus the firearms, with my good friend Michael Haynes, a man who was going to play an important role in my life, at the wheel of a hired Vauxhall Victor. We headed west from London as I had a fancy to see Devon and Cornwall again. I had been evacuated to Combeinteignhead in Devon at the beginning of the war and later, as the bombing got worse, to Delabole in Cornwall. There was a slate quarry close to Delabole and I remembered how easy it had been to get into a shed where the explosives were stored. What I planned to do with explosives I can't remember, but it was all rather academic, as long before we got to Cornwall the money had run out. So Mike and I decided to try a break-in or two with Charm acting as look-out.

Sadly, one snowy evening after a hair-raising chase through the tortuous roads of Swanage, our luck ran out and we were nicked. A string of charges followed, including my usual: 'driving away a motor vehicle without the owner's consent'.

Charm got her first – and only – taste of porridge in the women's wing of HMP Exeter and was soon up before the governor for smuggling in cash, which was strictly against prison regulations. Mike and I fared better. We were sent to HMP Dorchester where, as we were more experienced, our money wasn't found!

On 2 April 1958 we appeared before the judge at the Dorchester Quarter Sessions. A love story was presented to the court by our learned counsel, but the prosecutor declared us 'a threat'. Our fate was now in the hands of the red-faced judge. The court adjourned. Everything, I was told by my brief, was going to depend on whether his lordship's lunch had been satisfactory or not.

Stifling a burp, the well-fed judge returned to pass sentence. Charmian and Mike were put on two years' probation, while I ended up with two and a half years in prison – not a bad result, considering. With remission I was looking at twenty months, so Charmian and Mike would still be on probation when I got out.

And that's the way it turned out. I was sent to Norwich to do my time, but regularly, once a month, Charmian came to visit. We sat holding hands and making plans for our future. We were going to get married and 'settle down'. We exchanged long and passionate letters. I thought my sentence would never end.

I was released on a cold, foggy morning in mid-December 1959. I had been transferred to Wandsworth Prison in London to finish my time and Charmian was waiting outside the gate to meet me. We made a beeline for our favourite hotel and booked in as Mr and Mrs Biggs. Champagne and a double serving of bacon and eggs were sent to the room.

It was late evening when we emerged and caught the train to Redhill. I had arranged to stay with friends, John and Violet Goldsmith, until I could find a place of my own. It was good to see old friends again and we sat around drinking tea and laughing about old times. Charmian could not stay long as she was anxious not to infringe the terms of her probation. She didn't want 'Old Saddle-Bags' – Miss Sadler, her probation officer – to read her the riot act.

I got a job with the Reigate Borough Council working as a carpenter. Not very well paid, but plenty of tea and sympathy from the housewives. From my wages I managed to rent a small furnished flat where Charm and I spent as much time as possible together. We were more keen than ever to get married but Charmian's father, far less fond of me since he had had to fork out the £200 his daughter had pilfered as well as her legal fees, was dead against the idea of our union. In the end we decided to force the old man's hand. We would get Charm pregnant and present our case as a *fait accompli*.

The wedding took place at the Reigate Registry Office on 20 February 1960. For us it was the Wedding of the Year.

I changed my job shortly afterwards and started working for an elderly Redhill building contractor by the name of Sid Budgeon. Sid allowed me to get in as much overtime as possible as there would soon be a third Biggs to feed.

Nicholas Grant was born on 23 July 1960 at Redhill County Hospital. The proud and happy parents could be seen wheeling His Nibs through the streets of Redhill in an enormous plum-coloured baby carriage. The pram had cost an arm and a leg but 'Mother' had insisted that it had to be the very best.

I was happy with the way things were going. I was being offered so much work that I decided it was time to set up in business for myself, hiring help whenever necessary.

When Nicky was nearly one year old, our close friends Ron and Janet Searle invited Charm and me to spend a week with them in a caravan in Hastings. Although I couldn't really afford to take the time off I finally allowed myself to be persuaded to go. Janet was most enthusiastic about fortune-telling and things of that nature, things that at the time I considered to be nothing more than mumbo-jumbo.

We drove to Hastings in the Searles' car and for much of the time Janet was raving on about her pet subject, trying to persuade us all to have our fortunes told.

The second day in Hastings Charmian did go and see a fortune-teller on the pier. A certain 'Professor Cullen' was her seer. When she rejoined us some twenty minutes later she was visibly shaken. The professor had told her things which she thought only she and her mother knew.

'It really was remarkable,' she said.

Janet looked triumphant.

'You see,' she gloated. 'Now it's your turn, Ron.' I declined her invitation, still insisting that it was all hocus-pocus. The next morning, however, when everyone was asleep, I went into town and found myself a fortune-teller. Ten shillings she charged for her services. Half a quid! It was daylight robbery, I thought.

The fortune-teller was a frail-looking old lady of seventy odd. She invited me to put my hands on her crystal ball and told me straight away that in later years I would suffer with 'kidney problems'. This, it turned out, had nothing to do with fortune-telling – she deduced it from my sweating palms. She then went on to tell me that I was a self-employed carpenter and that when I had worked for other people I had always had 'foreman trouble'. She said that I was on holiday in Hastings but could ill afford to take the time off because of pressing work commitments. I was with a wife – nine to ten years younger than myself – and had an only son who was just one year old. She saw me forming a partnership with a man who worked with 'bricks and mortar' (at that time I knew of no bricklayer that I would take on as a partner).

Until that point everything she had said had been totally correct. How, I wanted to know, out of all the trades and professions in the world could she know that I was a carpenter – and a self-employed one at that? Her credibility took a tumble, however, when she told me that I would 'travel extensively around the world and that I would have a child with a woman with long, black hair'. Now, I thought, we were really in the realms of gypsy flim-flam. But I was impressed. She told me I would never be rich but I would always be a good 'breadwinner'. Then, as I was leaving, she called me back.

'I have some advice for you,' she offered. 'If you want anything out of this life, be sure you pay for it.'

A year passed and one day over lunch Charm told me that she had run into an old school chum, Janet, who had moved into the neighbourhood with her husband, Ray Stripp. They would be coming along on Saturday evening for drinks. Ray was a bricklayer and Charm had told her friend that I might be able to fix him up with some weekend work. As history shows we became partners, splitting the expenses and profits down the middle. We went from strength to strength, taking on more workers until we had a gang of ten. On paper we were making a substantial profit, but some of our clients were slow to pay and there were times when I found it difficult to meet my half of the payroll.

Christopher Dean, our second son, was born on 24 March 1963. A little beauty – and the image of his dad. Christopher brought with him additional expenses and one weekend in June I found myself particularly strapped for cash. I decided to phone my old pal Bruce Reynolds and see if he could lend me £500 – that would be about £6000 today – to tide me over.

'Normally, as you know, I would be only too happy to help you out,' Bruce said when I called him. 'But at this exact moment all my dough is tied up in a piece of business, something that I'd like to talk to you about, only not over the phone.'

We made an arrangement for him to visit us at the weekend. He arrived with his wife Frances and his baby son, by coincidence also called Nicholas. While the girls were in the garden cooing over the kids, Bruce said he was in a position to put me into his 'piece of business', details of which he could not give me right then. I thanked him for the offer but pointed out that I was now working for a living and was very happy with married life. I also wasn't keen to put my liberty at risk.

'I'm pleased to hear it,' Bruce said, 'but if you want to make one I can guarantee you a minimum of forty grand for your whack.'

'Jesus!' I replied. 'Can I have some time to think it over?'

'You can, but there's one condition. If you want to take part you'll have to come up with someone who knows how to drive a diesel train.'

As luck or fate would have it, I was working for an old train driver; I was renewing the front windows of his house in Redhill.

I found it hard to sleep that night. Forty grand was a lot of money even to dream about. It was enough money to buy four new four-bedroomed houses in the best part of Reigate. I phoned Bruce the next morning and put my name on the list.

'I'm in,' I said. I gave him the train driver's address and told Bruce I would be working there for at least another week.

A few days later Bruce drove down from London with his brother-in-law, John Daly. They wanted to get a close look at the old man. The train driver – let's call him simply Peter, although I believe he is dead by now – saw Bruce and John pull up in Bruce's sporty Lotus. We went off to a nearby pub to discuss a plan of action.

My first priority was to see if the old boy would join the gang. All he would have to do was drive a diesel train for a mile or so for a straight £40,000 (nearly £500,000 at today's rates). When I returned to the house Peter was watering his garden – his pride and joy.

'What would you do for £40,000?' I asked casually.

'£40,000?' he repeated. 'Blimey, I'd do just about anything for that kind of money, although I wouldn't hurt or kill anyone for it. Why are you asking?'

'Would you rob a bank?'

'Yes, I would,' he affirmed after a moment's thought. 'Are you serious?'

'Suppose I was to offer you £40,000 for your share, would you join me in a robbery?'

'I would. If you wanted me to help you with anything like that I'd be in like a shot.'

'But what if you were to get caught?'

'I'd keep my mouth shut, if that's what you mean, and if I got time I'd tread it out. But what's this all about? Are you really thinking of robbing a bank, Ron?'

'I can't tell you anything yet. But if I ask you to join me, you will?'

Peter put his hand out and we shook on it. His interest in his roses had wilted somewhat. He kept asking questions – most of which I honestly could not answer – and he wanted to know if it had anything to do with the people he had recently seen in the white Lotus.

The first time I met the whole gang was in Roy James' flat in Nell Gwynn House in Chelsea. I have to say they looked a pretty formidable bunch. With a few exceptions they were all big men and even though they were well dressed the majority still had the distinctive look of villains.

The basic plan for the robbery had already been well established when I entered the scene. Jimmy White was the 'quartermaster' responsible for the provision of army uniforms and overalls to be used in the raid. Charlie Wilson was chosen to stock the hide-out with food and drink. Roy James and the man I will call Mr One, a member of the gang who would never be caught, would take care of transport. And so forth.

Bruce formally introduced me to the gang and I was invited to tell the assembly what I could about the train driver. They asked questions about him. What kind of trains was he working on? How well would he hold up if he got nicked? No stone was left unturned.

Most decisions taken by the gang were made on a show of hands and a vote was called for as to whether the old man should be brought in or not. All hands were raised with the exception of one, Roy James. The gang listened intently as Roy argued that the old man had no experience in the world of villainy.

'It's all very well for the old chap to say that he'd keep his mouth shut,' Roy went on, 'but he's never been trampled on by a fifteen-stone copper.'

It was a strong argument and I knew from experience how ugly Old Bill could get during an 'interrogation'. But where would we stand, countered one of the gang, if the actual train driver refused to co-operate? We had to have a back-up driver, it was that simple. On a second show of hands yours truly and the old man were voted in.

Now that I had been formally accepted, Bruce filled me in on the details of the plan and when the robbery would take place. I would have to take Peter to Euston Station and let him see the kind of train that he would be expected to handle.

'He's got to be sure that he knows how to drive this particular train,' Bruce emphasized.

A couple of days later Peter and I went to Euston Station. I bought a platform ticket and sat on a bench at the far end of the platform close to the sleek diesel engine of a train preparing to leave. I hid behind a copy of the *Daily Mirror*. After a minute or two Peter came along dressed in his railwayman's blue dungarees, an oily rag hanging from his jacket pocket. He gave the driver of the train a cheery greeting.

'What-ho, mate. I'm going on one of these big buggers next week – I wonder if you'd like to give me a few tips?'

'Sure,' replied the driver, clearly only too happy to help one of his colleagues, 'hop up.' Twenty minutes later I 'bumped into'

Peter in a café near the station. He was confident and clearly enjoying the part.

'It's a piece of cake,' he said. 'There's almost no difference to the engines I'm working on in Redhill.'

It was all arranged. Bruce would meet Peter and me at Victoria Station at 8 a.m. on Tuesday 6 August. So that we could get away from our homes for what might be as much as two weeks I concocted a story that I had been contracted for a tree-felling job 'somewhere in Wiltshire'. Peter was 'invited' to go with me as a cook and applied for two weeks' leave of absence from his job. Charmian was disappointed that I was going to be away from home for my thirty-fourth birthday, which fell on 8 August, but I convinced her with the argument that I was going to be well paid for my labours and that we could celebrate in style upon my return.

Monday 5 August was a bank holiday. I had promised to take Charmian and the children to Brighton for the day. Early that morning my partner, Ray, appeared at the house with a £50 cheque for some work we had done in a nearby house. He was to give me half the value of the cheque, but only had £15 in cash. Before he arrived I had been studying the form and looking over the many runners and riders scheduled for the races that day. Ray lived above a betting shop, and on the spur of the moment I decided to make a bet with the £10 he owed me. I wrote down the details on a piece of paper. It was to be a £5 each-way double. Dameon and Rococco. Two horses at different meetings. Ray thought I was mad to be gambling such an amount, especially on two horses that appeared on paper to have little or no chance. I said nothing to Charm, either, as she had no faith whatsoever in my gambling 'hunches'.

We travelled to Brighton by train and had what appeared to be a happy family day. The fact that I was going off on 'the business' the following day was very much on my mind and I wanted us to enjoy ourselves to the full. It just could be our last day together as a family for quite a long time. I tried to push these negative thoughts from my mind – I should be coming back from my trip with forty grand!

I took Nicky for a ride in a speedboat, followed by ice-cream, toffee apples and the inevitable flop in a deck-chair on the pier.

There was horse-racing in Brighton that afternoon and after looking over the runners and riders in the midday newspaper my 'special selection' was the favourite in the last race with Ron Hutchinson up. I tried to get Charm interested in a ten quid 'investment', but we settled for a fiver. I went off to place the bet. After a dinner of fish and chips I bought the late evening paper to see if the nag had obliged; it had, and there was eight pounds to collect.

Standing in line at the betting shop to collect my winnings, I found myself looking at the day's racing results, which were chalked up on a number of blackboards. The name Rococco caught my eye. It was one of the horses I had asked Ray to bet on and it had won at odds of 10 to 1. Then I saw Dameon, a 9 to 1 winner.

If Ray had placed the bet I had won £500, about £6000 in today's terms, which was the bookmaker's limit on any one bet. I said nothing about it to Charm, but when we got home I urgently telephoned Ray to check that he had in fact placed the bet. He said he had and asked if I had won anything. I told him, and loud enough so that Charm could hear me in the kitchen, that I had indeed won and £500 to boot. I asked him to go over to the bookmaker in the morning and pick up my winnings. My partner was dumbfounded.

'You jammy bastard,' he said.

My devoted spouse was not in the least bit dumbfounded, but was considerably less convinced.

'That will be the day when you win £500 on a bet. I know you and your little games. Don't think you can fool me.'

I rose early the next morning: I had a train to catch! A light breakfast, hugs and kisses and a final reminder not to forget to write when I got there.

'And behave yourself,' were Charmian's parting words.

At Redhill Station I was glad and relieved to see that Peter was among the early morning travellers to London. We had previously agreed not to travel together. At least not as a pair.

During the journey to Victoria I was deep in thought. I had set out to borrow £500 and I had won exactly that amount. I remembered what the old fortune-teller had said: 'If you want anything out of this life, be sure you pay for it.' But the die was cast and there was no turning back. In truth, I knew I didn't want to.

Bruce was waiting for us in a café in Wilton Road, close to Victoria Station. He was with his brother-in-law, John Daly, and two other members of the gang whom I had met at the gathering in Roy James' flat. They were Jimmy White, the quartermaster, and the biggest man in the group, the man who coshed the train driver; he was one of the four men never to be caught, and I'll call him Mr Three.

After a cheese sandwich and a cup of tea we climbed into a green army Land-Rover which was parked nearby. Soon we were on the open road and heading for Bucks. The weather was still good and the day seemed full of promise. We were generally lighthearted, laughing and joking as we went along. Peter was sitting next to me in the back of the Land-Rover and appeared quite relaxed.

'Nice vehicles, these Land-Rovers,' he said at one point. 'Who do they belong to?'

Jimmy White, who was driving, responded, 'Don't know, Dad. We nicked it the night before last in the Strand.'

'Nicked it?' exclaimed the old man, losing his smile. 'Christ! You can get pinched for that kind of thing!' We all cracked up and Peter joined in, happy to be the cause of our merriment and the centre of attention.

It was mid-morning by the time we arrived at our destination, Leatherslade Farm, a small farm located off the B4011, close to the villages of Brill and Oakley in Buckinghamshire. We were the first of the gang to arrive; the rest would be arriving at staggered intervals. We explored the two-storey farmhouse and the various outbuildings. Precious little had been left behind by the former tenants. A rusty generator seized the attention of Jimmy White, who immediately set about trying to get it to work. Mr Three and I volunteered to fix a lunch of steak, chips and runner beans. Old Peter, for his part, found a deck-chair and relaxed in the sun, puffing away at his pipe and blending in with the pastoral surroundings. He might have been in his own back yard.

During the afternoon, the second group turned up in an Austin army truck. Among them were Tommy Wisbey, Jim Hussey, Bob Welch, Buster Edwards, Mr One and Mr Two, two other

members of the gang who were lucky enough never to be caught
or even suspected. On the way to the farm they had stopped off to
buy further provisions. Bobby Welch, who liked a drink or two,
bought a number of pipkins of ale, an act that subsequently led
to his arrest and conviction.

Roy James and Charlie Wilson arrived soon after in a second
Land-Rover, bringing yet more supplies. John Daly had thoughtfully brought cards and games to while away the time and I was
one of the first to start a game of Monopoly with John, Tommy
Wisbey, Charlie and Roy. Soon enough the game turned into an
unruly riot with much shouting and laughter. Charlie was the
runaway winner.

Peter – 'Dad' to the gang – was happy to be the tea boy, quite
taken with the friendliness shown by one and all.

It was just after dark when Roger Cordrey got to the farm
carrying a large suitcase. He was popular with the gang and
received a vociferous welcome. By now there were fifteen of us
at Leatherslade Farm – only Gordon Goody was missing.

At the time, Gordon was at the home of a solicitor's managing
clerk, Brian Field, in nearby Pangbourne. He was waiting for
a phone call from a certain Post Office worker in Carlisle.
Described as the 'Ulsterman' in the media and in various books
about the robbery, this person was in league with the gang and
the call that Goody was waiting for would tell him when the
extra big load of registered cash had been despatched. Who the
'Ulsterman' is – or was – I cannot say, but when the loot was
eventually split up into shares, the Ulsterman got his whack.

Leonard 'Nipper' Read, who at the time of the robbery was
an officer in New Scotland Yard's Murder Squad, wrote in his
autobiography *Nipper – The Man Who Nicked the Krays* that
'an Irishman was responsible for planning robberies and then
selling them on to the perpetrators . . . I am sure from all the
information I had that he [the Irishman] drew up the plan for
the Great Train Robbery, but it was Bruce Reynolds who honed,
polished and fine-tuned it.'

We were not certain what day the big load would be sent to
London after the bank holiday weekend, so we had arrived at
the farm on Tuesday (6 August) just in case we had to 'go to
work' in the early hours of Wednesday morning.

Goody arrived at Leatherslade Farm just before 11 p.m., making rather a dramatic entrance, swigging from a bottle of Johnnie Walker.

'You can all relax,' he announced, as he caught us trying on our army uniforms. 'There's nothing doing tonight.' Groans greeted this piece of news. We had been raring to go.

Few of us felt like sleep that night. We sat around in the kitchen, chatting, playing cards and drinking warm beer. It was late when we finally stretched out our blankets and sleeping bags in the various rooms of the farmhouse.

Dawn broke with the promise of another warm and sunny day. I got up and made breakfast for the early risers – eggs and bacon, of course. Rural sounds were coming in through the kitchen window, a mixture of livestock and the mechanical noises common on farms.

It had been decided on the previous day that we would show as little movement as possible at the farm. For that reason we were 'confined to barracks' and only allowed out to make use of the privy, situated some thirty yards from the house.

During the morning that plan changed after a visitor turned up and knocked on the front door. Everyone slipped silently out of view and Bruce went to take care of the caller. It turned out to be a Mr Wyatt, a neighbouring farmer who had become accustomed to hiring a meadow which formed part of Leatherslade Farm. He wanted to know if he could make a similar arrangement with the new 'owner' of the farm. Bruce gave the visitor some cock-and-bull story about being at the farm to take care of redecorating the premises before the new owner moved in. He promised to pass on Mr Wyatt's request.

The day seemed endless. There was little interest in cards or other pastimes and it was difficult to concentrate to read a book. Towards late afternoon we assembled in the kitchen to go through the plan one last time to make certain that everyone knew exactly what they had to do. Subject to getting the green light from the Ulsterman, we would leave just after midnight and travel as an army detail on night manoeuvres. Bruce would be dressed as the officer and would be carrying 'official papers' to show in the unlikely event that we were stopped by Old Bill. Bruce's driver would be 'Corporal' John Daly and the rest of us (extra)ordinary soldiers. At Bridego Bridge, where the railway goes over a quiet country road just off the B488, two miles north of Cheddington Station, we would put dark blue boiler-suits on over the uniforms and go about our various tasks.

As night fell we sat around in the dark swapping anecdotes and dirty jokes. Goody told us about an encounter he had once had with a gorgeous chick in a swanky London restaurant. She was alone – and so was Gordon. He beckoned the waiter over and had him invite the young lady to his table. It was almost love at first sight. They wined and dined by candlelight, they danced cheek to cheek, they kissed. Gordon paid the bill.

'Your place or mine?' he asked.

In the cab on the way to the young thing's flat, Gordon started to slide his hand up under her skirt and between his companion's legs. She stopped him. She had something to tell him: 'I'm not a girl!'

Gordon then gave a graphic description of how he ejected, somewhat prematurely, his perfumed partner from the taxi – whilst it was still in motion. More a question of crying shame than *Crying Game*.

During the fun, Bruce lit up one of a number of cigars he had in his top pocket. Bobby Welch, who was sitting nearby, asked Bruce for one and Bruce obliged.

'Give one to Pete,' suggested Bob.

'No, no,' said our stand-in train driver. 'If I wanted one you'd give me one, wouldn't you, Bruce?'

I could almost see Bruce smiling in the gloom.

'Don't worry, Dad,' he said, taking a long drag at his cigar. 'If you wanted one – I'd give you one!'

Everyone laughed, including the old man.

'I like your friends,' Peter confided in me. 'They're such a jolly crowd.'

Just before 10 p.m., Goody slipped out of the farm to phone Brian Field from the phone-box in nearby Brill. He was soon back with the news we had been waiting to hear.

'There's an unusually big load on the train tonight – and, gentlemen, it's on its way.'

# 2. Thursday 8 August 1963

Midnight came and went. I hardly had time to remember that it was my birthday, yet by the end of the day it would certainly be the one to remember!

The night mail train from Glasgow, consisting of a high-powered diesel engine and twelve coaches, had left Carlisle en route for London. It was now our turn to leave Leatherslade Farm and meet it. We finally got on the move slightly after midnight. From what I remember it was a cool, dry, moonlit night with just a few scattered clouds. More importantly there was no sign of rain.

The gang set off in convoy and looked every bit the part of the army patrol on night manoeuvres we were meant to be.

I was in the lead Land-Rover, which was driven by Mr Two. Mr One drove the truck. Besides the driver my Land-Rover was carrying Bruce, John Daly, Roger Cordrey and, of course, Peter, who was my responsibility for the night. Most of the rest of the gang piled into the truck, with Roy James bringing up the rear in the second Land-Rover with Gordon Goody and Jimmy White.

The country lanes were deserted with not a sight nor sound of anything during the fifty-minute drive to Bridego Bridge. We dropped John Daly at the distant signal and backed the lorry up between the bridge and a pond so that it was in place to receive the mailbags. The Land-Rovers were parked close by.

Our first task was to put our blue overalls on over our army uniforms, overalls being more appropriate for our trackside duties should we be spotted from a passing train or car. I then scrambled over the protective fence and up the bank to

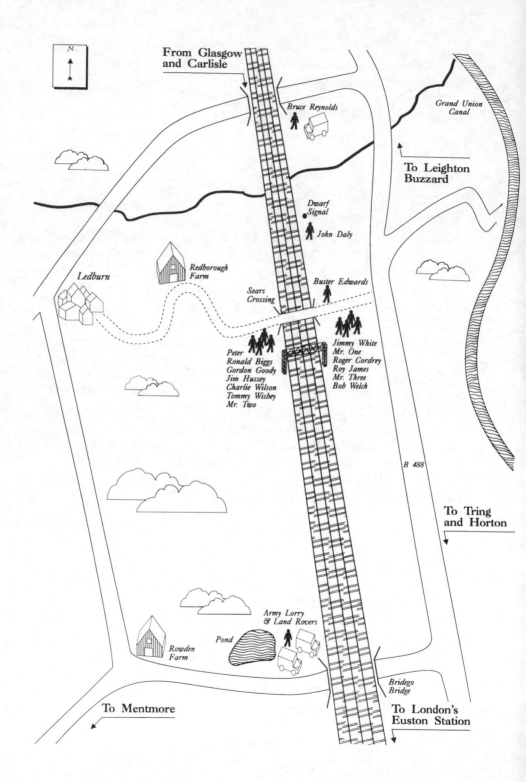

N

From Glasgow
and Carlisle

Bruce Reynolds

Grand Union
Canal

To Leighton
Buzzard

Dwarf
Signal

John Daly

Ledburn

Redborough
Farm

Buster Edwards

Sears
Crossing

Jimmy White
Mr. One
Roger Cordrey
Roy James
Mr. Three
Bob Welch

Peter
Ronald Biggs
Gordon Goody
Jim Hussey
Charlie Wilson
Tommy Wisbey
Mr. Two

B 488

To Tring
and Horton

Army Lorry
& Land Rovers

Pond

Rowden
Farm

Bridego
Bridge

To Mentmore

To London's
Euston Station

the track with Bruce and Peter. Markers were unrolled which would show Peter exactly where the train had to stop for unloading. We made our way up the track towards the gantry and Sears Crossing, a bridge which went over rather than under the track. Roy James left us to cut the telephone wires from the trackside boxes and went off to help Bruce cut the public telephone lines that linked two nearby farms, Rowden Farm near Bridego Bridge and Redborough Farm near Sears Crossing, to the outside world. Bruce then went back to get one of the Land-Rovers so that he could take up his position further down the track, where the road to Ledburn crossed under the railway, a mere 800 yards from Leighton Buzzard Station, from where he could warn us of the train's imminent arrival.

John Daly and Roger Cordrey had the most to do at this time. To them fell the responsibility of stopping the train. John's signal with an amber light would slow the train at the distant signal, the dwarf signal, while Roger's red light would stop the train altogether by the home signal on the gantry. The dwarf signal and gantry were separated by a distance of some 1300 yards.

We spent nearly an hour and a half trackside waiting for the train. During this time other trains sped by and one, a freight train, came to a stop directly under the gantry. Roger hid behind the signal while the rest of us crouched down on the bank listening to the conversation between the driver and his mate. Old Peter was so relaxed that he lit his pipe as he sat on the embankment. The match flared into the night sky. Charlie Wilson came scurrying over from the other bank, but hadn't the heart to yell at Peter.

'Look at the old fucker. You'd think he was on his holiday,' was all he said.

It was just after three o'clock when Bruce's voice crackled over the walkie-talkie to warn us that the train was on its way. The light on the gantry switched to red and Roger scrambled down to join Buster, Jimmy White and Roy James on the other side of the track to where I was waiting with Peter, Charlie Wilson, Gordon Goody, Jim Hussey and Tommy Wisbey.

'My word!' said old Peter, as he saw the light turn to red. 'Your mates have thought of everything.'

The train came slowly, almost silently, to an 'armchair stop'. From where Peter and I were hiding there was only the sound of the diesel motor ticking over. A light went on inside the driver's cab, then a door opened and a shadowy figure descended from the train and headed to the foot of the signal gantry. It was David Whitby, the fireman.

Whitby went to the gantry to call the signal box and must have discovered that the line had been cut. He was starting back to the train when he saw Buster Edwards who he must have assumed was working on the track. He went over to talk to him and was grabbed by two members of the gang and unceremoniously bundled down the bank where he was handcuffed and told to keep quiet. We were on the move.

Roy James and another member of the gang took up their positions to start uncoupling the locomotive and the High Value Package (HVP) coach from the rest of the train. The biggest member of the gang, Mr Three, stormed the cab. The train driver, Jack Mills, must have reacted automatically and threw himself on the intruder. He was coshed once and once only and fell sideways to his knees, striking the back of his head against the cab wall.

Other members of the gang now swarmed into the cab from both sides.

'Get the old man up here!' a voice called. I recognized it as Gordon Goody. I led Peter across the track to the iron ladder leading to the cab. The driver was back on his feet by now, looking groggy and bleeding from a head wound; Charlie Wilson, ever the gentleman, was mopping it with a white handkerchief and seeking to console him.

'You're okay, Dad,' I heard him say. 'You're not badly hurt.'

Peter had also witnessed the scene and threw me a troubled look – he hadn't bargained for anybody getting hurt, but then neither had I. The coshing was regrettable but it was one blow and not the heavy beating that the media likes to portray. It has been manipulated by the authorities, both at the trial and ever since, to turn public opinion against the train robbers. While force was certainly used to break into the HVP coach, you could never call the train robbery a violent crime compared with much that has gone on before and since.

The blood coming from Mills' injury seemed to have made people nervous in the cab and Goody took Peter by the arm and hustled him into the driving seat.

'When I give the word, pull away,' he shouted. 'About a mile down the track you'll see the white marker. I'll tell you when to stop.'

Behind us Roy James and other members of the gang were waiting for the signal to complete the uncoupling of the engine and HVP from the other coaches; these housed some seventy Post Office employees who were busily going about their business of sorting the regular mail, oblivious to what was going on just a few feet away.

The word was passed forward that the uncoupling was complete but during the procedure, and unknown to any of us in the cab, there had been a loss of brake pressure. Goody gave Peter the order to get the train moving. The old man just sat looking steadfastly at the controls.

'I'm waiting for my brake pressure to build,' he said by way of explanation. It was now a case of too many chiefs and not enough Indians.

'What's the problem?' barked Bob Welch. 'Let's get going.'

'I can't take the brake off until I've got sixteen inches of pressure,' Peter added, quite matter-of-factly.

'Get him out of here and get the driver,' Goody exploded.

Peter began to protest, referring again to the necessary brake pressure.

'Fuck the brake pressure,' stormed Goody. 'Get the driver up here.'

Peter was pulled out of the seat and Mills took his place. Goody waved his cosh under the nose of the injured driver.

'Listen,' he said. 'Get this thing moving – but not too fast – and stop when I tell you.'

The pressure built and in more ways than one. Finally the large diesel lurched into life and began to move slowly forward. Peter was not looking happy.

'I could have driven it. Why didn't they let me?' he protested. I told him not to worry, it was going to be all right.

Roy, who was riding on the outside of the cab, saw the markers first and shouted for us to slow the train. The large locomotive glided to a halt and the gang spilled out from the train on to the track.

Bruce was already standing waiting for us, cutting an elegant figure in his army officer's uniform rather than our blue overalls.

'Well done, chaps!' he said.

We stopped the train exactly at Bridego Bridge, which we knew was little used at night.

'Take Peter and wait for us in the back of the Land-Rover,' Bruce told me. 'And make sure the old chap doesn't take off into the boondocks.'

Peter and I did as Bruce said, scrambling down the grass embankment to the road and over the tailboard into the back of one of the Land-Rovers. At the same time members of the gang were taking Mills and Whitby off the train and getting them to lie down on the grass embankment.

From our position Peter and I had a clear and unobstructed view of the bridge and the paralysed train. There was the sound of glass shattering.

'My word!' said old Peter for the umpteenth time that night.

We sat in awed silence, witnessing the sacking of the train. The gang worked swiftly, passing the mailbags by way of a human chain to Jim Hussey and Bob Welch who were loading the truck. I knew then that I was a privileged spectator to a historic moment, although at the time I did not know just how historic it was to be. The Great Train Robbery was now fact.

Dawn was approaching and Bruce called a halt to the plundering, even though a few mailbags still remained. We removed our overalls and reverted to the role of soldiers. The 'work party' returned to the vehicles breathing heavily from their labours. The whole robbery – from the stopping of the train to our leaving the scene – had taken less than forty minutes.

Our small convoy made slow progress back to the farm, the truck sluggish with the weight of the mailbags and the gang. As I had had it comparatively easy I was given the task of being radio operator and tuned in to Old Bill's wavelength on the portable VHF radio we had brought along.

In comparison with recent events the drive back was uneventful and as we drove up the lane leading to the farm a rooster crowed. As far as I was concerned it was a new day in beautiful, bucolic Bucks.

As we reached the gate to the farm the radio crackled into life for the first time that morning. It was a general call. A train had been robbed near Linslade. The time was around 4.45 a.m.

The truck backed up close to the door of the farmhouse and was quickly and quietly unloaded, the mailbags and their valuable contents dumped unceremoniously on to the floor of the empty living room. One hundred and twenty bags in all – nearly ten bags each! Later we learned that it had been eight bags that were left behind on the train.

I assumed we would have our work cut out separating the 'wheat from the chaff' and made a comment of this nature to one of the others. By way of an answer he opened a pocket knife and slashed open one of the bags. He took a tightly wrapped bundle and ran his knife down the length of it, laying it open and exposing a wad of blue five-pound notes.

'It's wedge, Ron,' he said with shining eyes and an ear-to-ear grin, 'it's all fucking wedge!'

The truck was parked in a lean-to shed – squashing a can of yellow paint in the process – and the Land-Rovers placed out of sight. From the air or from the main road nobody would have been able to tell that the farmhouse was inhabited, certainly not by sixteen villains and some 120 mailbags.

Members of the gang were selected to go to various vantage points in the house and keep an eye out for unwanted guests. It had already been decided that if Old Bill did come calling they would be 'taken care of' and tied up. The coshes were hung up on a row of hooks near the door.

Charlie Wilson and Roger Cordrey were appointed 'accountants' to take care of the counting and distribution of the cash, but first it was decided that we should empty the sacks on the off chance that a homing device had been planted in any one of them. It took Bruce, Mr Two and myself close to three hours to empty the sacks and pass the money to Charlie and Roger.

Old Peter was much more relaxed by now and smiling at one and all. He set about making 'a nice cup of tea' for 'his boys', as he now fondly called us.

When the accountants reached the magic million we were all called in to admire the stack. Appreciative sounds filled the air and jokes were cracked.

'If only that prick on *Police 5* could see this lot!' said someone.

'Who said crime doesn't pay?' added Roy James.

Gordon Goody was crooning one of his favourite Tony Bennett pieces, 'It's the Good Life', while Charlie Wilson was twisting to a rousing version of Gerry and the Pacemakers' 'I Like It'.

Although there was general euphoria our guard didn't drop. There was always somebody monitoring the police traffic on the radio until Old Bill took to using a code after suspecting that we might be listening in on the line; even then we constantly monitored the news broadcasts.

Some of us not on look-out duty returned our attentions to the Monopoly set. A costly mistake, as it turned out. Charlie was once again the runaway winner, offering £5000 for a 'Get out of Jail Free' card. Jovial Tommy Wisbey quipped, 'Bank error in your favour. Collect one million quid.'

The original plan was for us to sit tight at the farm for some time – possibly a week or more. We certainly had the supplies for it and the farm was well off the beaten track. Police broadcasts and news bulletins were to change all that.

It was around midday when we heard on the radio that the police suspected that army vehicles had been used in the robbery. Another report spoke of the likelihood that we were holed up in a farmhouse somewhere in the vicinity of the robbery, perhaps 'within a thirty-minute drive or thirty-mile radius of Bridego Bridge'. A 'senior police spokesman' announced that a systematic search of farms and outbuildings would take place immediately.

For whatever reason, the police told the press that we had got away with 'over £100,000'. By late afternoon we were staring at a pile of over £2,500,000 and that did not count the ten bob notes. According to the *Guinness Book of Records* our total haul that night was £2,631,784, of which only £343,448 was ever recovered. That represented over US $7 million at the time and is the equivalent of over $30 million at 1993 Sterling rates. I am reliably informed by the Isle of Man Bank and the National Westminster's Economic Unit that if we had invested the money in a bank it would now be worth £48.6 million and if we had taken a gamble on equities it would have accrued to some £84.8 million.

The money was split into seventeen equal 'whacks' after Peter's £40,000 had been deducted. The extra whacks were for the Ulsterman and Brian Field. Each person took his share and packed it into kit-bags, hold-alls and suitcases. My whack filled two army kit-bags, more money than I had ever dreamed of, over £147,000, nearly £1.8 million pounds at today's rates. I gave Peter his money in a leather hold-all.

'My word!' said the old man. 'Is this all mine?' His retirement was suddenly looking a bit more promising than the fifteen bob a week promised by British Rail.

Decisions were still being taken as to what we should do next. As time might not be on our side we started to throw the empty mailbags down into the cellar and cleaning of the house began. Wrapping paper bearing the names of various well-known banks was incinerated in a small stove in the kitchen until Roy pointed out that the column of smoke pouring from the chimney on a warm summer's day might attract the attention of Old Bill. The fire was put out.

It was also decided that after the story we had told the neighbour about being there to decorate there should be some signs of life at the farm, so two of the gang went to dig a hole in the meadow behind the farmhouse. Peter saw this activity from an upstairs window. There was more than a hint of concern in his voice when he asked me why the hole was being dug. I told him it was to bury the mailbags and rubbish.

'Oh!' he said with obvious relief, 'is that what it's for?' Peter was still troubled by the fact that he hadn't been given the time to drive the train and he assured me more than once that he could have done the job had he been given the chance.

Peter was a lovable old man and I am happy that he never had his collar felt by Old Bill. He would not have survived in the nick and it is nice to think that at least he and three other members of the gang got to enjoy the spoils of that night's work.

While it was felt to be unwise to use the Land-Rovers we decided to carry on with painting the truck in case it was needed as a last resort. Jimmy White and a helper set to with brushes and a can of canary yellow paint to disguise the khaki truck. This yellow paint would be the undoing of Gordon Goody at the trial after samples from the crushed can at the farm had been matched to those found on his shoes.

Quiet, chain-smoking Roger Cordrey put it to the gang that he could nip out on the bike he had thoughtfully brought along, to see what was going on in the neighbourhood and buy a newspaper and some more fags. He would also make a couple of necessary calls to set up his own escape. If Roger was anything he was unobtrusive, so there was no objection to him going for a spin, especially as we all had the concern of how we could get away from the farm. It was agreed he would return in the morning.

The gang gathered to discuss the options and what our next move might be. The original plan had been to lie low, passing a week or so in the sun. One thing was for certain. Old Bill was flat out on the case and the 'Heavy Mob' were involved. The unanimous decision was that we should get away from the farm and the general area as soon as possible.

As nothing could be done until the following day we sat around drinking warm beer. It was then that somebody remembered it was my birthday. Each of the gang ceremoniously presented me with a fiver and I was asked what it felt like finally to have made the Big Time.

It had been a memorable day. Many of us had been without sleep for nearly thirty-six hours. We bedded down for the night, but the atmosphere was not as it had been on the eve of the robbery. It was hot and it was difficult, despite our exhaustion, to sleep.

# 3. Aftermath and Capture

Roger Cordrey cycled to Oxford and booked himself into a small hotel. The evening paper told him everything he needed to know. He had been involved in one of the largest robberies ever. Given his reputation for being able to stop trains he knew it wouldn't be long before Old Bill was knocking at his door. And if Old Bill knew of his reputation, so did some of his friends, who went back on promises to help after seeing the papers and hearing the news.

Back at the farm the rest of us had awoken early from our fitful sleep. After a breakfast of eggs, sausages, bacon and more of Peter's tea, the 'cleaners' got to work washing everything with great care and attention.

Early on Friday morning Bruce and John Daly set off on foot to hitch-hike to Tring where they could arrange for some sort of transportation to come out from London. Luck was with them and they were soon picked up by an elderly man. Needless to say, the conversation turned to the robbery, about which the old man had some strong views.

'The scoundrels should be horse-whipped,' he declared vehemently.

'Too good for them,' replied Bruce in a similar tone. 'They need to be given a taste of the cat.'

During the day we continued to listen to the news broadcasts. The police were now certain that we were still in the area. All police units had been mobilized to take part in a massive search which would cover a thirty-mile radius from the robbery site. The farm was just twenty-seven miles from Bridego Bridge. The public were invited to get in touch with the police if they had seen or heard anything of a suspicious nature about the time of the robbery.

We were becoming more nervous and there was further speculation about what should be done in the event of Old Bill turning up on the doorstep. The most important thing would be to put out their radio – a pick handle would do the trick – cop for the cozzers and tie 'em up, then hide the car. But then what?

Suddenly a car came racing up the lane to the farmhouse. Everybody took up their positions as it stopped in a swirl of dust by the front door.

'I thought that might make you jump,' said a smiling Roger Cordrey as he emerged from a Wolseley he had bought in Oxford to replace the bike. Roger was back for his whack, but the news was mixed. 'Old Bill's flying about all over the place,' he reported, 'but at least there are no road blocks.' He spread the evening and morning papers on the kitchen table. 'Look, fellas. We've hit the headlines.'

After some discussion Buster decided we should club together and pay a man to take care of the farm after we had left – if necessary he should burn it to the ground. Sadly for most of us, the police got to Leatherslade Farm before the dustman. Without the evidence they collected at the farm the Yard would have had no case, just speculation.

First to leave the farm were Roger, Jimmy White and Mr One, travelling in Roger's new car. Jimmy returned later in the day and handed the Wolseley over to Mr Two, who headed for London and the good life. Just after dusk Bruce and John returned to the farm, driving an Austin Healey apiece. They were accompanied by a middle-aged woman at the wheel of a Ford Cortina. Bruce told Peter to get his bags; he would be travelling with John and the lady, who had been introduced as Mary Manson. I would go with Bruce and our dough in one of the Healeys; the other one was to be taken by Jimmy White.

We made our hasty goodbyes in the hope of never seeing one another again. And then we were on our way, the nippy sports cars growling along the country lanes. Not a sign of Old Bill.

Happy days were here again!

On the way to Redhill, Bruce and I talked about our plans

for the future. I visualized dribbling some money into my 'on a shoestring' building business. I needed plant such as ladders and scaffolding and perhaps, later on, a smarter looking van for Biggs & Stripp. And of course I wanted to make sure that my sons got a good education.

I asked Bruce if he was going to get out of the business.

'I don't think so,' he said with half a smile. 'I'll probably look around for something bigger and better.' He also spoke of the importance of a sound education for his son. 'I think I'd like him to become an eminent Queen's Counsel,' he joked.

We made a short stop near London Airport so that I could tell Charm that her loving lord and very clever husband was on his way home. In a relieved but anxious voice she asked me if I had recently been in the company of a friend who wore spectacles. I told her I had and that he was in the car.

'Now I know,' she said.

Mary Manson had followed Bruce's Austin Healey back from the farm and at Horley we stopped to go our individual ways. I shook hands with old Peter and wished him well. We agreed not to be in touch until the dust had settled.

Charm was wearing curlers and a pink housecoat when Bruce and I arrived. When she realized I was not alone she went scurrying off and reappeared minus the coloured rollers. She gave Bruce a shy hello and eyed the two kit-bags standing in the middle of her neatly kept kitchen.

'What's that?' she asked.

'Money. It's all money,' I replied, yanking open the drawstring on the kit-bag and pulling out a few bundles of fivers for her to see. 'What a clever husband! And what a clever friend!'

Bruce left, promising to give me a 'tinkle' in the near future. I wouldn't see my good friend for twenty-nine years.

I would not see my brother Jack, either. Charmian waited for Bruce to leave before telling me that my brother – fifteen years my senior – had died of a heart attack on the eve of the robbery. His wife, Winnie, had been in touch to ask if I could attend the funeral. Charm told her that I was somewhere in Wiltshire engaged in a tree-felling job, the story I had given her to account for my absence. Winnie suggested that Charm should contact the Wiltshire Constabulary to see if they could find me. All I had told Charm was that I would be in the vicinity of Devizes. A search had been carried out, but there had been no sign of Charmian's 'clever husband'.

The next morning after my first decent sleep in what seemed like weeks we tipped the contents of the kit-bags out on to the bedroom floor.

'What would have happened to me and the kids if you had been caught?' Charm asked as the realization of what had happened sank in. 'We can't keep it in the house, you know. Where are you going to hide it?'

I assured her that she had nothing to worry about and that everything had been thought of. It hadn't, of course. First, however, we had to check all the money to make sure that none of the notes had any kind of identifying mark on them.

'It smells awful,' she said.

'But it looks divine,' I countered.

We went through the pile note by note, setting to one side any that were in any way suspicious. With a little reluctance we had to burn more than £700 in the kitchen stove, later digging in the ash around the rose bushes.

I packed £40,000 in blue five-pound notes into one suitcase, £60,000 in mixed notes into another and the rest into a hold-all. I had three 'minders' whom I was hoping I could trust with my cash and made arrangements by telephone to meet these people the following day. Charm and I kept a modest amount to pay off some bills and to have a private celebration – for my birthday, if anyone wanted to know.

Charmian's sister Rosalind was invited to babysit for us so that we could have our night out. We took a train to London where for the first time ever I was quite happy to join Charm window shopping.

We were wandering around Soho when we saw a notice on a news-stand: 'Train Robbery Latest. Police Hunt the Weasel'. The Weasel did not turn out to be anyone I knew, so I was not unduly worried. I bought the newspaper anyway. The Weasel was described as a well-known figure in the underworld and, as usual, the police were 'acting on a tip-off'. The news was not sufficient to put us off a splendid Indian meal. Wined and dined, we caught the last train back to

Redhill without giving the robbery or the Weasel a second thought.

I was up bright and early on the Sunday morning and went out to buy all the newspapers, certain that they would give the robbery their full attention. From what I read Old Bill didn't seem to be making much headway with his enquiries, but much was being made of the 'battered' driver.

A friend in the building business turned up in his pick-up truck soon after 9 a.m. and the suitcase containing £60,000 was put in the back and covered by a tarpaulin. I also gave him a carrier bag holding £5000, which was the amount agreed upon for him to babysit the money 'until further notice'.

I arranged to meet a second friend just after noon in the saloon bar of his favourite pub in Horley, a short distance from Redhill and not a million miles from old Peter's home. I called a mini-cab and casually handed the driver a suitcase holding £40,000 to put into the boot of the car. When we got to the pub my friend was waiting, greeting me with a strong handshake and a warm smile. He was also to receive a £5000 'drink' for his troubles.

I felt like a drink myself, so after the delivery I dropped in on one of my favourite watering-holes in Redhill. Sally, the barmaid, was ringing up a sale on the cash register as I approached. She was looking closely at a one-pound note that a customer had handed her, comparing it with a list of serial numbers by the side of the till. The fellow wanted to know why.

'I've got a list of numbers of notes that were stolen from the train and this might be one of them,' she told him.

'I wish it was,' he laughed.

I complimented Sally and asked her for a double Scotch, handing her a recently 'earned' five-pound note. She tucked the fiver straight into the till drawer and was just preparing my change when the other customer pointed out that she had not compared my note with the list.

'I don't have to check money that Ron hands me, I know him too well,' she said.

With the money out of the house I started to feel more relaxed. I told Charmian to go and buy herself some new clothes and shoes from the £500 that I had won on the horses.

On the Monday I was back at work, lying furiously about the tree-felling job that had paid so handsomely. My partner, Ray Stripp, had told our motley crew of workers about my good fortune on the horses and it was pints all round at lunch. There was a lot of joking about the train robbery and, like most of the country, we toasted the robbers.

That same Monday the police had been contacted by a farm labourer and told about a suspicious-looking truck parked in a farm not thirty miles from the scene of the robbery. At first the police merely added the information to their list of calls, but the caller was persistent. On Tuesday 13 August the police found the farm.

'The place is one big clue,' they told reporters.

The following evening we heard on the news that Roger Cordrey had been arrested in Bournemouth.

Roger's capture was a blow, but I still felt comfortable that I would not immediately be among the suspects. Charmian did not altogether share my confidence and when, a few days later, a suitcase containing £100,000 was found in the woods near Dorking -- scant miles from where we were living – she really got an attack of the 'nadgers'. Worse was to come, as four days after the Dorking find the police discovered a substantial sum of money concealed in the panelling of a caravan in nearby Box Hill – and Jimmy White's fingerprints to boot.

In August 1963 it seemed as if everyone was talking about the train robbery. Mick Boone, a paper-hanger who had worked for me on several occasions, sidled up to me one day; he knew that I had been in prison.

'I bet you wish you had been in on that train business, Biggsy,' he said. 'Two and a half million quid! Old Bill will never catch those blokes, they're bloody pros – they're all out of the country by now and bloody good luck to 'em. That's what I say!'

Exactly two weeks after the robbery, on 22 August, Charlie Wilson was arrested at his home in London. The arrest came on the same day that Scotland Yard was circulating mug-shots of Bruce, Jimmy White, Roy James, Buster Edwards and Charlie to the press. Now Charm and I were tuned in to all news broadcasts on the radio and television. Families and friends of the men whom the police were hoping could 'help them with their enquiries' would most certainly be investigated and visited, and as I knew that I was on Bruce's prison record as one of his 'associates' it would not be long before Old Bill came calling.

Inspector Basil Morris and Sergeant Church were from Reigate Police Station.

They came to see me on 24 August just to make a few 'routine enquiries'. I tried to look pleased to see them and invited them through to the living room. Charmian offered to make a cup of tea and gave me a glum look as she went to the kitchen.

Inspector Morris lost no time in getting down to the nitty-gritty of his routine enquiries.

'Now, Ron, when did you last see this chappie Bruce Reynolds we're looking for?'

'Bruce? I haven't seen him for about four years or more,' I said, lying through my teeth. 'The last time I saw him was when we were both in Wandsworth. Bruce went out before I did and I haven't seen him since.'

The questions flowed and so did the lies. The inspector told me that the local police had been keeping tabs on me and that he, for one, was glad to see that I had 'settled down to life on the straight and narrow'. He said he didn't have a search warrant, but would I mind if he had a look around?

He was a 'friendly' policeman with a disarming manner. He admired our kitchen but took the opportunity to check in the Bendix washing machine which, he said, he had been thinking of getting for his 'better half'. He also checked out the stove where Charm and I had recently sent 700 quid up in smoke.

He checked the bedrooms, opening cupboards and wardrobes, then expressed a desire to take a look in the loft. I got him a step-ladder and a torch and held the ladder while he climbed up into my workshop.

'Any sign of Bruce, Mr Morris?' I joked.

'No, Ron,' he answered evenly. 'No sign of Bruce.'

Next it was the garden that attracted Morris' attention and he made a beeline for the coal shed. I had recently had half a ton of coal delivered and upon seeing it the friendly inspector gave me a probing look.

'You wouldn't be trying the oldest trick in the book, now, would you, Ron?'

I admit a delivery of coal in early August may have been a little strange, but my coal was clean, so to speak.

'I think you're on the level, Ron,' Inspector Morris concluded. 'But I am going to ask you for a little favour. If this fellow Reynolds should get in touch I'd like you to string him along. He's on the run and he's going to need somewhere to hide and I think there's a good chance he'll be calling on you. If he does, give me a bell at the station. I'll make it worth your while. You help me and I'll help you. Have we a deal?'

I breathed a sigh of relief as they went on their way. I thought I had handled the situation rather well. Charm was less impressed by my performance. She said I had gone a rather interesting shade of green when I had opened the door to our visitors.

Soon it was September and there was less and less mention of the train robbery in the media. As far as Charmian and I were concerned no news was good news. I went about my business as normally as possible, returning to work on converting a house into three flats. Biggs & Stripp were in action on anything from 'penthouses to pussy-flaps'. The days were still warm – these were almost the halcyon days.

On the night of 4 September one of my painters, Joe, asked if he could borrow the company van to take his wife to the pictures. I had no objections as long as he dropped me home and picked me up in the morning.

He dropped me off outside my house. Alpine Road was deserted as I walked down the side of the house and went in by the back door. Two men were in the kitchen. Old Bill!

One of them reached behind me and locked the door, putting the key in his pocket.

'We are police officers,' he announced matter-of-factly. 'We are in the process of searching your house – we have a search warrant. We want you to be present when we take up the floorboards in the front room.'

This was not a time to be clever. It is the sort of time when silence is often golden. I caught a glimpse of Charm looking very distressed. She tried to say something, but was told to keep quiet. I could hear Nicky kicking on the door of his room and calling for me. It should have been play-time.

Burly cops with their shirt sleeves rolled up were attacking the living-room floor with crowbars. The policeman who had greeted me in the kitchen identified himself as Detective Chief Inspector Frank Williams and began a search of my person during which he appeared to find nothing of interest.

'I want you to show me the contents of a cupboard on the landing upstairs,' he said. 'I believe that's where you keep the tins of paint?'

Slightly bemused by this request, I was none the wiser after he showed a particular interest in yellow paint. A number of gallon tins were taken from the cupboard and marked up.

Nicky could hear me talking outside his room and was now shouting for me to open the door. Like his father he did not like to be locked up. I asked Williams if it would be okay to say hello to my son.

'No,' he said firmly. 'You are to be taken to the police station to make a statement.' Another cop was told to fetch a car which was parked close to the entrance of my house. Then, wedged between Williams and another beefy detective, I was bundled into the car and driven off.

Later I discovered that one of the policemen to visit my house that day was a young sergeant called Jack Slipper. A name that I was going to get to know rather well in the coming years.

After leaving Alpine Road we took the wrong turning to go into Redhill where the local police station was located. I pointed this out to Williams.

'I know,' he said, with just the slight trace of a smile. 'We are not going to Redhill, we are going to Scotland Yard.'

We drove along Frenches Road and past the Jolly Brick-makers. How long, I wondered, was it going to be before I saw these familiar sights again? I was clearly nicked. They don't send a car unless you're nicked.

'You're very quiet, Mr Biggs,' Williams said sarcastically as we sped towards London. 'Nothing bothering you, is there?'

At the Yard I was taken directly to see the recently appointed chief of the Flying Squad, Detective Chief Superintendent Thomas 'Tommy' Butler, the so-called 'Grey Ghost', who was now in charge of the train robbery enquiry. He pointed to a chair in front of his desk.

'Sit down,' he said. 'I have here a questionnaire. I'm going to ask you the questions and write down your answers.'

I told Butler not to waste his time.

'It's only for your antecedents,' he added, hoping to make it all look routine. 'Have you ever heard of Leatherslade Farm?'

'Of course I have heard of Leatherslade Farm, it's been on television every night for the last month.'

'Do you know Buckinghamshire well?' he pressed.

'Yes, I was stationed at two different camps in Buckingham-shire when I was in the Royal Air Force,' I admitted.

Butler started writing. Williams was at his side as a witness.

'Look,' I repeated, 'I told you I'm not answering any questions.'

Butler looked mean and leaned forward. 'All right, I know it's a big one and you've got to keep your mouth shut, but I'm going to charge you with the train robbery. I've got you by the bollocks, lad, and what I don't know I shall make up – do you understand what I mean?'

'Perfectly,' I nodded.

A fast car was ordered and Williams was told to 'take this bugger to Aylesbury and charge him'.

Charged I was, and photographed and fingerprinted and locked in a dark, dank cell.

'Turned out nice again!' I thought to myself.


'Act smart!' hissed Mr Butler, 'while you've got the bleeding chance.
A prison cell's awaiting you, not the South of fucking France.
Now, turn against your mates, lad, and I'll get you off with ten,
Just write down their names for me – here, use my fountain pen.'
'Do you know what you can do?' I said, scared shitless, grey but grim.
'Go and write a letter to your favourite fag,' and I pushed it back to him.

42

'All right, I'm going to charge you with – er – conspiracy to
rob.
I know the phrase sounds fancy – but then, so was the job.
You're going to prison for twenty years!' His voice rose to
a shout.
'You'll be fit for Sweet Fanny Adams by the time they let
you out.'
Well charged I was – and printed, my soul suffused
with pain.
I'd gone from rags to riches – and back to rags again.
Then swiftly off to Bedford nick, into the flowery dells.
Late night, sombre silence, foul, familiar smells.

Ronald Biggs

# 4. The Trial

And earthly power doth then show likest God's – when
mercy seasons justice.

William Shakespeare

'Anyone for Anti-wank?' calls the cocoa-boy called Smart.
'It's made with milk and sugar tonight – cross me fookin'
'eart!
Evenin' chocolate's noorishin', the bromide meks the boobles.
Guaranteed to cure the 'orn and all yer dickey troobles.'

Ronald Biggs

The next morning I was up before the beak at Linslade
Magistrates' Court, where I was remanded in custody to Her
Majesty's Prison, Bedford. So convincing was Tommy Butler's
manner when he gave his 'evidence' that he almost had me
believing the things I was supposed to have said. Under oath,
he declared that when I had been asked about the farm I had
replied, 'No. Never heard of it. I've got no interest in fucking
farms.' He also told the magistrate that he had no idea why I
had refused to sign my 'statement'.

As I was led away to my cell I heard a news report on the
prison radio. It said that 'Ronald Biggs, a thirty-four-year-old
carpenter of Alpine Road, Redhill, appeared before the Linslade
magistrate . . .' I did not catch the rest as the screw conducting
me down to the cell butted in.

'We've got one of your mates here, Charlie Wilson,' he said.

'Charlie Wilson? Never heard of him,' I replied.

The next day when we were unlocked for exercise I saw both Charlie Wilson and Roger Cordrey in the yard. We ignored each other until exercise was over. Charlie then said in a voice loud enough for all to hear, 'Aren't you the bloke who's been charged with the train robbery?'

'Yeah,' I said, 'but I had nothing to do with it.'

'Incredible,' said Charlie. 'I've been charged with that too. Bloody liberty.'

One by one the ranks of the 'innocents' swelled. First Jimmy Hussey, then Tommy Wisbey, who was quickly followed by Bobby Welch. None of us had any idea what evidence there was against us or how they came to pick our names. We were allowed visits, but we were all extra cautious as it was suggested that the visiting cubicles might be bugged.

Charmian came to see me and I was glad that at least by appearances she seemed to be weathering the storm reasonably well. During her second visit she told me that one of her friends, Jean Jarrard, was having a fling with a cop attached to Scotland Yard. He told Jean, after a bit of priming, that the evidence against us was the fingerprints found at Leatherslade Farm. Bob, Tommy and Jim, who had been three of the 'cleaners' at the farm, wouldn't hear of it.

'It's all bollocks,' said Bob firmly. 'If Old Bill produces fingerprints, then it's a fit-up.' Jim and Tom agreed, swearing that nothing had been overlooked during the clean-up operation.

They were almost right, as even the forensic boys have admitted since that the house was remarkably clean from having housed a gang as large as ours. It was only after they had dusted the more unlikely places, such as the Monopoly set, which we could easily have taken away with us, that they found anything of worth.

The three members of the gang who arrived at the farm wearing gloves and who had the sense and discipline not to remove them were never caught. What prints Peter may have left behind could not be traced as he had no previous record for them to be matched against and the Old Bill did not know they were looking for a second driver. The fact that they did know which prints to look for, however, raises a few questions. It is almost certain that some disgruntled person who knew about the job but had been left out pointed the finger. A finger that pointed to Bruce and by association to me.

A 'fit-up', by the way, is the introduction of false or manufactured evidence at the scene of a crime. Back in the mid '60s a certain detective by the name of Harry Challenor had grabbed three young lads during a street disturbance and charged them with 'being in possession of an offensive weapon', the weapon being a piece of brick. The kids denied the charge, saying that they had not had pieces of brick in their possession when they were taken into custody. Not to be made a liar, Mr Challenor produced a brick and a hammer and broke the brick in front of the boys.

'An offensive weapon for you,' he said. 'One for you. And one for you.'

At the trial an alert lawyer noticed that the three 'offensive weapons' fitted neatly together. What did not fit very neatly together was the fact that until they were arrested the three boys hadn't known each other, as they came from different parts of London. They were sent home and a little later Harry Challenor took his turn in the dock. He had been overworking, the court was told, and he really was a very fine officer who had been awarded this, that and the other for his dedication in the fight against crime. He was sentenced to a spell in a rest home – which just goes to show that while we are all supposed to be equal in the eyes of the law, a few, as many in Los Angeles know, remain more equal than others.

Gordon Goody was the next to feature in the news. The police had taken him in for questioning early on, but produced no case or charges against him and he was released. He then surprised us by turning up in Bedford to visit Charlie. I'm not certain to this day why he took the risk, but he had a message for me from Bruce and that was to let his solicitor, George Stanley, take care of my defence. Until then, as a poor, struggling carpenter, I had been granted Legal Aid. But I decided to take Bruce's advice.

During the time in Bedford I tried to get the group interested in an escape. The prison wall was not very high and there were more than enough of us to take care of the screws who supervised our exercise period. But everyone still thought that they had a good chance of 'slipping out of it' – even when told about the fingerprint evidence – so the opportunity was lost.

Somebody was obviously reading my thoughts, because very soon after my proposal to escape we were transferred *en masse* to Aylesbury Prison. The hospital wing had been cleared of patients and we were put into cells which had barred observation flaps on the doors. Experienced screws were selected from different prisons around England to take care of us. Security, at first, was tight.

Just after the transfer, the solicitor's managing clerk, Brian Field, and his boss, John Wheater, were arrested in connection with the sale of Leatherslade Farm and joined us in Aylesbury. Security was relaxed somewhat and we spent our time playing cards and chess, listening to the radio and getting to know one another rather better than had been possible at the time of the robbery.

At the beginning of December, Bruce's brother-in-law, John Daly, was arrested in a house in Eaton Square. After a brief court appearance he too was sent on to Aylesbury. A week later, on 10 December, it was the turn of Roy James to fall into Butler's hands, after what was reported to be a dramatic roof-top chase.

We were all visited regularly by our legal representatives. George Stanley also had the professional pleasure of taking care of Johnny Daly's defence. Stanley confirmed that the main evidence against us was the fingerprints found at Leatherslade Farm. It was suggested that I should admit to having been to the farm prior to the robbery, but only in my capacity as a carpenter, to construct a whipping-post for 'kinky' parties. He told John to plead guilty and hope for leniency.

'George is right,' said John after we had spoken to him. 'If fingerprints have been found at the farm we haven't got a leg to stand on. I think I'll take his advice: plead guilty and hope to cop a shorter sentence.' We all begged to differ.

'You'd be potty if you pleaded guilty,' said Bobby Welch. 'Plead not guilty and you've got a chance – we might be able to nobble someone on the jury. If you plead guilty, you're fucked!'

We really had to work on John to make him see that he was making the wrong decision. Finally he agreed to plead not guilty. The only one among us who was obliged to plead guilty was Roger Cordrey, as he had been caught 'bang to rights' with his share of the loot.

The majority of the gang thought that they still had a reasonable chance of slipping out of the charges against us, a view that was not shared by Gordon Goody, Charlie Wilson and Ronnie Biggs! We began to put together an escape plan.

God knows how or why, but Charlie had been put to work in a small kitchen in the hospital wing. His job was to prepare snacks and hot drinks for the screws. Two officers patrolled the prison yard at night and were accustomed to getting a mug of cocoa passed out to them through the bars of one of the cells. It was decided that these two screws would have to be drugged to facilitate our plan. Once the guards were in the Land of Nod, friends would come over the wall and Bob's your uncle. Roger Cordrey, who had spent a large part of his life in the horse-racing world, was consulted for information as to the best type of dope for the job in hand. He knew exactly what was required and where it could be obtained: tasteless and colourless, satisfaction guaranteed. Charlie was enthusiastic: knocking the screws out by hand – or by dope – would give him great pleasure. That was until Brian Field appeared reading from his *Archbold's Criminal Law and Practice*: 'For administering a stupefying drug: up to fourteen years' imprisonment.'

'Fuck that!' said Charlie. 'Back to the drawing board!'

The screws who took care of us in Aylesbury Prison were changed every month. Most of them were an unhappy lot and being away from their homes didn't do much to improve their humour. One exception was Paddy, a fine fella from County Cork. One evening when he came on duty he looked into my cell and saw that my table was laden with a selection of cold meat and cheeses plus a couple of bottles of Carlsberg 'Special Brew' lager.

'Sure, you fellas are livin' like lords,' said Paddy, 'I think I'm in the wrong game.'

'Hello, Paddy,' I greeted him, 'fancy a beer?' The Irishman

took the slender bottle and slid it into a pocket at the side of his trousers where his truncheon should have been. He thanked me, saying that he would drink it later.

'Y'know,' he said, lowering his tone, 'I've got a lot of admiration for you and your mates.' I felt I knew what was coming next. 'I'd be prepared to help you lads – if you needed anything. But I wouldn't bring in any guns or dope.'

'Come off it, Paddy. You know that we're not into anything like that. But I would be interested in getting hold of a miniature radio.' So we talked about a price and a place where the deal could be done. As I knew Aylesbury fairly well from my days in the RAF I was able to arrange for a friend to meet Paddy outside a certain cinema at eight in the evening. He would pass over a tiny 'Ruby' radio and receive an envelope containing £100, around £1200 by today's standards. Paddy was delighted – and so were Gordon and Charlie when I told them that we had a sympathizer in our midst. A contact was made with a legendary keymaker known as Johnny the Bosh. He only had to know the make of the lock to come up with a blank key that was sure to fit. This information was duly passed out and the key was produced and handed to one of Gordon's pals. During the next couple of weeks, hacksaw blades, a one-inch wood chisel, a watch, the blank key and a set of needle files were smuggled into the Maximum Security Wing of HMP Aylesbury. All that we needed to put our plan into operation was to make the blank into a key that unlocked the doors to our cells.

Security slackened off during the months we spent on remand. The hearings at the Magistrates' Court were over and we had all been committed for trial. We associated most of the day, only locked in our cells during lunchtime and after 9 p.m. The screws were generally easy to get along with, although some were not very happy about the amount of 'freedom' we were given. Friendly screws often played games of cards or chess with us and it was during one of these fraternal moments that Goody was able to exercise his artistic skills.

As a guard and I sat facing each other, pitting our wits over the chessboard, Gordon came along, sketch-pad in hand, and asked the screw if he had any objection to being drawn in this somewhat remarkable pose. Permission granted, Goody started sketching away, telling us how he planned to publish a book of his drawings 'when he got out'.

'Make a bomb!' he predicted.

The screw sitting across the chessboard from me was so engrossed in the black and white armies in front of him that he paid no attention to the bunch of keys hanging from his belt: in the meantime Goody was filling in the details, from time to time complimenting my adversary on his strategic expertise. With the aid of his sketches and the needle files, Goody produced the key we needed overnight. The following morning, while someone kept the screws occupied with some trivial matter, Goody tested his handiwork on the door of my cell. It turned the lock first time! It was a 'goer'.

Roger Cordrey, Billy Boal (whose only crime had been to give Roger a lift and help him hide the money and who had been arrested at the very beginning along with Roger) and Brian Field shared a dormitory at one end of the first floor of the hospital wing. The door was not like the cell doors, which were faced with sheet metal on the inside. The dormitory door was fitted with a flimsy mortise lock and there was no metal facing. Anyone on the inside would have little trouble cutting the wood and removing the lock altogether. As Roger and Brian were not anxious to participate in the planned escape, we reluctantly decided to invite Boal to join us. Ever worried about the welfare of his wife and children, Boal was only too ready to 'make one'.

All the arrangements were made. Charlie's 'firm' would leave a car at a spot near the back of the hospital. Bill would quietly cut the lock from the dormitory door and get out, unlocking Gordon's cell, which was next door to the dormitory. Gordon would then unlock Charlie – who was on the same landing – and they would cop for the night-watchman, tying him up. Then they would go down to the cells in the basement and unlock me.

Lying under a blanket, fully dressed, I heard the night-watchman shuffling around, making his rounds. I could just imagine good old Bill Boal at work on the door – using the chisel as I had shown him. Somewhere a clock struck eleven, then twelve . . . one . . . two. At three o'clock I took my clothes off and got into bed: something had obviously gone badly wrong.

For whatever reason, Boal chickened out and laid wide the plot to the chief screw. The screws moved in with a massive search of the cells and their occupants. 'Association' came to an abrupt end and the screws were no longer friendly. Most of the items that had been smuggled in were found and confiscated. The cops were called in and wasted their time asking us questions. All privileges ceased, visiting time was curtailed and foodstuff coming into the prison was restricted to the permitted amount. And for good measure, a pig of a Principal Officer came to the nick to take charge during the Christmas period.

God Rest Ye Merry Gentlemen!

The trial proper began on 20 January 1964. The judge was one Mr Justice Edmund Davies, a Welshman not known for his leniency in dealing with the likes of us.

As the crime had been committed in the county of Buckinghamshire, the venue for the trial was set to be the county town of Aylesbury. The town's Assize Court was far too small to accommodate such a large number of accused, so the local Rural District Council Chamber was converted into the courtroom. A team of carpenters was called in to construct an enormous dock that would be big enough to seat all of us and then as many again in the shape of the accompanying policemen.

Every morning, Monday through Friday, we would be handcuffed and locked into small individual compartments in a police bus, commonly known as a Black Maria. Then with a massive escort which consisted of at least four police cars and a dozen or so motorcycle cops, we would make the ten-minute journey from the prison to the council chamber.

School-kids would wave and give us the thumbs-up as we went to and fro; in complete contrast, the more elderly inhabitants of the area would shake their fists as the bus passed.

Never had the town of Aylesbury seen anything quite like it, and I doubt they ever will again.

After the morning hearing we would return to prison in much the same fashion for lunch. At the time we were having our meals brought in from one of the town's better restaurants and served by the proprietor. One prison officer was heard to grumble, 'Isn't it bloody marvellous! You blokes are eating roast pheasant and jugged hare and here we are, lucky if we get some beans on bloody toast.'

At around 2 p.m. the routine would be repeated and we would be cuffed up and sent off to court for the afternoon session. On our arrival in the courthouse there was always one officious uniformed superintendent who would fuss around us like some giant mother hen, telling us to do this and do that, to stop talking, to sit up straight. On and on he went. At one point, early in the proceedings, he produced some squares of cardboard with strings attached which he had numbered from one to twelve. He held one of the cards out to Tommy Wisbey.

'Here, hang this around your neck,' the beefy superintendent instructed, 'so that you can be easily identified.'

'Easily identified?' replied Tommy indignantly. 'What do you think this is? A fucking cattle show? Shove 'em up your arse!'

And that, so to speak, was that, at least as far as the cards were concerned.

The trial proceeded.

The court, packed with reporters, coppers, the public and the accused, would often become stuffy, particularly during the afternoon sessions. A string of bank clerks were early witnesses and they would be led painstakingly through their earlier statements to the police by the junior prosecutor, Howard Sabin. The aim was for the prosecution to prove beyond any question of doubt that the train in question had been carrying a large sum of money which was subsequently stolen. At times it was hard to stay awake and more than once I saw members of the jury nodding off. My solicitor, George Stanley, had engaged Mr Wilfred Fordham, a barrister, to defend me. Fordham was a kindly old gentleman, highly respected in legal circles.

At one point Fordham's absence from the proceedings, as he catnapped in court, was noted by His Lordship, who sat drumming his fingers as he waited for my defence counsel to rejoin us. Charlie Wilson spoke to me about the matter.

'It's really nothing to do with me,' he said, 'but old Wilfred spends every afternoon having a kip. Your liberty is on the line. If I was you I'd get myself someone who's a bit more on the ball.'

Charlie was right, so I spoke to George Stanley about it. Stanley argued in favour of sticking with Fordham – a fine man if it should come to making a plea for leniency, he said – but it was finally decided that a QC would be brought in and Mr Fordham would stay on to assist.

I remember feeling distinctly more optimistic after my first meeting with Michael Argyle, QC. At that time he was the Recorder for Leicester – dishing out bird! A young man, obviously well bred, exuding efficiency and Old Spice. This was more like it!

A hush fell over the court when Jack Mills, the train driver, entered to give his evidence. The judge glared in the direction of the dock as Mills made his way to the witness box and took the oath. He was invited by the judge to give his evidence seated and accepted the invitation. Aided by the prosecutor, Mr Mills described his misadventure when his train was stopped at a point on the line known as Sears Crossing. The hordes of reporters scribbled away furiously, not wanting to miss a word of the driver's whispered and damning testimony.

Mills was the key figure in manipulating the 'monstrous' nature of our crime. Without him it would have been nigh on impossible for the judge to get away with the sentences he later handed down. I never met Mills personally, so I can only base my impressions on hearsay, but I do know that when the robbery was planned there was never any intention that anyone would get hurt.

One of the people most troubled by Mr Mills' performance in court was not a member of the gang but the wife of my lawyer, Peta Fordham. Mrs Fordham, who went on to write a book, *The Robbers' Tale*, revealed that before his death Mills had admitted to her that he had been warned that his pension would be at stake if he showed any sympathy in court to the gang or suggested that we had treated him 'like gentlemen'. He was also not to admit under any circumstances that his worst head injury came from his fall and not from a blow to his head from Mr Three. (Though as we were all wearing masks, Mills would not actually have any idea which of us did cosh him.)

After Mills' dramatic court appearance it was left to the guard of the train to provide the court with reason for laughter. He was a talkative witness and the prosecutor had his work cut out to stop him from rambling on about 'railway procedure' and like matters. Describing his duties in the event of his train coming to an unscheduled stop, he told the court that he had left the guard's van and gone to place detonators on the line by way of a warning to any train that might be approaching in the same direction. But the gang also knew a thing or two about railway procedure and one of our number had already put detonators on the line.

'When I walked back down the line to place my detonators, what do you think I found?' asked the guard.

The prosecutor smiled politely.

'I am quite certain that the court is itching with curiosity to learn what it was you found.'

'Detonators! Someone had already laid detonators!' There was something else the poor man found; when he hurried to the front of his train he found that the engine and the High Value Package coach were missing!

On the fourteenth day of the trial, my old friend, Detective Inspector Basil Morris, appeared to give evidence. The cross-eyed cop stepped smartly into the witness-box, seized the New Testament in his right hand and held it aloft.

'Detective Inspector Basil Morris,' he announced in a loud, clear voice. 'Surrey Constabulary, Reigate CID.'

It was the first time the gang had seen Mr Morris, and Tommy Wisbey, always ready to see the funny side of things, cracked up at the sight of the Inspector.

'Jesus Christ!' he said, *sotto voce*. 'It's Ben Turpin!' – referring to the cross-eyed comedian in the old Mack Sennett movies. He dropped his head into his hands and began to shake with suppressed laughter. Those of us who had heard Tom's crack tried to keep straight faces. Once more the judge glared in our direction. The prosecutor was taking the inspector through the evidence he had given before a magistrate when I was first charged.

'Did you, Inspector Morris, ask Mr Biggs if he knew any of the men wanted for the train robbery in Buckinghamshire?' he asked.

'I did,' affirmed the inspector.

'And what did he say?'

'He said, "I know Reynolds, I met him when we were doing time together." '

This reply took the prosecutor by surprise; it was not what he was expecting or wanted. To enable the jury to return an impartial verdict, it is essential that there must be no indication that the accused has previously been to prison. Telling the court I had 'done time' was quite wrong. Those in the courtroom who were aware of this looked at Inspector Morris in disbelief, especially the Old Bill who were in charge of the investigation!

Brian Field, who was sitting behind me in the dock, laid a hand on my shoulder.

'Ronnie! You lucky so-and-so!' he said excitedly. 'That entitles you to a retrial!'

Gordon Goody grinned. 'You crafty bastard, Biggsy,' he said softly. 'You had that cozzer straightened!'

My lawyer hurried over to the dock to confer with me about the inspector's 'unfortunate remark'. I didn't hesitate to tell him I wanted a retrial. I imagined that if I stood accused alone I would have a better chance than if I was cheek by jowl with a bunch of obvious thugs. My counsel went off and entered into a whispered conversation with His Lordship, returning to say that the judge did not think that the jury had 'picked up' the inspector's reference to my having previously been to prison. But I insisted. I wanted a retrial.

The judge gave the order for the jury to be taken from the court, then, when the last good man and true had left the council chamber, Mr Justice Davies turned his attention to the hapless detective inspector. I almost felt sorry for him, such was the dressing down he received from the judge.

I was then discharged from the present trial without a verdict and ordered to be held in custody until the date of a new trial. I nursed a hope that my lawyers could arrange for the venue of my trial to be changed – perhaps to the Old Bailey – where friends could possibly 'get at' someone on the jury to hold out for a not guilty verdict. But it was decided that to try such a move might well be prejudicial to my situation. It wouldn't do to piss His Lordship off.

So the next day, when the gang were carted off to court, I stayed at the prison, once more the odd man out. I was allowed to pass my days in the company of Roger Cordrey, who was also not attending the trial because he had pleaded guilty. He was interesting, intelligent company, with an endless fund of anecdotes about his capers before the train robbery.

Three days after Inspector Morris had made his blunder, the case for the prosecution was closed. It was now up to the defence to make submissions to the judge and jury, offering arguments with regard to the innocence of their respective clients.

On Friday 14 February the defence began. The gang told their stories and produced their witnesses. If they were to be believed, few of the defendants should have been accused in the first place. Gordon Goody, for instance, couldn't have participated in the raid because he had been going about his business smuggling watches. Roy James, late on the night of 7 August, had engaged in a long conversation with a friendly taxi driver which took them into the wee small hours of the morning of the 8th. And so forth. The trial drifted on into March.

One mid-morning Roger and I heard the main prison gate opening. We went to the window of the dormitory and saw a police car drive in. Minutes later Johnny Daly, the man who had wanted to plead guilty, came to the door, trembling and pale faced.

'What's the trouble, John?' I asked. 'Are you ill?'

'No, I'm not ill. I've been acquitted!'

'Christ! You've been chucked? That's fantastic!' said Roger, delightedly. 'How? Why?'

'Reaburn [John's counsel] made a submission to the effect that the Monopoly set could have been taken to the farm after I left my prints on it. The jury accepted that fact and acquitted me. I've just come back to pick up my belongings. I'm free! But I can't believe it!'

Too bad I wasn't able to share the lucky Irishman's good fortune. My fingerprints were found not only on the Monopoly set, but also on a sauce bottle (I never thought they would 'ketchup' with me). It was the sauce bottle that tied me to the farm. A previous resident at Leatherslade Farm was the key witness and he swore that no such item had been left there.

Most of the explanations given by the gang during the trial for their fingerprints being found at the farm were, at best, ludicrous. Jimmy Hussey's palm print, for example, was found on the tailboard of the truck that was used in the robbery. His story was that an acquaintance had pulled up outside his home driving that very same vehicle. His friend was 'delivering some fruit and veg down the country somewhere' and invited Jim to go along for the ride. Unfortunately, Jim's poor old mum was not very well so he had to take care of her. However, thinking that there might be a nice apple within easy reach, Jim rested his hand against the tailboard ... the next thing you know, he's getting tugged in for the train robbery ... what a liberty!

My fairy story was even more pathetic. Charmian and I, the court were told, had been given the chance to buy the humble little house we were renting in Redhill. The owner, a retired policeman, had told us that if we could come up with £500 as a deposit we could pay the rest off weekly instead of paying rent. During a trip to London to visit my ailing father, I ran into an old prison chum named Norman Bickers. I told him about the 'golden opportunity' we had to buy our own home and that all we needed was the down payment. Norman was eager to help – after all, we had been cell-mates.

It so happened that Norman had been invited to join in 'a little piece of business' down the country somewhere. He was not at liberty to give me any details, but he was sure that I could take part in the venture. I would be away from home for four or five days, so it would be necessary to concoct some kind of a story to tell my wife. The tree-felling job was Norman's idea. He knew where I lived and he knew Charmian. It would be no problem to convince her that a few days away from home would provide us with the cash for the deposit on the house. It was arranged that I would tell my wife about the job and Norm would pick me up in his car on the morning of 6 August.

Charmian (who had agreed to play her part in my fairy story) waved us goodbye as we set out for 'somewhere in Wiltshire' to cut down trees. But instead of driving to Wiltshire we went to Leatherslade Farm in Buckinghamshire. The place was deserted when we got there, but we saw an army truck parked in one of the outbuildings. Inside the house, which was unlocked, we found a great amount of food, sleeping bags and army uniforms. I didn't like the look of it. I imagined that there was some kind of plan afoot to attack a military installation. I got cold feet and wanted out. But, much like Goldilocks in the house of the three bears, we fixed ourselves something to eat. Hence my fingerprints on the ketchup bottle and a Pyrex plate. After the snack we looked around and found – of all things – a Monopoly set! I opened the box; I hadn't played Monopoly since I was a kid. We decided to get out and go straight back to London, where I spent the next few days with Norman's friend, Brian Morse – another ex-con – arriving back in Redhill on Friday 10 August.

Later, when called upon to substantiate my story before the magistrate, Brian and Norm lied skilfully and convincingly, working hard for the £1000 apiece they were paid.

By now the gang, particularly Hussey, Wisbey and Welch, were feeling less confident about their chances of 'slipping out' of the case. There was some speculation as to what the sentences might be in the event of us being found guilty. According to *Archbold's Criminal Law and Practice*, the maximum term of imprisonment for robbery was fourteen years, but there appeared to be no limit for 'conspiring to rob', the second charge against us. 'Conspiring to blow up a bridge', however, carried a maximum sentence of fifteen years, so it was thought that our conspiracy charge was infinitely less serious. Bob Welch, a shrewd, inveterate gambler, sadly hit the jackpot.

'If we go down,' he predicted, 'we'll get thirties – mark my words.'

It was while I was awaiting my retrial, on 26 February, that I lost my prized radio. I was lying in my bed quietly listening to Sonny Liston defend his world title in Miami against the then Cassius Clay. Clay won the fight and the title after the sixth round when Liston refused to come out for the seventh. When he did I gave a little whoop of joy, as not only did I like Clay but I had money riding on him with other members of the gang. Unfortunately the screw outside the door heard my little cry and wanted to know what it was all about. At first I pretended that I could hear the radio being used by the screws in the yard outside my window, but I didn't think he was at all convinced. He wasn't, and the next day they started pulling my cell apart to look for things that had been smuggled in. They found the radio.

The closing speeches for the defence began on 10 March and ended on Saturday 14 March. The following Monday the judge began his summing-up. It took six days.

On Monday 23 March the jury retired to consider their verdicts, deliberating over their task for two whole days. With the exception of John Wheater, the solicitor Brian Field worked for, all the accused were found guilty on the conspiracy charge. Roy James, Charlie Wilson, Gordon Goody, Jimmy Hussey, Bobby Welch, Tommy Wisbey and Bill Boal (who was nowhere near the train or the farm) were also found guilty of robbery with violence. After hearing the verdicts, the judge decided not to pass sentence until my retrial had taken place.

On the morning of Wednesday 8 April I appeared once again before His Lordship Mr Justice Edmund Davies, but with a different jury. The prosecution went through all the evidence, some but not all of the witnesses being recalled.

Michael Argyle, peering over the top of his half-moon glasses, addressed the court with charm and eloquence in my defence, describing how I 'took fright' at the sight of the army uniforms at Leatherslade Farm. My case was looking reasonably good until Norman Bickers was called to support my alibi. He had mysteriously disappeared. A private detective was hired to find the missing witness, but to no avail. In the meantime, the foreman of the jury seemed to have taken a distinct dislike to me. The feeling was mutual – whenever I caught his eye I returned his sneer. With my key witness missing I could see my chances of acquittal were becoming less and less.

In his closing speech to the jury, Mr Argyle made a splendid effort to convince them of my innocence. But, in view of the fact that I had pleaded not guilty, Mr Arthur James, QC, prosecuting for the Crown, had the right to the famous 'last word'. And that word was 'Bullshit!'

The foreman lapped it up. There was no doubt in my mind what the verdict was going to be if it rested with him alone.

Mr Justice Davies finally summed up, eulogizing at length my learned counsel's manipulation of the English language.

'But, ladies and gentlemen of the jury,' he went on to say, 'let us keep our feet firmly on the ground. What the Crown says is so-and-so. And what the Crown says is this, that and the other.' The jury gaped. Then off they went to deliberate. It didn't take them long to come back with the verdict: guilty on both counts.

The next morning, 15 April, just over eight months since the robbery, we all left Aylesbury Prison in the Black Maria. This time we were not taken to the Rural District Council Chambers but instead were driven to the old Assize Court and locked into chilly cells beneath the courtroom. A steep, narrow staircase led up to the dock where, one by one, we were called to receive our sentences. Roger Cordrey, who had pleaded guilty, was the first up.

'Roger John Cordrey,' said the judge. 'You are the first to be sentenced out of certainly eleven greedy men whom hope of gain allured. You and your co-accused have been convicted of complicity, in one way or another, in a crime which in its impudence and enormity is the first of its kind in this country. I propose to do all within my power to ensure it will be the last of its kind; for your outrageous conduct constitutes an intolerable menace to the well-being of society.'

The judge went on at length with a prepared text which was obviously aimed more at the general public's perception of the case than at the man in the dock. He referred to the robbery as a 'sordid crime of violence' and he did not miss the opportunity to mention the 'nerve-shattered engine driver' whose treatment by the gang had had such a 'terrifying effect on law-abiding citizens'.

Mr Justice Davies did, however, recognize that within the gang there were two exceptions, one of whom was Roger, which hardly prepared Cordrey for what came next.

'In respect of the four counts,' the judge announced, 'you must go to prison for twenty years.' Prison officers hustled Roger from the dock and down a second flight of steps to a different line of cells as the court took in what the judge had said.

Little Billy Boal, who was neither a conspirator nor one of the robbers, was next to be called for sentence.

'William Gerald Boal,' said His Lordship, 'you who are substantially the oldest of the accused, have been convicted of conspiracy to rob the mail and of armed robbery itself. You have expressed no repentance for your wrong-doing, indeed, you continue to assert your innocence, yet you beg for mercy. I propose to extend to you some measure of mercy. The concurrent sentences you will serve are, upon the first count, twenty-one years and upon the second count, twenty-four years.' Boal was the second exception.

Charles Frederick Wilson followed. The judge, now warming to his task, told Charlie, 'It would be an affront to the public weal that any of you should be at liberty in anything like the near future to enjoy any of those ill-gotten gains. Accordingly, it is in no spirit of mere retribution that I propose to secure that such an opportunity will be denied all of you for an extremely long time. On the first count you will go to prison for twenty-five years and on the second count you will be sentenced to thirty years.' Charlie was taken down to join Roger and Billy Boal. It was my turn.

'Ronald Arthur Biggs, yesterday you were convicted of both the first and second counts of this indictment. Your learned counsel has urged that you had no special talent and that you were plainly not an originator of the conspiracy. These and all other submissions I bear in mind, but the truth is that I do not know when you entered the conspiracy, or what part you played in it. What I do know is you are a specious and facile liar and you have this week, in this court, perjured yourself time and time again, but I add not a day to your sentence on this account. Your previous record qualifies you do be sentenced to preventive detention; that I shall not do. Instead the sentence of the court upon you in respect of the first count is twenty-five years' imprisonment and in respect of the second count, thirty years' imprisonment. These sentences to be served concurrently.'

The old boy's totally off his rocker, I thought to myself. Only spies get locked away for thirty years. With remission for good behaviour, I calculated, it meant that I was looking to do at least twenty years in the nick. Twice the amount of bird you might get for bumping somebody off, for Christ's sake!

Charmian stood above in the public gallery, pale and shattered. As I was led in the direction of the 'down' staircase I looked up and gave her a wave and a smile. I may have lost a battle, but I knew the war was far from over.

'What did you get?' asked Charlie as I joined him, Roger and Billy Boal in the cells.

'Thirty!'

'Same as me. Bill got twenty-four and Roger got twenty on a guilty plea, for fuck's sake.'

Wisbey, Welch and Hussey, all sentenced to thirty years, joined us in swift succession. Then came Roy James, bewildered with his thirty-year sentence.

'Who's dead?' he asked. 'Did we kill somebody?'

Swashbuckling Gordon 'Checker' Goody came down from the court tight-lipped, also with thirty years. Bobby Welch had been right.

Brian Field was sentenced to twenty-five years' imprisonment for conspiracy with a concurrent five years for obstructing justice. Lennie Field – no relation to Brian – who was paid £500 to 'buy' Leatherslade Farm received a similar sentence. John Wheater, Brian Field's boss, who had been only marginally involved in the conveyance of the farm, was sent down for three years.

The gang was demolished. The villains had got their just deserts. Newspapers sold like hot cakes. Meanwhile, back at the nick, they were waiting for us. We were only given time to pick up our personal belongings and shake hands with each other. Then, handcuffed and under heavy police escorts, we were taken individually to different prisons around the country.

I wasn't told where I was going but from road signs I gathered that my new home – at least for the time being – was to be Her Majesty's Prison in Lincoln.

At 'reception' I exchanged my sports jacket and cavalry twill pants for an ill-fitting 'Special Watch' prison uniform. The cons working in the area were friendly, almost reverent – never before had they seen anyone with a thirty stretch. I could even feel a certain sympathy from the screws, and the prison medical officer made a joke that he and I could change places – for the right price.

At the time, it was recognized that Lincoln was a 'cushy' nick. The next morning I was presented to the prison governor, who turned out to be none other than the discipline-minded Commander Cook, governor of Lewes jail when I had been sent there in 1949. It saddened him to see me in front of him under such unhappy circumstances, he said, and it was his unhappy duty to inform me that my earliest possible date of release was 16 February 1984.

I laughed. 'The time will soon pass, sir.' I would be fifty-four.

'Really, Biggs,' said the commander in a voice I had never heard back in the old days. 'It's hardly a laughing matter. Now look, if there is anything you need, don't hesitate to ask – I'll help you all I can. And Biggs, keep the chin up!'

For quite some time there had been various mentions in the newspapers about the possibility of a parole scheme being introduced into the British penal system. Under this scheme prisoners would be eligible for parole after serving just one third of their sentence. Remission, on the other hand, offered a third off the total sentence for good behaviour. Although it was clutching at a straw, I told myself that such a scheme was obviously about to be introduced, and that this had been taken into consideration when the thirty-year sentences were dished out. Perhaps I would see a light at the end of the tunnel after I had served ten years or so.

On the day we were sentenced, our respective counsels lodged appeals against the severity of the sentences. I didn't entertain high hopes that there would be any reduction – in fact, we were running the risk of having the sentences increased. For the time being, I decided to play it cool.

I was allowed to exercise with other Special Watch prisoners and offers to help me escape were soon being made. The main wall around the prison seemed much lower than ones I had seen at other nicks, and it appeared to be reasonably easy to put an escape plan together. But I decided to wait until the appeal had been heard before making any moves to 'have it away'. In any case, after less than two weeks in Lincoln I was transferred without explanation to HMP Chelmsford.

At Chelmsford the wall was higher, but the food was better. A friendly prison officer, who was the physical training instructor, noticed that I was pretty much 'out of shape' and arranged for me to have daily work-outs in the gymnasium. A fellow Special Watch con, 'Spider' Webb, showed interest in my get-fit sessions and approached me with an escape plan that 'couldn't fail'. It sounded good, but I told him that I was going to wait until my appeal had been heard before thinking about going over the wall.

Early in July, once again under maximum security conditions, the gang was reassembled in HMP Brixton. On arrival we were immediately placed on Rule 43, which meant that we were to be held incommunicado. We were allowed to exercise, but never more than two or three of us in the yard at any one time. We were supposed to walk separately, in silence, but we took little notice of the screws trying to impose this order. On one of these exercise periods, I found myself in the company of Gordon Goody and Jimmy Hussey. We kept 'bunching up', as the screws put it, and from time to time one of them would stop us to spread us out.

'Now keep a space between you, lads,' one said. 'If the governor comes by and sees you all walking together, I'm the one who's going to drop a bollock.' Spacing us out for the fourth or fifth time, the screw said, 'I've been standing here thinking: you three blokes are facing ninety years' imprisonment between you!'

'That's right, guv,' said Jimmy with a straight face, 'and half a million fucking quid!'

One member of the gang who decided to play it even cooler than I did was Charlie Wilson, who didn't even bother to appear at the Court of Criminal Appeal when the hearing began. Charlie had a plan and that plan included staying put in HMP Winson Green, Birmingham. If he attended the appeal he ran the danger of being transferred to another prison.

The appeals were over, Roger and his friend Bill Boal had their sentences reduced to fourteen years. In Boal's case, the court saw that his physique and temperament did not fit him for a part in the robbery.

The two Fields were 'lucky'. Their appeals against conviction on the conspiracy charge were allowed and they left the court facing only five years. The rest of the appeals were dismissed – including Charlie's, which was heard in his absence. But the best was yet to come. The next day I was transferred to HMP Wandsworth, Britain's answer, at the time, to Alcatraz. As far as HM Government was concerned this was to be my home for at least the next twenty years. In 1994 that would mean contemplating the idea of being locked up in a small room until the year 2014. Not a happy prospect if you want to get out with all your marbles intact. In the event, as history records, Wandsworth was to be my home for just a few days over one year.

> The same old screws with the same old bull;
> 'All correct, sir! Three bags full!'
> The same old chief – still scratching his balls,
> The same old wit on the white-washed walls;
> 'McGinnis was here, ten years hard labour,
> Do thy bird and love thy neighbour.'
> The same sharp cons, the same old slags.
> The same old stench of mailbags.
> The same old padre with the same old text:
> Make peace with God! – you might be next.
>
> Ronald Biggs

# 5. Escape – The Making of a Legend

All too soon the shouts of the screws:
'Unlock the ones! Unlock the twos!
Empty your piss pots then bang up your doors.
Unlock the threes! Unlock the fours!
Downstairs transfers to Dartmoor and Norwich.
'Old out your plate lad. 'Ere comes your porridge.'

Ronald Biggs

I have much patience and equanimity but I am rapidly losing both and, quite frankly, rather than finding it more difficult to escape, I am finding it difficult not to!

Prisoner 2731, Biggs, in a letter from Wandsworth Prison<br>to Marcus Lipton, Labour MP for Brixton

Had I not escaped from Her Majesty's Prison in Wandsworth, South London, there would never have been a 'Ronnie Biggs' to talk about and this is something that is sometimes overlooked.

At the time of the train robbery no one person involved was any more famous than any other. That is at least as far as the general public were concerned, although I am sure that the Yard had its favourites. Admittedly some of us did get a head start with the media: Roy James for being a promising driver, myself for the mistrial, and Bruce and Buster for still being at large at the time of the trial.

But while the man in the street could name the gang to a man during the trial of 1964, thirty years on – and thanks mainly to the media – the names to stick are Biggs and Buster. Those of the right age may remember Charlie Wilson for his escape to Canada and his murder in Spain, and Bruce Reynolds as the brain, but the other names have mostly been forgotten with the passing of time.

In just the same way, in 1966, the British public could name England's World Cup side. Today the players who are remembered are remembered not so much for what they did on the day but for the combination of other moments that marked their career. One of the moments that marked my career was the escape from Wandsworth Prison in 1965.

Now you don't have to be a contestant on *Mastermind* to realize that any man sentenced to thirty years behind bars is going to think at least once about how to escape. Normally the thought went as far as getting over the wall; what you did after that as one of Britain's most wanted criminals was a bridge to be crossed when you came to it.

When I was first sentenced I was given about five minutes to talk to Charmian before I was taken off to the cells. She was upset and crying, but I told her not to be like that as she, more than anyone, should know that I was not going to stick around and spend a lot of time in prison if I didn't have to. I would be out the first chance I got.

I wasn't being totally sincere with Charm or myself, however, as at the time I honestly did believe that a parole scheme would come about and if it only meant doing ten years then I was going to do those ten years and get them out of the way as fast as I could. The only way to do that was to keep my nose clean. That is what I tried to indicate to the authorities when I got to Wandsworth, but I think they took it with a pinch of salt; given my record, the idea of Biggs keeping his nose clean was a little hard for them to contemplate.

I think all the members of the gang knew that whoever escaped first would have the best chance of getting away with it, as once a couple of us had got out the security around the rest would become much tighter. Yet at the time, all of us would have considered that escaping from an HM Prison was something of a doddle. If it was easy to stop and rob a train, it was even easier to escape from the nick. It was not a question of 'if' we would get out but 'when'.

Charlie Wilson was the first to walk. And walk he did after being abducted from Winson Green Prison in Birmingham on 12 August 1964. Three men, described as 'strangers', somehow got him over the prison wall and into a waiting car – wearing only his vest – without leaving the vestige of a clue. He was on the run for over three and a half years before being recaptured in Canada. It was the capture of Bruce and Buster and the recapture of Charlie that kept my picture and name in the press, just at the time when I was hoping to slip into a life of Australian obscurity.

On the same day as the appeal was turned down I was transferred from Brixton to Wandsworth, a prison I knew well and hated. But being sent to Wandsworth had its advantages and I certainly knew its ropes.

In a very short time I had a miniature radio smuggled in and every Saturday afternoon Joe, the landing cleaner and a fellow con, would deposit a bucket of murky water with a floor cloth and scrubbing brush outside my cell door with a view to having a 'scrub out'. Down in the depths of the inky water would be lurking a tin of crab, lobster, corned beef, peanuts and half a bottle of whisky. The empty tins and bottles went out the same way.

I was first put to work – for a few brief hours each day – in the mailbag shop, hand-sewing mailbags for the GPO. I was considered a 'security risk' and categorized as a Special Watch Prisoner. There were thirty or more cons in this category, most of us with a history of having broken out of one nick or another. We had coloured patches sewn on to our jackets and trousers and we were denied certain 'privileges' such as evening classes and 'open' visits. We worked immediately in front of a watchful prison officer. To relieve the tedium I became a bookmaker.

Almost as soon as I arrived in Wandsworth I began receiving offers from various cons to help me escape, but I turned them all down. One of these offers came from the prisoner who was working beside me, Paul Seabourne. Paul was at the tail-end of a four-year sentence, with less than a year to serve. He had a good reputation among the other cons and was known to be 'as game as a bygone', having escaped from Wandsworth during the sentence he was serving.

Paul and I became good friends. I liked his dry sense of humour. I turned down his first offer to get me out, using my argument about the introduction of a parole scheme and getting out legally after ten years or less.

'You're dreaming,' Paul said. 'There has been talk of a parole scheme for donkey's years. In any case, you can't be serious that you're prepared to face ten years' bird?'

I assured him I was.

It eventually got to a point where Paul and I started to annoy one another, him wanting to get me out and me refusing. Finally he told me that he was simply against the idea that I had been handed a thirty-year sentence for robbing a train.

'It's a fucking diabolical liberty, that's what it is,' he said, 'and I intend to get you out. I don't want any of your lousy train money, either. I'm a thief and I'll steal my own money.'

Paul loved the idea of getting me or anyone else out of Wandsworth. The idea of my escape really turned him on. I think to him it was a way to fuck with the authorities. To stick it to them on a grand scale.

On the Glorious Twelfth Charlie was 'spirited away' from Winson Green. I was delighted for Charlie and not in the slightest bit surprised that he had 'had it away'. The Home Office was far less elated and orders were given to double up on the security with regard to the train gang.

A screw was posted outside my cell door full time and would peer at me through the Judas flap at fifteen-minute intervals. I could hear him coughing, sneezing, farting and humming to himself. His chair creaked with every movement, he would have conversations with passing screws or the night-watchman and I could hear him messing with his Thermos flask and sandwiches. At first I asked him politely to make less noise but to no avail, so I became more abusive.

As a result I started being subjected to frequent 'changes of location', sometimes at midnight or later – the idea apparently being that this would confuse would-be rescuers. Nobody seemed to consider that it would have been all too easy for me to have hung some kind of marker from the window ledge to show my new location!

Wherever I went in the prison during the day I was escorted by two screws. I couldn't even take a crap without one of my vigilantes checking me out from time to time.

After a few weeks of the 'extra security measures' I felt that my health was being affected, so I asked the governor, 'Gusty' Gale, to relax the pressure, showing him my trembling hands.

The governor was very sorry, he said, but his orders were from the Home Office and those orders were quite clear.

'I have to detain you in this prison, Biggs – and detain you I shall. About turn. March out.'

Later, in the exercise yard I told Paul that if the offer was still open I wanted him to get me out.

From that moment in the yard Paul and I started plotting, considering every possible angle to put together a plan that was going to work. Every exercise period would be taken up exploring the ways and means of getting me over the wall. I had to curb some of my friend's enthusiasm: at one point he suggested storming the gate lodge at night, tying up the screws and releasing everybody!

In the middle of our scheming an old friend, Dennis Stafford, came to Wandsworth with a six-month sentence to serve. Dennis had achieved notoriety when he escaped from the grim confines of Dartmoor Prison back in the fifties. He was a very bright chap and a helicopter pilot.

Without knowing that Paul and I were already hatching an escape plan, Dennis was soon offering his professional aviation services. I passed this information on to Paul, who glowed with the idea of 'riding shotgun' on a helicopter break-out of the exercise yard. But some time before I had been transferred to Wandsworth, during my short sojourn at Chelmsford, a helicopter had flown low over the jail during an exercise period. In an instant two screws were at my side and my stroll around the flower garden of HMP Chelmsford came to an abrupt end.

I have to admit that I rather liked the idea of an airborne exit from Wandsworth, but I was looking for something a little bit more practical and with fewer risks. Then one day the idea of a removal van came to mind and I asked Paul just how tall the average van was.

'Not tall enough to reach the top of the wall, if that's what you're thinking' was his immediate answer. 'But I like the idea.'

We made some calculations using my experience in the building trade to work out the exact height of the prison wall by counting the number of brick courses. It was over twenty-five feet high.

'What about a platform on top of a furniture van?' I suggested.

'Charming,' he scoffed, 'Old Bill seeing us heading in the direction of Wandsworth nick in a removal van with a platform on top is never going to wonder what we're up to!' But he thought about it.

At this time another friendly face appeared in the Special Watch section of the mailbag workshop. His name was Eric Flower. Eric was a pal from my early days in the boob. We had been Young Prisoners together at Lewes in 1949 at the time when I had met the Post Office sorter by the name of Kitson.

Eric had been sentenced to twelve years for robbery and had lodged an appeal against the severity of his sentence, while knowing full well that he stood little or no chance of having it reduced. As a prisoner on appeal, however, he was able to receive visitors on a daily basis and I immediately saw that this could be very useful with regard to passing messages in and out of the prison.

At first Paul was reluctant to let anyone else in on our plan for fear of a possible leak. But I convinced him with the argument that if we didn't include Eric he would soon organize a plan of his own which could very well harm ours.

I didn't have to twist Eric's arm to 'make one' on our piece of business and I was more convinced than ever that with him aboard we were going to pull it off.

During the weekdays, Special Watch inmates were exercised in a yard that was flanked by the main prison wall. On the other side was a narrow service road which ran around the prison and on to the main road and freedom.

Exercise took place in the afternoon in two one-hour periods: two o'clock until three and three until four. A senior prison officer was always in charge and he would appear in the workshop just before 2 p.m. to make a random selection of half the Special Watch cons for the first exercise period. Those passed over at this time would automatically be taken into the yard at three o'clock as the first batch returned to the workshop. As we could not guarantee being picked for the first period, in order to ensure that we were in the yard at a pre-arranged time we would have to be 'missing' from the workshop at 2 p.m. on E-day.

As soon as I had decided to go over the wall I embarked on a get-fit routine as I was quite a bit overweight. I obtained some books from the prison library on yoga and physical training and had a one hour work-out every evening. At night I listened to my miniature radio which was tucked under my pillow and only just loud enough for me to hear. An Australian pop group, the Seekers, had a hit at the time which was my inspiration: it contained the line 'There's a new world somewhere they call the promised land.' Years later I was to meet them in Melbourne when I was working as a carpenter at the Channel 9 TV station.

Charmian knew about the escape plan and was very excited at the possibility of seeing her loving lord in liberty. A month or so before Paul was due to be released, Charm received a communication from a friend of ours, Brian Stone. Brian was in Brixton Prison on remand facing some spurious cheque charges and needed financial assistance. I gave Charmian the green light to arrange a lawyer to defend our friend and soon enough there he was sitting beside us in the mailbag shop!

Despite the circumstances of our meeting Brian was 'over the moon' with the four-year sentence he had received, as he had been expecting to go down for a much longer stretch.

'If I can help you in any way,' he said as we shook hands, 'don't hesitate to ask.' He was to prove as good as his word.

I had figured that Eric and I were going to need a little help on E-day. There would be four screws in the exercise yard and it was a certainty that they would come running as soon as we started scaling the wall.

I talked it over with Eric and Paul and we decided to ask Brian to mind us as we went into action. Brian didn't think twice when I put it to him, but he suggested that there should be a second 'minder' to tangle with the screws. Paul was already uptight about too many people knowing about the escape, but he agreed that two minders were better than one.

I decided, at Brian's suggestion, to have a wee word with a young lad from Glasgow. I told him that I needed someone to help me go over the wall. I stipulated that I didn't want any violence and all he would have to do would be to grab a screw and hang on. I offered him £500, the equivalent of close to £6000 today, for his help.

'I don't want your money, Biggsy,' said the Scot. 'I'll do it for the prestige.' The brotherhood of prison life really does exist.

Days before Paul's release we were doing dummy runs, rehearsing ways and means of avoiding the first exercise period. Dwelling in the bog seemed to be sound, and a 'sudden excruciating pain in the gut' was another sure-fire way to be taken to the prison hospital for a dose of 'white mixture', a concoction that was administered for practically everything. 'Guaranteed to cure coughs, colds, sore holes and pimples on the dicky,' as the hospital orderlies were wont to say. But a hospital visit was a good enough excuse to be missing from the workshop for half an hour or so.

As Eric was able to receive visitors every day, he got his friends and family to arrive at 1.30 p.m. on the dot, thus avoiding the first exercise call. There was also a storeroom in the workshop where one could go to have a pair of scissors sharpened or get more mailbag thread and 'not hear' the first call for walkies. On one of his visits Eric was able to smuggle in the business part of a small ladies wristwatch that was to be vital for timing ourselves in the exercise yard.

It had been arranged that on the day Paul would go into action at exactly 3.10 p.m., giving us enough time to make sure we were in the yard. We discovered that it took approximately half a minute to get from the toilet block to the main wall at a point between two screws.

The yoga started to pay off nicely. One evening a screw named Armstrong opened my cell door and saw me doing press-ups.

'What are you doing, Biggsy?' he gibed. 'Getting ready for your release?'

I smiled at his little joke. 'Something like that, Mr Armstrong.'

'I bet you wish you were!' he guffawed as he walked on.

Not long afterwards a certain Mrs Armstrong witnessed us coming over the wall 'full of the joys of spring', as she put it.

When I had finally given Paul the word that I wanted to escape he made two stipulations. Money to cover his expenses and an introduction to 'someone you can call your friend'. I assured him there was cash available and he would be working with a very staunch friend, Mickey Haynes.

The eve of Paul's release arrived and there was the customary leg-pulling by the screws. 'You'll be back!' and so forth. The cons were sorry to see him go; he had been good company, distinguished by his humour and indomitable spirit.

Paul lost no time in contacting Charmian and we soon began receiving 'progress reports' via Eric's visitors. Our 'bird' was dragging. E-day was set for Wednesday 7 July 1965.

As it turned out E-day was a typical English summer day. The forecast was rain!

When my cell was unlocked soon after 1.30 p.m. the screw found me doubled up in agony, gasping for medical attention. To say it must have been something I ate wasn't that far-fetched in Wandsworth! Two screws were summoned to escort me to the sick bay. The quack had seen it all before and, as I had expected, prescribed a good dose of 'white mixture'. Miracle of miracles, it worked and by 2.30 p.m. I was fully recovered and back in the mailbag workshop, sewing away.

Eric was smiling after having spent the last half-hour with his loved ones, while Brian was looking relieved after a similar length of time on the crapper. Wee Jock also looked confident as he emerged from the storeroom.

At 3 p.m., as expected, the call went up to put our work away and line up for exercise. Before five past three we were in the yard and, conforming to regulations, were walking around the footpath in pairs, Eric and I together, Brian and Jock a few yards ahead. The wall was almost within touching distance.

Dark clouds lowered above us and it began to drizzle.

Fuck!

The discipline officer – the screw in charge of the exercise – gave a signal to the other three screws to take us back into the prison wing for 'indoor exercise'. I protested, pointing out that it was only raining lightly, but as I was speaking the heavens opened and it started to piss down. Eric and I exchanged dejected looks.

At the very same moment the escape team was trundling towards the prison in their converted furniture van. But when Paul saw the rain he knew from experience that we would be taken off the yard. Given Britain's inclement weather we had foreseen the situation and it had been decided that should rain 'stop play' we would carry out the same procedure the following day.

Happily nothing we or the escape team had done had attracted any attention, so the escape was very much on. But there was still the frustration of knowing that we had nearly done it and would have to do it all over again. We would all have to be missing from our place of work the next day when the screws chose the cons for the first exercise period. Whether it meant having a crap, sharpening our scissors, going special sick or whatever, not one of the four of us could afford to be in the workshop until well after 2 p.m.

The delay had given Paul some extra time and he decided to tour the phone boxes in the direct vicinity of the escape and disconnect the mouthpieces to stop people telephoning our getaway to the police or reporting a suspicious-looking van. We only discovered later that not even a prison of the size and importance of Wandsworth had a direct line to the police. When I did go over the top the screws had to call 999 like everyone else and this meant a twenty-minute delay until the cops arrived.

Thursday 8 July, one year and eleven months to the day since the robbery, the sun rose brightly over London and I sensed that this was going to be the day. Charmian, who must have been fed up of traipsing off to museums with the kids as an alibi, set off for Whipsnade Zoo in Bedfordshire. She also thought that after the disappointment of Wednesday this would be the day.

Never had the exercise yard looked so good. I felt like peeing with pleasure, so we headed for the toilets, where – surprise,

surprise – Brian and Jock were to be found just shaking the drops off as Eric and I arrived.

'Tell me, do you boys hang around here all the time?' I said. With his back to the screw, who was watching closely to make sure that no one was having a crafty smoke, Eric checked the time by his watch and gave a nod. The four of us joined the other cons on exercise.

As we drew level with the wall I heard the sound of a heavy vehicle on the other side. I stopped to tie my shoelace, looking up at the wall. Suddenly, a head in a nylon stocking appeared. A split second later the first of the rope ladders came snaking down the wall. As Eric and I made for them the screws came running, blowing their whistles. Brian and Jock went into action.

As I cocked my leg over the wall Paul, the man in the nylon mask, greeted me.

'Hello, you big ugly bastard!' I gave him a slap on the back and looked down at the mêlée in the prison yard. My boys were hanging on to the screws as if they loved them.

'You're too late,' Brian shouted gleefully, 'Biggsy's away.'

The truck was parked close to the wall, something that would be unthinkable today, so it was an easy matter to drop on to the roof. A large rectangular opening had been cut in the van to allow a five-foot hinged platform to be pushed up through the roof, giving Paul those vital extra feet needed to reach the top of the wall and throw the rope ladders down. On the floor of the van were a number of old mattresses for us to jump down on to. A getaway car was parked nearby with Paul's trusty friend, Ronnie Leslie, at the wheel. Two other cons seized the opportunity to follow us over the wall and because of this Paul never got to burn the truck as he had planned.

Besides Ronnie Leslie, a motor mechanic who had worked on converting the van, there was a third member of the escape team, Ronnie Black, a Ron I had had my doubts about.

Ronnie Black had spent time with me in Wandsworth where he had proved to be a bit of a hothead. The last thing I wanted was to have any kind of violence. No guns and no violence was a strict rule and Paul had grudgingly agreed to go along with this. I was pissed off, therefore, when I heard that there had been a shotgun involved. But Paul just offered to put me back inside.

There is also a story that before we got over the wall Blackie had locked some screw's child in an outside toilet after he had emerged suddenly from a house.

As Eric and I scrambled into the car with Paul and the two Ronnies, the other two Special Watch cons came racing to the car looking for a lift.

'Let 'em in,' I shouted. They piled in and we zoomed off, full of the joys of being sprung.

We had made it!

We had done it!

We had fucking escaped from Wandsworth!

Despite the initial euphoria we still had a long way to go. The car raced around the perimeter wall, all seven of us piled inside. It was the only route to freedom and the main road. As we sped off our way was nearly blocked by a prison work party with a dust cart. Happily the screw, not knowing who we were, pulled them off the road and waved us through. If he had left the cart in the road our exit would have been blocked.

We drove on, four of us desperately trying to tear off our telltale Special Watch prison uniforms. A police car passed us going in the other direction, but there never seemed any danger of our being stopped.

Even without being chased or followed we went through with Paul's plan. It took us to a quiet cul-de-sac close to the prison where we dumped the first car and ran up a footpath leading to a second car. If Old Bill had been in pursuit we would have run down the alley and hoped that they did *not* have a second car waiting.

As the second car had been hired on a dodgy brief we told the two opportunists that they could use it after they had dropped us off and go as far as they liked until the next day, when a scream would go out for it. The first to be dropped off were the two Ronnies at Tooting Bec Station. The five of us then went on to Dulwich where Eric, Paul and I left the car close to our destination. Our final address was not something we wanted to broadcast to our uninvited guests who, without a plan, were more likely than us to get picked up.

When I was in hiding I read that our guests had been caught after three months. One of them, Anderson, had been one of my heaviest punters in the prison and owed me ten ounces of tobacco when we escaped. As he dropped us I asked, 'Hey! What about my ten ounces?'

'I'll pay you the next time I see you,' he replied with a wink. He still owes me.

Even after all these years I can't help thinking about the king-sized bollocking the governor must have had for the manner of my escape. That was just fine with me, because he had not believed me when I said I wanted to be treated like every other con. He had said that it could not be. When I told him that everything he was doing was going to drive me over the wall, he saw this as insolence. I was not trying to be insolent, I was trying to be perfectly honest, man to man, and show that it would be too much for me to endure. In the end I think I proved my point.

Charmian heard of my escape on the four o'clock news on the radio when they announced that four men had gone over the wall of Wandsworth, one of whom was 'believed' to be train robber Ronald Biggs.

# 6. On the Run: London–Bognor–Antwerp–Paris–Sydney

The hide-out was the upstairs flat of a semi-detached house in a quiet Dulwich road. On that lazy summer afternoon the road was deserted and Paul, Eric and I appeared to be just three young men going about their business. Suddenly Eric noticed the barrel of the shotgun sticking out from a sports coat that Paul was carrying under his arm. Oops!

Two young people were at the flat when we arrived: Paul's brother-in-law, George Gibbs, and his wife Jean. Eric threw me a furtive glance indicating that he was far from happy about 'unknowns' being on the scene.

'George is sound,' Paul assured us, 'and so is the girl.' It was now just after 3.30 p.m.

'Open up the champers, for Christ's sake!' I exclaimed.

We celebrated and toasted Paul. Another bottle of champers was cracked as we sat around the telly to catch news of the escape. Exit Biggs and co. – enter Mrs Armstrong! They announced that it had taken Old Bill twenty minutes to get to the nick.

'If I'd known, I would've made you buggers walk,' Paul remarked with obvious pride.

Although for the moment we were safe I could see that Eric wanted to arrange somewhere more secure for us to hole up. He had friends in East London and as soon as it was dark he slipped out of the house to make a phone call to one of them. He returned looking elated – his friends would be arriving in less than an hour. Now it was Paul's turn to be troubled. He wanted to know more about Eric's pals.

'I promised to get you out and I did,' Paul said, 'and I want you to stay out. You would be as safe here as anywhere.'

Eric could not agree. 'Paul,' he said, 'Old Bill is going to turn over every drum in South London. They must know that we're not far from the boob. My people will have us safely down in the country by tomorrow morning.'

I had to admit that the idea of getting off the manor appealed and I was certain that Eric wouldn't be putting us in the hands of mugs. We also knew that Paul would be the number one suspect for putting together the escape. In the prison workshop it must have looked as if we were Siamese twins at times, the way our heads were always locked together. Paul didn't seem too worried about the possibility of getting his collar felt, but as Eric was quick to point out, if the Old Bill were looking for Paul it would automatically lead them to us. We had also picked up that Paul and George's wife were on extra friendly terms, and George didn't look too happy about it. Ever super-security conscious Eric saw this as another good reason not to dwell in Dulwich.

With the arrival of Eric's friends the once spacious living room looked crowded. Both men were twice the size of Paul and unmistakably villains. Paul was wearing his worried look again. He had recognized one of the heavies. When the chance came he drew me into another room.

'Look,' he said, 'I know Alfie and I can tell you he's bad news. They're not here to do you any favours and they know you've got lots of dough tucked away.' He produced a Walther pistol. 'Take this to look after yourself. You're out, now make sure you stay out. Use this if you have to.'

I refused to take the gun. I told Paul I didn't need it and that I could take care of myself better without one.

'Do you know what you are?' he said. 'A big, ugly bastard!'

Alfie and his mate got into the front of the car which they had parked a short distance along the street. Moments later Eric and I slipped into the back and crouched down on the seat. We were tired. It had been a long and, to say the least, exciting day.

Morning noises filled the room but they were city noises. We were not 'in the country', but in a humble tenement building in Bermondsey.

An elderly docker by the name of Tom was our landlord for the next few days. We were provided with clothes, loads of good grub and booze and a record player, plus a pile of LPs which had been knocked off from a shop in the Charing Cross Road a few days earlier. Life was starting to look considerably better than it had done a few days earlier.

If Lady Luck was looking after old Biggsy, she wasn't as kind to the other people involved. Days after we moved on from Dulwich, as Detective Chief Superintendent Tommy Butler and his Flying Squad crew were raiding every hang-out where he thought Eric and I might be found, Paul was arrested. Paul was to serve four and a half years specifically for getting me out of prison, but many more indirectly for later crimes because the authorities were always out to get him for springing me from Wandsworth. Paul knew he would get caught, but he didn't care. My freedom was and is his reward. His only charges for getting me out of prison were expenses – which were virtually nothing – and some money for Ronnie Leslie. When I got over the wall I had to force £1000 on Paul as a show of gratitude, but he only took it because of his old lady.

Ronnie Leslie got three years for helping Paul, while Brian Stone and his mate Jock, instead of being picked for England and Scotland to strengthen their defence, were given an extra twelve months apiece for their rugby tackles on the screws.

A week or so later we were moved from Bermondsey to a new address, this time to a spacious apartment in Camberwell. While we were there we were introduced to a friend of Alfie's named George. This sharp-looking fellow represented an 'organization' capable of taking care of travel arrangements for people like Eric and myself. Thomas Cook they were not. With great self-assurance, George outlined a 'package deal' which consisted of temporary passports, a boat trip to the Continent, a car transfer to Paris, plastic surgery ('complete facial reforming by one of the most famous names in European cosmetic surgery' was how he put it), real passports in our 'new image' and airline tickets to 'anywhere in the world'.

The price?

A mere eighty grand. Close to £950,000 at today's prices. A bargain, George assured me, as a lot of people would have to be paid off. With a bit of haggling the price fell to £40,000. £20,000 down and the rest after the ops in Paris. There was also the question of a further £15,000 for the safe passage of Charmian, Eric's wife Carol and the kids to join us at our final destination. A cool £55,000 was spent, more than £650,000 at today's rates and roughly a third of what I had netted from the robbery.

The 'organization' I talk of had nothing to do with the train robbery – despite what people would like to believe – but is a body that helps those with the right connections. It almost certainly got Buster Edwards out of Britain and more than likely Charlie Wilson. But I am only guessing.

My contact with Charmian was at first restricted to calls to phone boxes in and around London, the numbers of which she had jotted down in the weeks before my escape. I have always assumed that Charmian's movements were monitored during this period, but, despite the escape, Scotland Yard never contacted her directly.

As the preparations for the move to Paris would take some time our minders decided that we should make yet another move. Once again, just after dark, we were picked up and spirited across London to our new digs. This time we would be sharing a room with a private detective! An Irishman whom, for his current peace of mind, I'll call Mick. The apartment was in a house somewhere between Putney and Richmond which belonged to a pleasant couple, also friends of Alfie. Everyone was in the villainy business, including the Irish detective, and, as Alfie noted, 'Here you are among your own.'

We were made very welcome by our host and the grog flowed. Mick entertained us into the wee small hours with hilarious tales about his clients and his work, which normally involved observing wayward husbands while he got pissed on Guinness.

Mick insisted that Eric and I should sleep in his double bed and that he would be quite happy sleeping on the floor with his faithful friend, Prince, a docile German Shepherd. The only window in the room had been blacked out by a thick curtain.

'Sure we wouldn't want the neighbours looking in now, would we?' was Mick's only concern. Indeed we wouldn't, and it meant that we could sleep late, more often than not being woken by the phone and one of Mick's more hysterical clients.

Now Mick was one of those people who had the knack of coming out of a deep sleep and being able to sound sensible and fully alert in an instant. He would come alive with the wildest line of bullshit imaginable.

'Mrs Parker? . . . Good morning, Mrs Parker . . . Yes, it's a wonderful morning. I've very good news for you. Your husband is not meeting another woman . . . No! I hope that puts your mind at rest, Mrs Parker. Believe me, nothing more than a few drinks with the boys and a game or two of darts . . . Thank you, Mrs Parker.'

With that he would roll over and show the true Mick we had come to know and love: 'God, my head! What's th' fuckin' time, Ron?'

Although we were enjoying the company of Mick and Co, we were not getting any exercise to speak of. It was still summertime and I was hankering to feel the sun on my body. As we were, we were only improving our prison pallor.

Leafing through a copy of the *Evening News* one day, I spotted an ad: Bognor Regis: 3 bedrooms; garden; quiet, secluded neighbourhood. I showed it to Eric and he was as enthusiastic as I was.

'If we could get that,' he said proudly, 'we might even be able to get the girls down to take care of our needs!' We were both looking forward to something a little more intimate than the telephone conversations we had managed to date.

We put the idea to Mick, who promised to talk it over with Alfie. Alfie growled a bit when he heard our request, but finally agreed to see what could be done.

All went well. After making the trip to Bognor lying down in the back of Alfie's car, we found ourselves in a comfortable, fully furnished two-storey house, a little old-fashioned but exactly what we had been hoping for. There was a small garden surrounded by a high wooden fence with flowers and plants galore. This, we decided, was more like it.

A plan was made for Eric's wife to come down to take care of the shopping, cooking and washing. Charmian would be brought down if and when there was a chance.

With the arrival of Carol to take care of the chores life became almost idyllic. After a hearty breakfast – Carol was a good cook – we would lie in the garden sunbathing and listening to the radio. The Dave Clark Five were also feeling pretty good at the time as their song, appropriately entitled 'Catch Us If You Can', was riding high in the charts.

Carol had arrived with their only child, Kim, a cute, blonde four-year-old. Eric was looking quite mellow and content with his lot. I must admit that I felt the odd twinge of envy in my celibate state.

One night the door to my room flew open and a body landed on top of me.

'You're nicked, you bastard!' It was Charm and the kids, all trying to get at me at the same time. My cup runneth over.

Once again we were one big happy family. The only thing we couldn't do was go to the beach – but the kids didn't even know there was one nearby. We talked and made plans for the future. One of Alfie's friends, whom we had met early on, had been to South Africa and from what he said about it we were leaning towards it as the place to wind up. But I still hadn't forgotten that 'new world somewhere they call the promised land' I had heard the Seekers singing about.

The second anniversary of the robbery came and went.

George from the organization came to visit us on a couple of occasions to discuss details of the plastic surgery. He took photographs of Eric and me on the first visit and returned with suggestions from the surgeon who was going to wield the knife. Eric was only to have a nose job, I was going to have the works.

As you can imagine, I was somewhat apprehensive about the surgery and I asked George for more details.

'Don't worry about a thing,' he assured me. 'Liz Taylor has it done every couple of years. If you want to, you can even have the skin removed from your fingertips and then you could never ever be nicked!'

At a price today of around £12,000 a finger, I declined.

Our sojourn in Bognor was almost over, George informed us, so we started making the necessary preparations to move back to London.

Sure enough, in mid-September the 'holiday' came to an end and after three months of hiding behind net curtains it was time to move on. Little did I know that those early autumn days of 1965 were going to be the last time that I set foot on British soil.

Eric and I were transferred back to the flat in Camberwell, minus wives and kids. Now that we knew that we were on the point of departure the time seemed to drag. We wanted action.

Early one morning in October, Alfie turned up with two parcels of clothing. 'Put this clobber on,' he growled in his normal friendly manner. 'You're on your way.' The clothes were obviously second hand and consisted of flannel shirts, jeans, donkey jackets and gumboots. We were supposed to look like seamen.

We dressed quickly and were soon on our way in a black van which was parked outside the building. Alfie's hefty friend, whom we had first seen at Dulwich, was at the wheel and from him came the instructions.

'When you're dropped off, walk straight through the gate. The mate of the boat on which you're travelling will be waiting to meet you. He'll take you aboard and hide you.' He then produced an envelope which turned out to contain a couple of seasickness pills.

'Take these if you think you are going to have a problem,' he said. 'You'll probably have a rough trip across the Channel. Now however bad you feel, stay put. Even when the boat docks. The mate will tell you when it is okay to go ashore. When you leave the boat walk straight out of the dock gate and turn left. Keep walking. Someone will come along driving a yellow Daf and offer you a lift into the city. He will take you to a motel where George will be waiting for you.'

As we left the van he wished us well.

The mate, a Dutchman, was waiting for us just as Alfie's friend had said. He spoke little English but had enough international sign language to get us to follow him. Other than the three of us, there was no sign of life. We went aboard the cargo ship unchallenged. Down in the hold we scrambled over sacks of what smelled like rubber and with the aid of a torch the mate conducted us through to the bow where a small area had been left clear. He indicated that this was where we would spend the journey and shone the torch on a whisky bottle full of water.

'No smoke,' he said. 'No food — only water.' We got into our deluxe accommodation and the mate left us, barricading the entrance with sacks of rubber as he went. It was the first sea trip for both of us.

After what seemed like an age, the boat's engines began to throb and we were under way. The trip was not as rough as we had expected but it seemed to take forever, especially as we had no idea of time.

Finally we became aware that the boat had docked and after a time the sacks began to fall away. It was our friend the mate.

'Come. Leave now!' he urged in his faltering English. We clambered over the sacks and up on to the deck on stiff legs. It was early morning and the boat was as deserted as when we had embarked. The mate smiled and shook hands, pointing to the dock gates as he did so. I don't know if he ever realized what, or rather who, his precious cargo was.

There was nobody to be seen and the dock gates were wide open just as the organization had promised. We turned left, as per instructions, and before we had gone more than a couple of yards, along came a yellow Daf.

'Hello, boys,' called the driver. 'Going into town? Perhaps I can offer you a lift?'

His name was Peter and it turned out that he had been the captain of our vessel. With typically heavy Dutch humour he asked if we had enjoyed the crossing. He laughed when we told him we did not even know where we were.

'Antwerp, boys! You're in Antwerp. I'm sorry that we won't have time to stop and look around, but your friend is waiting for us.'

Further on we stopped at a set of traffic lights and our

attention was drawn to a pretty Belgian girl dressing a shop window. We made appreciative male gestures and the girl smiled and waved. We were also sorry that we couldn't stop and look around.

George was waiting at the motel. He was immaculately dressed with Lisa, his 'gorgeous piece of German crumpet', at his side. He wrinkled his nose as we approached. 'Christ,' he said disdainfully. 'You two look as if you've spent the night down a rat-hole.'

After a quick shower, a shave and some fresh clothing we were ready for action. The first step was a slap-up breakfast while George outlined the next leg of the journey, which would take us to Paris.

We would be travelling in two cars. Eric would be with George and Lisa in George's Mercedes and I would travel in a Ford Zephyr with an English couple – trusted friends of George – and their two young daughters. We were given false passports, mine in the name of Ronald King, a sportsmaster by profession.

'We'll drive ahead,' George told us. 'When we come to the frontier the gendarmes will only be interested in one thing – Lisa's legs – and you'll be letting them see plenty, won't you, darling?'

I was told that I would be in the back of the Zephyr with the kids and all of us were to be asleep.

George's friends, Bill and Veronica, and their children joined us at the motel in the early afternoon and after lunch in a swanky restaurant – 'This is on Mr King!' – we headed for France.

Crossing the frontier proved no problem. Bill presented the passports and a gendarme peered into the back of the car. It was by now way past midnight and the three innocents were fast asleep. Bless 'em!

We had made it to France, where I could only echo the thoughts of Maurice Chevalier: 'Thank Heaven for little girls.' After a brief pit-stop for a beer and a snack we pressed on for Paris.

Bill pulled up behind George's car in a tree-lined avenue with the Eiffel Tower looming high above us. A man stepped out of the shadows, went to George's car and got in. The

Merc pulled away and we followed it through the quiet Paris streets.

Our new hide-out was a fourth-floor apartment on the Rue Vivienne and the person who would be taking care of us from here on was 'Henri', the man who had recently emerged from the shadows. Henri was well dressed and appeared to be in his mid-fifties. He was powerfully built, not the kind of man you would choose to pick a fight with. He had a bone-crushing handshake, a big smile and an even bigger heart. He spoke English with a heavy American accent which made it impossible to pin down his origins.

'From here on I'm the boss,' Henri told us as we surveyed our new surroundings. 'Ya gotta do everythin' th' way Uncle Henri tells ya, an' I don't want to find you guys sneakin' out t' get laid.'

The apartment was small but comfortable and well stocked with food and drink. Henri was to visit us daily with bread, milk and the newspapers. Within a day or so George came calling and told us we would be taken to the clinic to discuss the forthcoming surgery.

It was cold and snowing heavily but Eric and I were thinking of sunnier climes, as after the ops we would be free to go anywhere. We both discussed the subject of where 'anywhere' would be, until one Sunday afternoon I read an article in the *News of the World* describing the pleasures that Australia had to offer and in particular Bondi Beach in Sydney and the sun-kissed sheilas. I handed the article to Eric and without hesitation we both agreed that we could do with some of that. So Oz it was.

Eric and I began to look forward to Henri's daily visits. We could hear him as he hauled his bulky frame up the wooden staircase to the flat, where he would arrive breathless. Every day he would follow the same routine, slumping into a chair from which would come the by now familiar phrase: 'God dammit boys! I quit!'

Henri was quite a man. He could converse in seven languages, including Russian and Chinese. He told us he had been everything from a prize-fighter to a pimp. At the time he had been asked to play nursemaid to us he was running a small

With Charmian in 1958.

On our wedding day in Reigate, Surrey, 20 February 1960.

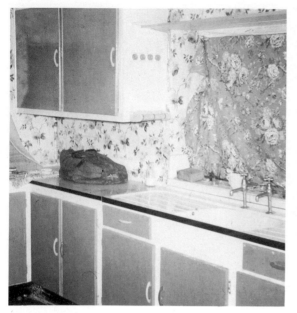

The kitchen at Leatherslade Farm, including the sink where we so carefully washed up all the plates and glasses – not carefully enough in the case of a Pyrex dish I had handled.

The larder at Leatherslade Farm where a bottle of tomato sauce with my prints on it was found.

Bridego Bridge shortly after the robbery.

Being taken to the Aylesbury court shortly after my arrest.

A

B

C

D

E

F

G

H

I

J

A. Bruce Reynolds, 'Prince of Thieves' and the brains behind the robbery.
B. Buster Edwards, who now runs a flower stall outside London's Waterloo Station.
C. Roy James, who helped arrange the robbers' transport and uncoupled the locomotive and High Value Package coach from the rest of the train.
D. Roger Cordrey, who together with John Daly was responsible for stopping the train.
E. John Weater, a member of the robbers' support team.
F. Charlie Wilson, who took care of the train driver after he was coshed.
G. Tommy Wisbey, who formed part of the human chain between the train and the truck.
H. Gordon Goody, who now runs a beach bar in Spain.
I. Bill Boal, who died in prison in 1970.
J. Jimmy Hussey, a member of the gang who loaded the mailbags into the robbers' truck.

Wandsworth Prison shortly after my escape. We dropped through a hole in the van roof and landed on a 'trampoline' arrangement of mattresses. The getaway car was waiting at the back of the van.

October 1965: with Charmian in Bognor after I had escaped from Wandsworth
Prison.

1966: together again in Sydney, Australia, after I'd had my facelift in Paris.

Raimunda and 'Michael Haynes' enjoy a pineapple on Copacabana beach before the arrival of Scotland Yard.

The Trocadero Hotel in Copacabana where Jack Slipper finally found his man.

My worldly possessions when I was taken into custody in Brasilia on 2 February 1974.

sand-blasting business and living beyond his means. He also collected money from a number of whorehouses for someone he affectionately referred to as his 'bors'. The boss, he told us, was the owner of the apartment we were using. He also liked to talk about the 'broads' at the houses where he picked up the takings, but declared that we would never touch any of them.

'The bors would bust my ass,' he added with obvious concern and respect for this unknown gentleman.

George turned up a couple of times, bringing mail and presents from home, where our wives were 'over the moon' with the progress we were making.

Although it was against our orders we did go out at night from time to time. We even went to see Les Folies Bergères, where Eric was nearly selected to join the girls onstage in the can-can. Mostly we would go to small bars and jazz clubs where we could pass unnoticed as a couple of British visitors enjoying the Paris nightlife. Sometimes Henri would arrive in the apartment and see some telltale sign that we had been out, like a box of matches. He would look at us suspiciously.

'Have you two been out tom-cattin'?'

'Not us, Henri!'

But one night I did go out tom-catting and the feline company I arranged was a little pussy. 'All the way from Greece,' she purred.

Finally we were taken to the clinic in Henri's old Citroën (what else!) and he was clearly nervous about his 'hot cargo'. Hunched over the wheel like the getaway driver in a bad B-movie, Henri's nerves took him through a red light on more than one occasion. Crack-driver Eric, crouched on the floor, could only grin and bear it.

Marcel, let us call him, would perform the operations. I had my doubts about him being 'one of the most famous names in European cosmetic surgery' but pressed on. He examined us and made a few notes. A date was fixed. We had three days to think about our new hooters.

When Henri came back for us on the appointed day he was beaming. 'Dis is it, you guys. Lambs t' the slaughter.'

Our 'cover story' for the clinic was that we were a pair of Canadian tax dodgers – not that anyone seemed to worry. While

I was being prepared for surgery a doctor spoke to me in French. I apologized and told him that I did not speak any French. He looked bemused: 'But it says on your card that you are from Quebec?' I put on my best sick smile and explained that my mother had taken me to the English-speaking provinces when I was a small child. I got a feeling the doctor did not altogether believe me.

My mobile stretcher was wheeled off to await my turn in the operating theatre. A sexy nurse dug a needle in my arm and hooked me up to some sort of contraption. She took my pulse; her hand was cool and efficient.

'You are very calm,' she said. 'That is good.'

'I am?' I swallowed.

'Yes, your pulse is quite normal.'

I was just about to invest further in this conversation when the doors to the theatre swung open and there was my old mate looking a very sad and sorry state. I wanted to laugh. Only his blood-suffused eyes were visible – and they were clearly distressed – and two bloodied prongs projecting from the area that had been his nose. A muffled voice came from behind the bandages: 'Don't let them tell you it doesn't hurt.'

Before you could say 'knife' or check my pulse I was on the operating table and starting to feel woozy. Bright lights, voices, someone breaking up the cartilage in my nose with what felt like a hammer and chisel. The blood was running down my throat. 'You won't feel a thing,' they had said. 'Liz Taylor does it all the time . . .'

Henri arrived the following morning to pick us up and take us back to the apartment. As usual he was smiling broadly, thanking and bull-shitting Marcel the surgeon. He looked at Eric and me, sitting sore and glum with the plaster nose-casts taped to our swollen faces.

'Hey! Ain't my babies lookin' beautiful?' We were not able to say much, but Eric made a supreme effort and pleaded with Henri not to make us laugh.

Back at the apartment Henri set out our antibiotic tablets and painkillers, fussing around us like a mother hen. 'An' you guys are gonna have t' start eatin' a lotta yogurt. Don't tell me you don't like it cos that's all I'm gonna buy for ya. You babies are going to look so goddam beautiful when them casts come off that I'm gonna kiss ya!'

We tried not to look at each other for fear of laughing, but in the end I cracked up when I saw Eric trying to eat yogurt with a table knife to avoid having to open his mouth. Then we both started laughing. They say laughter is the best medicine, but on that day I was not so sure.

The pain from the first surgery eased off after a couple of days and eating and drinking became less difficult. George paid us another visit to talk about the second part of my surgery. A permanent face-lift. He and Henri pooh-poohed my misgivings about further suffering. The worst, they assured me, was over.

'Anyone would think you were going to have your cock chopped off,' George added by way of encouragement.

It was about this time that Henri told us his name was not Henri.

'That's the name that George chose for me. For Christ sake do I look like th' kinda guy that would have a dumb son-of-a-bitch name like Henri? No! I'm gonna tell you guys my real name. It's Barney.' He gave us his best Anthony Quinn smile and stretched out his hand. 'Shake hands with Barney. An' don't forget it! Every time you guys called me Henri I felt like pukin'.'

Barney went with us to the clinic to have the casts removed and was very impressed. Looking at Eric in profile he said, 'It's amazin'. Ya went in lookin' like Jimmy Durante an' ya come out lookin' like Mickey Rooney.'

At first it was strange looking at and feeling my new nose. It wasn't and still isn't – after all this time – exactly what Marcel had promised, but if I had my reservations, Eric seemed to be more than happy with the results of his op. His nose had been quite a landmark.

Barney, who had suffered none of the pain, was in high spirits that everything was going so well and invited us out to lunch at his favourite Chinese restaurant. A second treat was in store. He insisted on taking us to see a movie. We looked in a newspaper and found a film that was in English with French sub-titles. It was called *The Brig*, the story of twenty-four hours in a US Marine prison. Early in the film it became clear that Wandsworth had been a holiday camp by comparison. Some of the scenes were so brutal that Barney was moved to rise from his seat and shout abuse at a particularly unpleasant Marine screw.

'You mother-fucker!' he shouted at the screen. 'You goddam mother-fucker – I'd kill ya.' We had to drag him back into his seat.

Far too soon I was back at the clinic getting a thorough medical examination before surgery. I could not help wondering why all the fuss if the worst was over. Suppositories were issued and administered with devastating results and once again I found myself in pre-op.

I regained consciousness at one point and found myself lying in a bed in a ward with the faithful Barney sitting beside me in a chair. Unbelievable pain was raging in and around my head. Pain such as I had never experienced before.

Barney was smiling. 'You look beautiful, sweetheart,' he said just before I vomited into his lap and went into oblivion again. When I came around the second time everything had been cleaned up and there was no sign of Barney. The pain was unbearable, any and every movement sending shock waves of agony through my head. I could see French windows at one side of the ward and I began to think about getting up and throwing myself into the street. Luckily, just trying to sit up was out of the question.

I made a supreme effort and managed to press a bell push that was suspended above the bed. Somewhere a bell rang and at the same time a light came on in the middle of the ward. A door opened an inch or so, then a hand appeared and switched the light off. I rang the bell again and the same process was repeated. I gave up on the idea of asking for help and tried to sleep. Only Edgar Allan Poe could do justice to the night of torment that followed. If only I had taken the gun Paul had offered me I might well have used it that day!

Two days later I was released from the clinic. Barney was all smiles again, conversing with the nurses and my favourite surgeon. I was given a huge supply of antibiotics and Barney wrote down in what order they had to be taken. It was four of this, six of that and two of those. And more goddam yoghurt.

When Eric saw the results of the operation he was very impressed.

'Christ,' he said. 'You look like a bloody Chink. Nobody would ever recognize you now.'

He was right, I did have an oriental look but as the days passed the swelling slowly left my face and I began to lose my Asian appearance. After a week I returned to the clinic to have some of the stitches removed – there were 140-odd in my face to tackle – and this was a fairly bloody business. The healing was a slow and painful process.

When the swelling and discoloration left my face, Barney took us out to have our hair cut, telling the open-mouthed barber that I had just undergone brain surgery. From there we were taken to a photographer to have pictures taken for our new passports. The scars on my face were still vivid and a black pen was used to give me some sideburns and hide the telltale marks. The photographs were sent on to George and he turned up at the apartment a couple of weeks later with the 'goods': the new passports, crisp and freshly issued by the Foreign Office, plus a one-way ticket to Sydney for Eric – it had been decided that he would go a couple of weeks before me as a trailblazer.

George also brought more mail from our wives, money and a Christmas present from Charm – a gold watch. She didn't know it at the time, but the organization had planned their own present and that was for her and the boys to spend Christmas in Paris.

Three days before Christmas it was time for Eric, now Robert Burley, to leave Paris. A day later he rang through from Sydney to say he had arrived safely.

'The place is fantastic,' he enthused. 'It's tailor-made for people like us. The beer's great and I've sunbathed on Bondi Beach already.' This was excellent news and I began looking forward to joining him.

Charm and the kids arrived safely in Paris. Barney brought me the glad tidings and told me that he would take me to meet them as soon as it was dark. Many precautions had to be taken to make certain that they had not been tailed.

Barney finally stopped the car near a cinema and pointed to

a car parked nearby. It was the same Ford in which I had made the trip from Antwerp to Paris.

'There's your old lady and your kids,' said my friend, reaching out to shake my hand. 'Merry Christmas! I'll see you guys later.'

Charm and the boys had driven from London to Dover, where they had caught the boat to Ostend before driving on to Paris. They were travelling on passports in Charmian's maiden name and did not attract any attention during the festive season.

It was wonderful to see Charmian and the boys again and there was much hugging and kissing. Nicky was a bit bewildered by his father's 'new look', but he was soon over it and chatting excitedly. When he could get a word in, Chris, now close to four years old, also had much to say. It was Christmas and Father Christmas was on his way!

We booked in to a modest hotel in the centre of Paris and spent the next five days having family fun. We went to the parks and the zoo. In the evening a baby-sitter would come in so that Charm and I could do justice to the night life of Paris. We did our Christmas shopping and Charmian bought me a pair of very expensive crocodile shoes 'to travel in'. The shop assistant told me to buy them half a size smaller than what I usually took, so that by the time I had worn them in they would fit more snugly. They felt tight, but I took the assistant's advice!

We were having a wonderful time: going to shows and eating at famous restaurants. This was the life, but I knew it could not last forever. Sure enough, just after Christmas, Barney appeared at the hotel with the news that it was time for me to move on.

Early the next morning, Wednesday 29 December 1965, George arrived with my new passport and the ticket to Sydney. I had some misgivings about the passport as it was quite obviously brand new and didn't have any stamps in it whatsoever.

'How did Mr Furminger get out of England and into France without a single stamp in his passport?' I asked George.

'You worry too much' was his only reply.

With a butterfly or two in my stomach I said my goodbyes to Charmian and the kids and reassured them that we would all be together again and hopefully soon. Nobody was looking particularly cheerful – least of all Nicky, who was coming down with measles.

I also took my leave of my very special new friend Barney. Wherever you are, Barney, thanks!

George and I set off alone for Orly Airport for the flight to freedom. It was goodbye Europe, hello brave new world. There seemed to be very few people at the airport that day and my misgivings about the passport returned. To make matters worse the official at passport control looked most unfriendly. George shook me warmly by the hand and I went to meet my doom.

To my surprise the official barely glanced at the passport and handed it back to me, wishing me 'Bon Voyage'. I gave George a wave and headed for my flight to Zurich – the first leg of my journey 'down under'.

I travelled as Terence Furminger, a man, I was told, who had been paid £1000, about £12,000 today, for the use of his documents. To all intents and purposes Ronald Biggs no longer existed. I had perfected the escape. The only flaw to the plan were the crocodile shoes. They were already starting to pinch and I hadn't even got on the plane.

# 7. Australian Days

After a stifling stopover in Darwin to go through immigration formalities, the plane finally touched down at Mascot Airport in Sydney. It was New Year's Eve 1965.

I crushed my swollen feet back into my crocodile shoes and limped to the customs area. All I could think about at that moment were all the more comfortable pairs of shoes in my suitcase.

'Anything to declare, sir?' said the official in an unmistakably Aussie twang.

'Yes,' I replied. 'These shoes are killing me. Please let me get at some old ones.'

I had already kicked off my crocodile shoes and was eager to make the change. Suddenly there seemed to be something more serious to deal with than my mutilated feet. Not only were the shoes made from crocodile skin – which put them in a special class – but even if they did let them into the country there would be import tax to pay.

'If you let me get at a different pair of shoes, you can keep these or throw them away,' I offered. 'I'll never, ever use them again.' The offer was enough. I was cleared through customs, shoes and all.

'Welcome to Australia, Mr Furminger!'

Now I was bouncing along in the old Hush Puppies. I had made it to the promised land. I was in bloody, beautiful Australia, a world away from Wandsworth Prison. Catch us if you can!

As I left the airport it started to rain, a sudden rust-coloured downpour. But I wasn't worrying about the rain or its colour – I felt like Gene Kelly even with my aching feet.

I took a taxi to King's Cross and found the Wentworth Hotel, where I had arranged to meet Eric.

'Mr Burley checked out two days ago,' the desk clerk apologized, 'and does not seem to have left a forwarding address.'

Worse was to come. The hotel was fully booked for New Year's Eve. With a lot of persistence the staff managed to track down a room at a hotel nearby after some kind soul had cancelled their reservation. I left a message at the Wentworth in case Eric should return. Mr Burley was to call Mr Furminger 'as soon as possible'.

There was no air-conditioning at the hotel other than an old-fashioned fan that whirred above the bed. But the room was clean and spacious – and the fridge was well stocked with cold beer. Still doing mental handsprings I opened a 'tube' and guzzled the contents. Happy New Year, Ron!

After a long and much welcomed shower and a shave I got dressed and decided to look around 'the Cross'. Light years before, when I was in Wandsworth, I had read a humorous book about the Australians called *They're a Weird Mob*. Now I would be able to judge for myself.

With my scars and Paris pallor I probably looked a bit weird to the Aussies. I visited a few bars and found out all about 'ponies' and 'schooners' and 'grogged on' into the evening. By midnight I had joined up with some British sailors and their girlfriends, singing and sharing their champagne. We went from 'Waltzin' Matilda' to 'We'll Meet Again' and back again.

I slept well and woke up early, the sun shining through the blinds on to my face. Today was a day to tour the city and get my bearings. I wanted to see some of the Sydney shoreline and especially the famous Bondi Beach.

I hailed the first taxi that came along.

'Where to, mate?' the driver asked.

'I'd like to hire you for the whole day,' I said. 'Perhaps you could show me all the places of note in Sydney, but especially the beaches.'

'I'm your man,' said the driver enthusiastically. 'The first thing we'll do is to turn off this bloody meter. I hope you'll excuse the smell of drink, mate, but I've been on the piss for most of the night.'

There were no worries. I had been on the piss too, so I appreciated the man behind the wheel as my kind of cab driver.

The cabbie's name was Stan. Born and bred in Sydney, Stan was a family man with four kids. He had a keen sense of humour and soon we were chatting away like old friends. His passions were horse-racing and Chinese food, so once it had been established that I shared both these enthusiasms we decided that after the tour of the city we would go to a track called Randwick and then on to one of Stan's favourite Chinese restaurants for dinner.

I told Stan I was a writer and that I planned to stay in Australia for about six months. As I didn't have a fixed abode at that moment, I asked my new friend if I could possibly have my mail sent to his home. He readily agreed.

'I'll take you to a pub near the Cross where us cabbies get together. I go there practically every day, so everyone knows me and that's where I can hand over anything that comes for you.'

It was a beautiful, sunny day and I enjoyed my tour. The beaches looked great! Stan gave me a quick lesson in 'Strine' – the way dinkum Aussies speak the English language. I picked up a lot more when he took me to the pub where the cab drivers hung out.

The races turned out to be something of a financial disaster. Neither one of us backed a winner, but Stan kept the schooners coming and I loved every minute of it. By the time we got to the Chinese restaurant we were firm friends and we agreed that it had been a bloody beaut day.

When I got back to my hotel there was a message from Eric with a telephone number where I could contact him. We had a brief but euphoric conversation on the phone and an hour later my friend was knocking at the bedroom door.

'Bob Burley?'

'Terry Furminger? You made it, you old bastard!'

When Eric's funds began to dwindle he had found himself a room in a boarding house and had even got himself a job as a petrol-pump attendant in a service station. He was a picture of health and already had a deep tan.

'I go to the beach every morning before work,' he said. 'We'll go tomorrow. Just wait until you see the crumpet.'

Eric was pleased to hear that I had already managed to establish an address where our mail could be sent safely.

It did not take us long to find ourselves a furnished house in Botany Bay (where else!) and settle in. Our next-door neighbours were the owners of the house and offered to take care of any chores. We bought an elderly Morris and spent some time tarting it up, Eric, who knew about these things, happily taking the engine to pieces.

Sunny and happy days, all that was missing were the wives and kids.

As cash was getting low I wrote to Charmian to send me more. We had decided that it was a bit unwise to transfer money via the banks for the time being, so we opted for the old prison trick of smuggling in money and letters. Banknotes or letters would be tightly folded lengthwise until they became narrow strips. The strips were then glued between two pages of a bulky magazine. Charm was no stranger to these little subterfuges and soon enough my Aussie chum Stan was calling to say that there was mail for Terence Furminger.

The second time my dutiful wife sent me a copy of *Country Life* it unfortunately seized the attention of Post Office inspectors, who were obviously interested to know why anybody would send money in this fashion. The first hint of trouble was a call from Stan.

'Look, Terry,' he said, in a slightly worried tone. 'I've had the bloody demons from the Post Office down here. They're looking for you.'

Although Stan did not have our Botany Bay address, he did have our phone number and that was enough to give Eric the nadgers. It was clear that we would have to 'shoot through', as Old Bill would certainly be wanting to have a little chat with Mr Furminger. Eric had thoughtfully bought the Morris in a false name, so there was no way the car could be traced, and we hoped that our landlord would not remember the car's registration number. We loaded up the Morris with our worldly possessions and headed out in the direction of Melbourne.

Eric was all for putting as much distance between us and the Sydney 'demons' as possible, so when we got to Melbourne we decided to press on.

It was late at night when we arrived at the outskirts of Adelaide. Eric, exhausted after the long drive, pulled off the road and we slept in the car until daylight.

I liked the 'feel' of Adelaide immediately. It had a certain atmosphere of calm, especially a beach area we found called Grange. We bought a newspaper and scanned a number of ads for room and board. One was for Surfside, a guest house owned and run by a young Australian called Gavin Jones. His price was five dollars a week – in advance.

The other guests were a pretty mixed bunch. English, Australian and New Zealanders, mostly young, mostly nice. I have many fond memories of the time spent at Surfside.

Eric had kept the name of Bob Burley, but I was now operating as Terence King. We both got jobs without any trouble, Eric as a service-station attendant and me as a joiner in a furniture factory where I sweated for peanuts. But I didn't mind – we were having a ball and as a lifestyle it was certainly more appealing than HM Prison. The only thing missing (apart from the wives and kids) was female company. Nobody could explain to me why, but there was a noticeable shortage of sheilas in Adelaide. You had to be built like Mr Universe just to get it on with any girl who appeared on the beach.

Money having changed hands in England, the organization was in the process of preparing travel documents and tickets for our families to join us. Charm would be travelling as Mrs Margaret Furminger, which worried Eric rather.

Having 'lost' the Morris in a road accident, I bought another car from one of Surfside's boarders, an English fellow called Mike. It was a Holden, an Australian car, and in reasonably good condition. Once again Eric 'did a job' on the engine.

Word reached us in April 1966 that Carol, Eric's wife, had arrived in Sydney with their daughter. Eric drove like a man possessed on the way to pick them up, clipping hours off the time it had taken us to get from Sydney to Adelaide.

There, at the Sunshine Motel, were Carol and Kim waiting to greet us.

Charm had taken the opportunity to send more funds and a letter indicating that she would be arriving in the next couple of months. We returned to Adelaide at a more leisurely pace.

It wasn't long before Eric moved out of Surfside and into a small flat close to the gas station where he was working. I stayed on and it was about this time that the cook was sacked for being drunk on duty. Her place was taken by a fearless Australian lady by the name of Anne Pitcher. Anne and I became good friends and not long after her arrival at Surfside we took over the management.

It was June when I got the news that Charmian was virtually on her way to Australia. For security reasons we had decided that it would be best for her to arrive in Darwin, where I would go to meet her. From an Australian motel guide I found the perfect place for her and the boys to book into, the Koala Motel.

The day that I was due to travel I was taken ill. I developed a high fever and arrived in Darwin feeling pretty groggy. I spoke to a number of taxi drivers but not one of them had ever heard of the Koala Motel. Later I discovered that the motel was still under construction. That's builders for you!

As there was some kind of convention going on in Darwin I considered myself lucky even to find a motel room. I flopped on to the bed and promptly fell asleep.

When I awoke it was already past the time when Charm's plane was due to arrive. I grabbed a super-quick shower, dressed and called a cab to take me to the airport. I was quite late and the passengers were already leaving the airport when I arrived. I looked about for Charmian and the boys, but there was no sign of them. I was thinking that they might have got a taxi and gone off in search of the Koala Motel when I saw her through the glass doors of an office. Charmian was standing by her luggage, talking to an airport official. There was no sign of Nicky or Chris. As I stood undecided what to do she turned and looked in my direction, but gave no sign that she had seen me. She was looking troubled.

I turned away abruptly, telling myself that she had been

detained. 'Jesus Christ!' I thought, 'now what?' I went out of the airport feeling sick and desperate. I hid behind a clump of bushes and waited. After what seemed like hours a van with some people in it came through a gate at the side of the airport. I was convinced it was Charm on her way to be locked up for the night. Back at my motel I spent a fretful night wondering what the hell I should do. If it had been discovered that Charm was using a phony passport, she would obviously be charged with something and possibly make a court appearance. Wild ideas were going on inside my head.

Early the next morning I called Eric in Adelaide and told him that Charm had been taken into custody. He was shattered by the news. If Charm had been nicked Old Bill must know that we were in Australia.

'What are we going to do?' he asked. I told him that I had been thinking about going down to the courthouse to see what I could find out. Eric didn't think that this would be a good move.

'Don't go anywhere near any courthouse, for Christ's sake – even if she is taken to court today there's nothing that you can do. Your best move would be to get back to Adelaide on the first plane out of Darwin.'

I told Eric that I would get back to him later and hung up. I had had an idea. I would call the airline and see what they had to say with regard to the whereabouts of one Mrs Margaret Furminger. I rang from the post office and got an efficient-sounding female on the line.

'Hello, I wonder if you could help me? I'm trying to find out if a Mrs Margaret Furminger arrived on the BOAC flight via Zurich last night?' There was a suspicious pause.

'Hello . . . Yes, Mrs Furminger did arrive and she is staying at the Fanny Bay Hotel.'

I thanked her for her help and hurried out of the post office. The woman had sounded a little too ready with the information for my liking and I had a sneaking feeling that she had not been alone.

Over a much needed beer I studied a map of Darwin that I had bought the day before and found the Fanny Bay Hotel situated on the edge of town. I made up my mind. I was going to go out to the hotel.

As I got out of the taxi the first thing I saw was Old Bill! There were plainclothes coppers everywhere! As I walked down the path to the foyer of the hotel I passed two beefy chaps with short haircuts. I was doing my best not to turn green. The receptionist smiled.

'Can I help you?'

I noticed other big men with short haircuts standing around talking. As soon as I asked for Mrs Furminger, I told myself, these bastards were going to pile on to me. 'Yes,' I found myself saying. 'Could you tell me if there is a Mrs Furminger staying here?'

'She is, sir. She's on the second floor – would you like me to call her for you?'

Nobody moved and a few brief moments later there were Charmian and the boys hurtling down the stairs and into my outstretched arms.

'Darling!'

'Dad!'

We hugged and kissed and cried with happiness, oblivious to the onlookers. Nicky and Chris were tugging at me for my attention, wanting to show me the drawings they had done on the flight.

I was right about the men with the short haircuts. Darwin was hosting a major convention for senior policemen and that was the reason all the hotels were full. When I had seen Charmian 'look through me' she had been preoccupied with the fact that there was nowhere for her and the kids to stay and there had been talk that she would have to pass the night in the local police station! A vacancy at the Fanny Bay Hotel was found at the last minute. Earlier that morning when I had been biting my nails with anguish, Charm and the kids had been enjoying themselves at the beach until they were scared off by a flasher!

It was fabulous being together again, all the agony of the previous hours now forgotten. We went to the beach where Charm had got her first glimpse of Aussie manhood. I swam and played with the kids, chasing them and giving them 'bear hugs' when I caught them. Back at the hotel I phoned Adelaide and brought Eric up to date with the glad tidings.

'Thank God for that,' he said, somewhat relieved. 'I was just starting to make plans to shoot through again.'

Charmian had arrived in Australia with all that remained of my share of the train robbery cash – a little over £7000 (about £70,000 today). After lunch we went to a number of banks, changed a couple of thousand pounds into Australian dollars and then went shopping for a car. We had decided that we would buy a station wagon and make a slow overland trip down to Adelaide. It would be our first holiday together since we had been to Hastings five years earlier.

It did not take us long to choose a vehicle. A brand new, gleaming white Holden station wagon took our fancy. As I didn't know how to drive a car at the time we went for a test drive with Charmian at the wheel. We would take it, we decided, and with all the extras. It came out at about $A3000, including the tax and insurance. We loaded up with an array of stuff we thought we might need for the trip: blankets, jerry cans, water bottles, an ice-chest, and so on. Then we went back to the hotel and picked up the luggage.

We finally drove out of Darwin as evening approached, the sky streaked dramatically with red and gold. We stayed close to Darwin on the first night, but the first big dot on the map was to be our target for day two. It was a place called Daly Waters.

As it got dark on our first full day behind the wheel we calculated that we must be somewhere near Daly Waters. We stopped where there was some light and sound coming from a bar of some kind. I went to investigate. The people in the bar stopped talking as I entered.

'Could you tell me where I might find the Daly Waters Hotel?' I asked politely.

The barmaid looked me over. 'You're in it, mate.' The laughs continued.

The Daly Waters Hotel made the Fanny Bay Hotel look like the Savoy. When Charm went to the Ladies she found somebody washing socks in the only sink. The 'somebody' was a truck driver, and a male truck driver to boot. Later as Charm pulled on the sheet I was hogging it ripped right down the middle. Welcome to Australia, Charm!

Early next morning we were on the highway and the sun was shining fit to bust. The station wagon had an automatic transmission so once we were out in the middle of nowhere I had my turn at the wheel. Soon I was zipping along – nothing to it – Charm gently nagging, 'You're doing eighty! Slow down a little.' The kids were loving it every bit as much as I was. It was hot and it was dusty but we didn't mind, we were having the time of our lives marvelling at the flocks of coloured birds, the billabongs, the 'roos and the emus.

'There are only two things wrong with Australia,' I said at one point. 'Too many flies and not enough women.'

We drove to Alice Springs where we stayed overnight. A cowboy town, noisy and lively and very popular with the flies. Charm turned a few heads with her Pommy accent and beehive hair-do. Looking at a map I discovered that the road across Queensland to the Great Barrier Reef would take us close to Mount Isa, a copper-mining town where I knew a couple of my friends from Adelaide had gone to work. On the spur of the moment I suggested that we should make a bit of a detour and give my chums a surprise.

It was early afternoon when we drove into Mount Isa. After we had booked into a small but comfortable motel, I left Charm with the kids and went off in search of my friends, Mel Kidd and Dave Stone. I had no trouble locating the mine where they had told me they were working, but I got little or no help from the personnel department.

The department that day consisted of one bloke who was sitting behind a desk, writing. He hardly looked up from what he was doing when I entered his office.

'Good afternoon,' I said, 'I'm trying to locate a couple of friends who work here – Mel Kidd and Dave Stone?'

'We don't give out information about our workers,' the man said flatly.

'But I'm a friend of these people,' I insisted.

'So you might be,' said the man, still writing. 'On the other hand, you could be a debt collector or a copper. Sorry, mate, can't help you.'

'Thanks very much! But if by any chance you should see either of my pals, would you please tell them that Terry King is staying at the Paramount?'

The man showed no sign that he had heard me or that he cared, so it was a pleasant surprise when later that evening Mel and Dave showed up at the motel.

Several years later, when I was hiding from the police in Melbourne, I considered making my way to Mount Isa. The policy at the mine, by then, rather appealed to me!

From Mount Isa we headed across to Cairns on the Great Barrier Reef. We stayed there for several days, going off on tours in the glass-bottomed boats, oohing and aahing at the coral formations and the brightly coloured fish. The kids played happily on the beaches, already tanned and glowing with good health. It was a big improvement on Bognor. The motel where we were staying had a baby-sitting service, and in the evenings Charmian and I could go out to dine.

Somewhat reluctantly, we left Cairns and began the long trip south to Adelaide. We took the highway along the coast, making overnight stops in Townsville and Mackay.

One early morning we 'discovered' a deserted beach at a place called Yeppoon. The tide was out and there was not a footprint to be seen on the sand. We couldn't resist. We changed into our bathing togs and raced across the virgin sand in the direction of the sea. 'Last one in the water is a bad egg!' I cried. The sea was crystal clear and shallow, with hardly a wave. We were spread out as we gleefully splashed into the cool water, Charmian bringing up the rear some twenty yards behind us.

Suddenly, she turned back towards the beach, screaming as she ran madly through the shallow water. Calmed down, but still white with fright, she described how a water snake had passed between her legs.

We continued our adventurous journey down the coast to Sydney, where we stayed the best part of a week, then across country to Adelaide via Melbourne. The trip had taken us just over a month – long enough for Charmian to get pregnant again!

We had a jubilant reunion with Eric and Carol, the kids resuming the brief friendship they had begun with Kim when we had been hiding in Bognor Regis. A good friend from Leeds,

Mike Cunnington, joined our company, as did Anne Pitcher, my partner in the guest house at the Grange. One big happy family.

Soon after our arrival in Adelaide, we rented a spacious house in an area called Glenelg and spent nearly all our remaining cash furnishing the place. Wall-to-wall carpets, 'Danish' furniture and so forth. It had been suggested that Charmian could take part in the activities at the guest house, but it was fairly obvious from the start that she wasn't going to get along too well with my Aussie partner. In the kitchen, Anne was the essence of efficiency, working quickly and snapping at anyone who might get in her way. Charm's job was to serve food to the guests and clear the tables, work that she clearly wasn't cut out for – and being pregnant didn't help. It didn't take her long to announce her early retirement from Surfside. In any case, the guest house was not paying, so I reluctantly passed on my share of the business to Anne and found myself a job as a carpenter.

The kids had taken to their new lifestyle like fish to water and soon made friends with other children in the neighbourhood. Nicky was six years old at the time and had accepted his new surname, Furminger, without question. We had told him that I was on secret government work and it was necessary to live under a different name. He was a bright little chap and caught on quickly, never making any reference to his life in England. One day, however, when he was playing with the kids next door, I heard him shout, 'All right, you be the police inspector and I'll be one of the train robbers.'

Life was almost a bowl of cherries. With plenty of overtime I was earning good wages, setting money aside for Charmian's forthcoming confinement. At weekends we would go with the 'Burleys' to one of the many beaches in the area or to 'hotels', as the pubs were called, and grog on while the kids ran wild, appearing every so often for another lemonade or more crisps.

As the months slipped by, Charmian became more and more conscious of her size and went out less frequently once she had decided that she was 'not fit to be seen in public'. Notwithstanding, Farley Paul, our third son, was born in Glenelg Community Hospital on 27 April 1967. After a few drinks with the lads to 'wet the baby's head' I went to the hospital to visit my wife and the latest addition to the Biggs family. Charm was sharing a room with another lady who had also recently given birth. When I arrived, the other happy father was in the room, gazing proudly at his handiwork cradled in his wife's arms.

'Terry King,' I said warmly, extending my hand to the fellow. 'Congratulations!'

Mrs Charmian 'Furminger' was quick to cover my blunder. 'You and your silly jokes, Terry! Why don't you tell the gentleman your proper name?' I laughed it off, but I saw how easy it was to slip up using an alias. I would have to be more careful.

Farl was a great kid. He rarely cried or made a fuss. We all loved him. But not long after Charm left the hospital we received a bit of a blow through the post. It came in the form of an anonymous letter. The police, it said in poor handwriting, were aware that I was in Australia. It was imperative that we should move out of Adelaide as fast as possible and change our names again. It was something of a mystery because we thought the only people who knew our address were immediate friends. I was all for ignoring the letter, but Charmian didn't want to take the chance. We discussed the matter with Eric and Carol. Charmian was right, they said, we had to 'shoot through'.

Heartbreaking though it was, I went out the next day and sold the station wagon for $900, getting gypped on the deal. At a different used car dealer's, I bought a furniture truck for 600 bucks that looked as if it had been fabricated soon after the discovery of Australia. But it suited my purpose and it left me with $300 for petrol and other expenses. Soon after dark that very same day, Eric backed the truck into my garden. Then, as silently as possible, so as not to alert any of the neighbours, we loaded the truck with the major part of our belongings and stole off into the night and out of Adelaide – destination Melbourne. Charm and the kids went to spend the night with Carol.

Early the next morning Eric and I arrived on the outskirts of Melbourne. Eric was just about wrecked after the 500-mile drive. Without too much trouble we found a warehouse where, at an exorbitant price, I was able to leave the furniture. After a meal and a wash and brush-up, we set about finding new accommodation for my family.

In a local newspaper I saw something I fancied. It was a two-bedroomed house with a 'beautiful garden' and a telephone. I rang a number and made an appointment with the estate agent.

I introduced myself as Terence Cook, giving my profession as architect. My wife and children, I said, were on their way to Australia from England and I was anxious to find somewhere nice and comfortable for them. I was very sorry, but I couldn't provide any references because I had only just arrived in Australia myself. The estate agent was uncertain, the owners had asked for someone who was able to furnish references, but as I looked like an honest person he didn't think that would be a problem. He picked up a pen and asked, 'What is your full name?'

'Terence King,' I replied.

The man looked up in surprise. 'I thought you said your name was Cook.'

'I'm sorry,' I stumbled. 'I have a double-barrelled name. It's King-Cook really. For practical purposes I mostly call myself Cook.' Mistake number two, but luckily the agent kept writing and an appointment was made to see the house in Hibiscus Road, Blackburn.

A pleasant Australian couple, Bert and Joan Shepherd, were the owners of the house. I told them much the same story as I had told the estate agent and was accepted as the new tenant without further ado.

I suggested to Eric that we pass the night in a cheap hotel, but he was all for getting straight back to Adelaide without a rest. We made better speed with the van now that it was unloaded. We had left a mattress and a couple of blankets in the back of the truck and I managed to crash out for a few hours. Eric woke me up when we were about halfway through the journey; he was unable to go any further. I would have to drive, he said. I had no experience of driving a vehicle with manually operated gears and I reminded him of this. I suggested that we should pull off the road into a lay-by and continue after Eric had slept a while. He argued that this might attract the attention of Old

Bill, we had to press on, he would show me how to drive the truck – there's nothing to it, he promised.

Sitting alone behind the steering wheel of the ancient furniture van, I found myself thinking of places where I would rather be. The headlights needed adjusting and on full beam I was blinding oncoming drivers and being blinded in return. Enormous semi-trailers would go screaming by, seemingly inches away. I would have settled for the worst kind of nightmare, even more plastic surgery in Paris. Never had I been so happy as when the dawn broke.

Miraculously back in Adelaide, we both slept through the rest of the day at Eric's flat. That same evening we were going to pick up the rest of our goods from the house at Glenelg and repeat the performance. And, after another 500 bone-shaking miles in the 'beast', with Charmian, Carol and the kids following in Eric's elderly car, we trundled into Melbourne a second time.

Mrs Shepherd, our new landlady, had left the house spick and span and by the time we got the furniture arranged our new home looked very cosy. We had told the boys that they were going to have a new surname, Cook, and before they went off to explore the neighbourhood we gave them a briefing. The next day, leaving Charm with the children, I returned to Adelaide with Eric and Carol. On arrival we took the truck to the dealer I had bought it from and swapped it for an automatic Ford Falcon, whose flying days, it soon became evident, were long past. But somehow I got it – and myself – back to Melbourne.

As Charmian was such an unusual name and we wanted to break off as many ties as possible with Adelaide, we decided that Charm would change her name to Sharon. So we became known as Terry and Sharon Cook. We made friends with some of our neighbours. Lawrie and Rhona Black, who lived next door, were particularly friendly and helpful – always ready to baby-sit if Charm and I wanted to go out for the evening. The Williams family, neighbours on the other side of our house, were quite the opposite. Soon showing a hostile attitude to the 'bloody Poms' who had moved in next to them, they would continue to be unfriendly to Charm long after I had gone. But we took the good and the bad in our stride. We had settled in nicely. The kids were in a school just around the corner and I had found myself a job as a carpenter. We acquired a friendly yellow Labrador bitch whom we named Sadie, and it looked as if we were set to live happily ever after.

We expanded our circle of friends. At work I palled up with other Brits, Aussies and the odd Greek (aren't they all!) and we held some wild parties – the Williams being startled from their slumbers at three o'clock one morning by the Phantom Bugler. As time went on we exchanged the much maligned Falcon for a smart green Holden – that too, coming and going, had annoyed our neighbours. Sometimes I would pick up the boys after school and drive them home, doing 'screamies' à la Batman, much to their delight.

To 'help out with the housekeeping' Charmian bravely took on evening work, which varied from biscuits to bog-rolls. She was none too keen on the work, but I think she liked the chance to have a natter with the other women.

Perhaps foolishly, we drove down to Adelaide to spend Christmas 1967 with Eric and Carol. A surprise was awaiting us. Eric's two hefty mates were also paying a visit, the same ones who had taken Eric and me off Paul's hands when we first escaped.

'Nice to see you fellas again!'

It was getting a little too warm in Adelaide. So after a jolly New Year's Eve party, we made our goodbyes and went back to muggy Melbourne.

The old fortune-teller in Hastings had been more right than wrong to date and, just as she had suggested, I still had 'foreman trouble'. Much to Charm's distress, I changed my job on a number of occasions. I had a stint as a maintenance carpenter at the television studios of Channel 9. At weekend beach events, the hard core of the maintenance crew, Bert and I, would erect the camera stands, perving shamelessly at the sunburned sheilas.

It was our economic situation that finally dragged me away from Channel 9 where there was rarely any overtime to be had. I found myself another erecting job, this time office partitions. The pay was better and the hours were longer. Another year slipped by.

During the time we had been in Australia, we had seen a number of news items regarding the train gang. In 1966, Buster Edwards had given himself up to the police and had subsequently been sentenced to fifteen years' imprisonment. Jimmy White was also nicked the same year and was probably delighted to cop 'only' eighteen years. Mighty Paul Seabourne, who had been given four and a half years for getting us out of Wandsworth, didn't stay free for very long after his release. He went back with ten years for holding up an armoured truck. And about the same time, 'Gentleman' George, the Mr Fixit who had made all our arrangements, was also given a long stretch for a piece of business that had gone badly wrong. Then, after we had spent a happy Christmas and New Year, we heard the bad news that Charlie Wilson had been captured in Canada. That was 25 January 1968.

As 1968 got underway, I was working on suspended ceilings at an immense shopping centre that was under construction. I had teamed up with a likable Dutch carpenter named Martin and we were on piecework, working flat out. One morning I noticed two men carrying a large sheet of glass. The fellow at the back looked a lot like my very good friend, Mike Haynes. I got down from the scaffold where I had been working and went to get a better look at the bloke. Sure enough, it was Mike. I couldn't believe it. I sneaked up behind him, grabbed his arm and said, 'You're nicked, Haynes!'

When I first got to Australia, Charmian had been so elated that she had gone to visit Mike and Jessie Haynes to tell them the good news. But before she could say where I was Mike had stopped her. No one should be told, he had said wisely. The fewer people who knew of my whereabouts, the better.

We were both completely knocked out by our amazing chance encounter. Mike and Jessie and their two children, Tracy and John, had emigrated to Australia only a short time before we met. During the lunch break we got together, still 'mind-boggled' by our encounter. That evening we all got together at Hibiscus Road – there was a lot of drinking to do and the girls had plenty to talk about! It turned out that the Haynes had a flat not very far from where we were living, so we got together quite frequently, becoming better friends than ever.

But there was more bad news to come. On 8 November 1969 Bruce Reynolds was caught in Torquay. Now I really was the odd man out. Bruce's fingerprints, like mine, had been found on the Monopoly board and a bottle of tomato ketchup. He pleaded guilty and received a sentence of twenty-five years' imprisonment. In March 1969 Bruce's wife Frances had her story published in the *Sunday Mirror* in London and subsequently in an Australian women's magazine.

The magazine in question, *Woman's Weekly*, had been delivered to our home with the newspaper and Nicky was leafing through the pages.

'Look, Mum,' he said. 'Here's a picture of Dad!'

Charm hastily relieved Nick of the magazine, telling him that it was just somebody who looked like me. But she was worried – and so was I when I got home from work and saw the article.

A bright young Australian girl called Marjorie, who had been one of my guests at Surfside, also saw the story and she too thought that Terry King looked a lot like the photograph of one of the wanted men in the article. She showed it to Anne Pitcher's son-in-law, Max Philips, who agreed that there was a strong resemblance. Max was a newscaster with a small radio station near Perth and decided to announce his suspicions over the air, which resulted in a visit from the local 'demons', who were more than interested in hearing whatever Philips could tell them about Mr King.

While we had been doing our thing in Melbourne, Eric had gone into business with his two heavyweight chums. They had set up a trucking company in Adelaide and were doing very nicely. The article in *Woman's Weekly* didn't please them.

Without knowing that our clever little guest at Surfside had recognized me, they assumed that somebody would. It was just a question of time, they said, before Old Bill found out that I was in Australia. Eric and his two friends – who also had good reason to avoid contact with the police – decided that it would be prudent to abandon everything and shoot through, advising us to do the same. But even though we knew that other people in the neighbourhood would see the article, I was all for riding out the storm. The months crept by and we started to relax again. Eric and friends were by now holed up in Sydney.

I changed my job again. Still in the office partitions and suspended ceiling business, but this time as a foreman, cracking the whip over a fairly motley crew of thirty-odd carpenters and labourers. I tried to be a good foreman. I didn't dock anyone's time for being late or absent if they had a good excuse. I had been one of these poor buggers myself once. We played nine card brag almost every lunchtime, frequently going over the allotted break time, especially if there was a big kitty that had to be won.

'You're very popular,' said my boss one day. 'Everyone's asking to be put in Terry Cook's gang.' But our output must have been satisfactory, as we were chosen to take on a big job at the new Melbourne Airport.

Charmian, who was still working at the toilet-roll factory, was accustomed to leaving the house just before six o'clock each evening, leaving Nicky in charge. More often than not she would leave a written note for me with instructions for making the kids' dinner. Her messages would nearly always end with the words, 'Farley is sleeping. Try not to wake him!' I usually arrived home soon after six, looking forward to my nightly 'playtime' with the kids. Soon enough, Farley, now a fun-loving two-year-old, would begin rocking his cot against the wall of his room, demanding my attention. Most evenings we would all end up in the bath together, the kids clamouring to be the next 'depth charge'.

One October evening, during the fun and games, I received a telephone call from an Australian friend who was aware of my true identity. He asked me if I had seen the six o'clock news. I told him I had arrived home too late to catch the headlines.

'Make sure you see the nine o'clock edition,' he said seriously. 'It concerns you – and the news is not good.' I got the boys to bed before nine and sat on the edge of a chair to watch the news.

Earlier that day, a Reuters correspondent named Reeves had dropped in at Melbourne Police Headquarters snooping around for news. He happened to see a memo on a desk to the effect that it was suspected that I was living in Melbourne with my wife and children. Mr Reeves sent out this little gem of information as a news item and in no time the rest of the media picked it up.

Channel 9 showed mug-shots of Eric and me, together with

general descriptions of us. The train robbery story was rehashed and the public was invited to contact the police in the event of having any information that might lead to our capture. This time, the shit had well and truly hit the fan.

Charmian paled when I told her the bad news. 'What are we going to do?' she asked. Once again I was all for 'sweating it out'. I was sick of running. But Charmian wouldn't hear of it. 'I'm going to pack a bag for you,' she told me. 'And as soon as it's light you're going to get out of here!' We made a plan. Early the next morning Charmian would drive me to a motel on the outskirts of the city. There I would wait to see if the situation got any worse – or otherwise. In the event of little or no reaction to the news item, we would meet at eight o'clock at a certain Chinese restaurant.

We hardly slept that night and we were both awake long before dawn. A good foreman to the last, I filled in the time-sheets of the workers I was responsible for and took them to a fellow foreman, Andy, who lived close by. I was taking a chance as he may well have seen the news the previous evening. But Andy, a Scottish ex-commando, and I were pretty good mates, so I didn't think there was a chance that he would 'dob me in'. We often drove to work together and he was surprised that I was calling on him at the crack of dawn. Without preamble I told him that I was leaving town for a little while, perhaps for a long while, and there was a strong chance that I would never see him again.

'Look,' he said, 'it's a bit early in the day for this kind of stuff. Sit down and have a cup of tea, and tell me what's going on!' But I shook hands with him, said goodbye and left him standing open-mouthed.

Our lovely little boys were still sound asleep when we left for the motel. I hoped and prayed that I would be able to come back to them.

Charmian drove me to a motel in an area called Essenden, not far from the airport where I had been working until the previous evening. I kissed my tearful wife goodbye and watched her drive off, then turned and booked in at the motel under the name of Arthur Robert Carson. The news at lunchtime was more or less a repeat of what had been aired the previous night. The newspaper also added nothing to what I had already learned. I went out for lunch but discovered that I didn't have much of an appetite. On the way back to the motel I dropped into a shop to pick up a copy of the afternoon newspaper. A glance at the counter where the papers were laid out told me everything I needed to know. My picture was on the front page.

Charmian had returned immediately to Hibiscus Road, soon to witness a posse of armed policemen arrive at the house. They wanted me 'dead or alive', they said. Charm got cross at the sight of the firearms.

'My husband isn't here,' she told them. 'And put those guns away – you're frightening my children.' She was locked up in a police station and the children were put into a home.

Back at the motel, I emptied out my briefcase and packed it with clothes and personal items. I planned to leave the motel when it was dark and keep my appointment with Charmian at the Chinese restaurant. I didn't intend to return. When there was no sign of Charm by nine o'clock I guessed that she had been taken into custody. Now what?

I thought of turning up on Mike Haynes' doorstep, but dismissed the idea instantly: Old Bill was probably grilling him at that very moment. Finally I decided to grab a cab and pay a visit to the Australian friend who had tipped me off the night before. He was not expecting me. In fact he got a bit of a fright when I tapped on his bedroom window. But he was more than ready to help and two days later I found myself in a cosy little holiday home called Blue Waters, high up in the Dandenong Mountains that flank one side of Melbourne.

I was provided with plenty of food, magazines and a radio. Much to my joy, I heard that Charmian had been released and reunited with the children. Then my friend came to visit with some further good news. Charmian had sold her story to the Packer group of newspapers for $65,000. The not-so-good news was that the hunt was very much on. Chief Superintendent Jim Milner of the Melbourne CID was in charge of the operation. He made frequent statements to the public – and me – via radio and television, telling us what moves were being made to catch the train robber. Railway stations and airports were under close watch. Road blocks had been set up at strategic points. Biggs was desperate and without friends, according to Mr Milner, who promised that I would be locked up in the City Watch-house 'within twenty-four hours'.

'Fresh evidence' was presented to the news-hungry press corps when detectives discovered the clothing I had left behind at the motel and a little later a much publicized home movie was shown on television in which – according to Mr Milner, who made the dramatic presentation – the wanted man could be seen on a beach in Spain, puffing away at a cigar. How either of these incidents could have been of any help in getting me into the City Watch-house I never discovered. Furthermore, I am a non-smoker and I have never set foot in Spain. But the net was tightening.

A few days later my favourite cop came on the radio and telly to say that the search was going to swing in the direction of the Dandenong Mountains, the 'perfect place' for someone to hide. My Aussie pal had also heard Jim Milner's pronouncement and soon showed up at my little hideaway in the hills. It was too bad, but I would have to find another refuge.

It was a Sunday evening when I knocked on the door of Mike Haynes' flat.

'Christ Almighty!' exclaimed my old mate as he opened the door, 'I thought it was the law! Come in!' They had kept up with the news, of course, and thought that Old Bill would be paying them a visit any moment. It would be very risky for me to stay with them. But they were friendly with a young English couple whom Mike thought could be asked to put me up for a week or two. He would speak to them the next morning before they went to work.

The couple, George and Janet, agreed to let me stay with them until the heat was off and that evening, when it was dark, I walked to my new digs. My hosts were clearly quite nervous about their lodger but, said George, they were taking the chance because I was Mike's friend. Janet prepared the spare room, hoping I would be comfortable, and then showed me where to find everything that I might need. They both had jobs and would be out of the house all day. I would have to fend for myself.

The 'demons' were still very active in the area. Through the net curtains in the kitchen I could see patrol cars cruising around the neighbourhood. Then, much to my delight, a couple of desperados escaped from Pentridge, Melbourne's grim old jail, and the police turned their attention to the capture of their home-grown fugitives.

Eric Flower, alias Bob Burley, was arrested in Sydney on 24 October. More bad news. Then, days later, Alfie's big friend met a similar fate. Soon it was Alfie's turn. He had been spotted by a neighbour sunbathing in the back garden of a rented house. The good lady, mistaking Alfie for me, phoned the cops and 'Biggs' was pounced on. Sorry about that, Alf!

About the same time, a certain Mr Ronald Biggs planned a sea trip. A trunk bearing his name was delivered to the port awaiting the arrival of the owner. When he turned up to travel he, too, was pounced on and dragged away to the slammer. Sorry about that, Ron.

As the weeks passed the police pressure eased off. As the Haynes had not been visited by the police, we decided that it would be safe for me to move in with them. There was more room, a garden that wasn't overlooked by neighbours and I would be with people whom I considered to be 'family'. My plan at that time was to lie low for a few months, then make my way up north.

Thanks to the attitude of the personnel department in one of its mines, I was seriously considering Mount Isa as a place to head for.

Although Charm had been charged with illegally entering Australia, she was still permitted to go about her business. The police kept watch on her, following her wherever she went, and a squad car could always be seen close to her house. But, with the help of friends, we managed to communicate. I was thinking particularly of Charmian and the kids when Christmas came. Although there was a fine 'Christmas spirit' at the Haynes' and an abundance of everything, it was difficult to be merry. New Year's Eve was even less jolly, as my friends went off to spend the evening with Charmian. At midnight I raised a glass of champagne to absent friends and loved ones, listening to the neighbours singing 'Auld Lang Syne'.

It was during this period that Mike Haynes very generously offered me his passport.

'It's yours,' he said, 'if you think you can do anything with it.' Well, that literally opened new horizons. Mike and I were quite similar in general appearance and height; the only real difference was the colour of our eyes, his being brown and mine blue. But it was an offer I couldn't refuse.

Once again I was in a position to go anywhere in the world. But where? Mike, Jessie and I discussed the subject for hours while we played cards. I would have to think about a suitable disguise if I was hoping to get out of the country. I had gained quite a bit of weight since I had gone to ground, so we decided that I would become a fatty. From then on, much to Mike's delight, we ate spaghetti bolognese practically every day.

I was still in a dither about where to go until one evening Jessie arrived in the house with a pile of travel pamphlets.

'Here you are, Ron,' she said, dropping them on the dining-room table. 'See if you can find a place you fancy in this lot!'

I picked up the brochure that was on the top of the pile. It was a Varig Airline leaflet showing the beautiful Bay of Guanabara and Sugar Loaf Mountain. 'I want to go there,' I said, without looking any further.

Mike looked at the pamphlet over my shoulder, 'South America!' he exclaimed. 'Of course! Why didn't we think of it before? There's 100,000 Nazi war criminals hiding over there – that's the place to go!'

All three of us knew precious little about South America. All we knew was what we had learned from the *Mission Impossible* television series: cruel dictators, corrupt officials and incompetent soldiers. So it was decided. I was going to try to get to Rio de Janeiro.

A map was produced to work out the best way to get there. A boat to Panama, then a plane down to Rio – Mike made it sound so easy.

I needed a haircut and Mike, who had been in the army and had a bit of barbering experience, offered to do the honours. Soon I was sporting a 'short back and sides' that would have gratified the most demanding Company Sergeant Major. Jessie giggled, 'Now you look more like an escaped con than ever!'

Returning to the passport, I found – as good luck would have it – that Mike's photograph was quite loose and easy to remove. The difficult thing was going to be reproducing part of the embossed Foreign Office stamp which appeared on the bottom right-hand corner of the picture. That evening, under the cover of darkness, Mike and I went to a shopping mall where I made a couple of dozen passport pictures. The next morning, at my instigation and expense, the Haynes family went off camping for the weekend. I needed to be alone to work on the passport. Having got Mike to stock up the refrigerator with beer before leaving, I set to work as soon as they were gone. I had never considered taking up forgery for a living, but by Sunday afternoon I was satisfied with my labours. The new Michael John Haynes had a passport. When Mike saw the result he was very impressed. It was bloody near perfect, even if I say so myself.

Charmian had been able to lay her hands on some of the cash that she was to receive for the story she had sold. She had been told of Operation Rio and managed to get $2000 to me without too much trouble. With part of the money Jessie went to a travel agency and booked a sea passage to Panama in Mike's name. I would be sailing on the SS *Ellinis*, a Greek liner of the Chandris Line, in less than a week.

# 8. The Pacifics:
# Melbourne–Rio

As I had left most of my clothes at the hotel, I had precious little to put in the much travelled suitcase which Mike produced for the trip. My bits and pieces just about covered the bottom of the suitcase but little else, so Mike threw in a sleeping bag and all the old clothing that he and Jessie no longer needed. Thinking that it might come in handy I packed the magnifying glass which I had been using to work on the passport. One of the locks on the case was broken, so we secured it with a piece of cord on one side. Not exactly what the well-dressed traveller would use, but at least it was functional.

When the day arrived for me to embark on the SS *Ellinis* – 5 February 1970 – both Mike and I were more than a little apprehensive. Fortunately, the ship was to sail in the evening, so we would be able to leave the house under cover of dark. The plan was for Mike to go through passport control as the passenger, while Jessie and I went aboard as visitors to see him off. I had stuck Mike's picture lightly back into his passport. Once we were all on board I would take the ticket and passport, swap the photographs and assume my new identity. We opened a bottle of brandy, 'to calm the old nerves', as Mike put it. I had a last get-together with Charmian to say goodbye. She was enthusiastic about the plan, but sad to see me go. It was nearly four agonizing months since the police had raided the house.

Charmian and I had no idea when we would meet again. We kissed and hugged each other.

'You'll meet other women,' said Charmian unhappily, 'but don't forget about us.' It would be four years almost to the day

121

before I next saw Charmian and that was under very different circumstances.

Everything went according to plan. Mike had no trouble with passport control and the ugly suitcase was taken from him to be stored in the cabin. Wearing horn-rimmed glasses and a checked cap I went up the gangplank of the *Ellinis* with Jessie steadying herself on my arm. We met Mike on deck, all of us nervous but flushed with success and brandy. I took the ticket and passport from Mike and went off to find the cabin I would be sharing with three other people. As luck would have it, it was empty. I locked myself into the toilet and swapped the photographs in the passport, taking particular care about how I stuck down my photo. This was in the days before there was plastic film over the photo, so I didn't want anyone to be able to see the pencil marks on the reverse. I flushed the torn-up pieces of Mike's picture down the toilet bowl and rejoined my friends on deck. Not for the first time, Mike said softly, 'Now make sure you keep your bins on at all times – we know you hate the bloody things, but keep 'em on. And keep yourself to yourself – play the part of a hermit, don't mix.' Sound advice from a caring friend, my 'brother' as Paul Seabourne had called him.

The Haynes could not stay very long. They had made plans with Charmian to see the Modern Jazz Quartet and didn't want to miss the concert or the alibi. We said our fond farewells.

'Have a good trip, Mike, and don't forget to write!'

I watched and waved my friends ashore, then mingled with the other passengers on deck. They were a mixed bunch as the *Ellinis* was bound for Southampton via Sydney, Auckland, Tahiti and the Panama Canal. The ship's siren blew and a general call went up for visitors to go ashore. Families and friends left the ship and gathered on the quay calling last-minute messages to their departing loved ones. As I walked to the rail to look down at the throng I found that right beneath me and looking up was a foreman called Les, with whom I had been working a short time before I went to ground. He saw me, perhaps saw through me, but he didn't show any signs of recognition. I turned away from the rail and went to my cabin. The world was turning out to be far too small for my liking.

My cabin-mates were a lot younger than me: two Aussie

university graduates, Bill and Greg, on their way to Canada, and Peter, a wiry Italian-Yugoslav, also Canada bound. Greg produced some 'coldies' and opened up the conversation. He was more talkative and humorous than his friend. Peter was quite a card and friendly as only the Italians can be. He had been working as a labourer in Australia and rolled up his shirt-sleeves so that we could see his rock-hard muscles. It soon became obvious that Peter was sex mad.

The boat would be stopping at Tahiti and the vivid description Greg gave of the exotic delights awaiting us left our Italian friend with flared nostrils. Soon we were under way and the coast came to life; the evening meal was served and the bar was open. We opted unanimously for a liquid dinner and grogged on into the night, finding out about each other. After half-a-dozen tubes we were all getting along like long-established chinas, and before the evening was over, Greg paid me the highest compliment that any Australian can pay to an Englishman: 'You're not a bad bloke – for a Pommy.'

I rose early the next morning and went on deck for a walk – I had to meet the public some time. Other early risers smiled and said good morning; the disguise seemed to be working. A bell sounded to announce breakfast. After the walk I fancied a nice cup of hot coffee. The only person sitting at the table to which I had been assigned was a pretty young lady with fluffy blonde hair, blue eyes and great tits. She reminded me of the sexy nurse in Paris.

With the *savoir faire* one would normally associate with Gregory Peck, I joined her.

'Mike Haynes,' I said, extending my hand.

'Blondie,' she said with a firm grip. 'At least that's the name I'm using while I'm on this boat.'

She was as Australian as Ayers Rock, the kind of a girl who would have happily told Gregory Peck to go play with his marbles. On a scale of one to ten she probably saw me at that moment as a one, a right one, a four-eyed, piss-weak Pommy bastard. I raised my cup to take a sip of coffee. For a moment I wondered what had happened – I couldn't see a thing, my glasses had steamed over. Blondie thought it was hilarious as I groped around the table to find my napkin.

All too soon we were joined by Frank, a shy Spanish fellow on his way to Caracas to join his brother in a restaurant business. Then along came an elderly English couple, the Harrisons, polite and kindly folk who had spent many years fruit-farming in Australia but who had not lost their frightfully posh Pommy accents. They were going back to England 'for one last look at the old place'. Miss Carey was the last to make up our group at the table, a crochety old Irish lady, who, understandably, appeared to have 'missed the bus' at some point in her life.

It was heating up in the dining room and my glasses started to slide down my nose. The faster I pushed them up, the faster they slid down again until finally, with a crash, they fell off my face altogether and clattered on to my plate. I didn't say what I wanted to say, I simply wiped the glasses on my napkin and put them into my pocket, never to be used again. Fuck the glasses, I thought!

We were steaming towards Sydney, the first stop on the voyage. Greg and Bill were full of plans to go ashore and have a last gut-full of fair dinkum Australian piss. But I feigned sickness, making appropriately nauseating sounds in the bathroom.

'Sorry, boys,' I groaned, 'I wish I was well enough to go with you.'

Before I had gone aboard the *Ellinis*, I had imagined that my chief obstacle would be the Master at Arms. I had visualized an unpleasant snooper, in all probability an ex-detective, who would recognize me instantly from wanted notices sent to the ship. I needn't have worried, there wasn't a nicer person on board. He was an easy-going young Dutchman, courteous and friendly, who occasionally joined us for our informal parties in the cabin prior to dinner.

Well sloshed, my cabin-mates returned to the ship just before we were due to sail, abusing piss-weak Poms in general and me in particular. A little later, when I heard the blast on the ship's horn advising visitors to leave, I started to feel 'much better'.

'Typical of you useless Poms!' Greg ventured.

Crowds of people were on deck as the *Ellinis* slowly drew away from the quay. Other passengers had joined the ship and there was a similar scene to the one in Melbourne, with well-wishers waving and shouting from the dock.

There was a certain feeling of excitement in the warm summer evening air now that we were leaving Australia and New Zealand would be our next stop. A singsong started up as we passed beneath the Sydney Harbour Bridge and it was not long until it seemed that the whole ship was singing 'Waltzin' Matilda', roaring out the words of the Australian 'national anthem'. I couldn't sing. I had a problem with a lump in my throat. I had a feeling that I would never see this lovely land again – and I was going to miss it.

The next morning volunteers were invited to participate in various cruise activities. Jimmy, as camp as a row of pink tents, was in charge of deck recreation and was allocating small jobs to anyone who was interested.

'Hmmm, you look nice,' he said when I stepped forward to be interviewed. 'I wonder if you would like to take care of ladies' deck sports?' How could Jimmy have known that this was exactly the kind of job I had been born for? The next morning I was handling a bunch of lovelies wearing brief tennis skirts and 'Gorgeous Gussie' knickers, leaping and cavorting under the approving – and roving – eye of their 'sportsmaster'.

I was not keen to go ashore in New Zealand either. It was still too close to Australia for comfort. But my cabin-mates and other people I had chummed up with were going off to do a bit of rubber-necking and I was obliged to join them. It was a sunny afternoon, so I was able to put on a pair of shades for the outing. Blondie saw me leaving the ship and told me the 'sunnies' gave me a sinister air.

'You look like a Mafia hit-man,' she declared.

Back on the ship again Peter was all but doing handsprings; we were en route to Tahiti. That evening, so that the people could get to know each other for the Pacific crossing, the official 'Captain's Party' was held with everyone turning out in their crumpled finery. I stood at the side of the dance-floor with Greg and Co, swigging Greek plonk from a paper cup, checking out the sheilas. Greg summed the ladies up as a 'fuckin' grim-lookin' bunch', but an unaccompanied girl in a white dress caught my eye. Unmistakably English, almost prim – not unlike a young Joyce Grenfell to look at. Her name was Molly. When I asked her to dance, she warned me that she was not a very good dancer. She was not much of a drinker either and, a little later, she warned me again; she was not very good in bed. She was frigid, she told me.

We found a secluded spot on an upper deck and sat looking at the stars. Molly thought it was the right moment to tell me about 'John', the love of her life until a tiff had sent her running off to Australia. She missed him dreadfully and knew that he was missing her, so she was on her way back to England to see if there was a chance of a reconciliation with her erstwhile lover. But, she sighed, she felt physically attracted to me – and Johnny boy was on the other side of the world!

The weather was perfect. Most mornings we would lie around one of the decks sunbathing and knocking back coldies. The dirty jokes out of the way, we turned to more profound subjects. A conversation arose about Australia's national hero, the outlaw Ned Kelly, who was hanged in Melbourne jail. I remarked that I thought it was odd that one of our colonies had chosen a criminal as their national hero. Greg, who was from the state of Victoria – 'Kelly' country – was swift to defend the Irish renegade.

'So I don't want to hear anyone havin' a shot at Ned Kelly . . . like this bloke Briggs (*sic*) they're lookin' for back in Melbourne, no self-respecting Australian would ever dob him in.'

'I read somewhere,' I interrupted, 'that an Aussie news-caster near Perth was the person who put the police on to Briggs.'

'You're missing the point, mate,' responded Greg. 'I said no "self-respecting" Australian. Nobody back there wants to see him caught, even the Chief of Police is helping the bloke; he comes on telly all the time, telling Briggs his next move! It's a bloody comedy.'

A day or so later, sunbathing with Molly after a swim, she suddenly surprised me by whispering in my ear, 'I know who you are!'

Warning bells were clanging.

'Really? So do tell me, who am I?'

'You're Bruce Reynolds!'

'Bruce Reynolds! I think you'll find he's in jail for the train robbery.'

'Well,' Molly insisted, 'if you're not Reynolds, you're Charlie Wilson!'

'And if I'm not Charlie Wilson, I must be Ronnie Biggs?'

'Yes! That's who you are!' she said, as her eyes brightened. 'But don't worry, I won't tell anyone, Mike – and I'll help you if you need money or anything.'

What a sweet girl. What an amazing girl!

It was just before dawn when the ship docked in rainswept Tahiti. The Aussies and I felt that we needed more sleep, but Peter was up and dressed, pacing the floor of the cabin, waiting for the gangplank to be lowered so that he could get to the girls. When the time came he was the first person off the ship.

Molly and I mooched around the island in the rain until we got bored and went back to the ship early for afternoon tea. To our surprise, Peter was sitting in the dining room, looking a picture of abject misery, nearly knee-deep in empty beer cans. I approached him.

'Hey! Peter. You make good fucky-fucky?' He looked disgusted.

'Don't make fucky-fucky. Don't make any fucking thing. All the Tahitian girls are fat pigs! One looks at me and says, "Hey boy, let's make fuck. Only five dollar." I tell her, "Fat pig! I don't pay five cents to fuck you!" '

The voyage progressed. We were on our way to Panama where I would be saying goodbye to all my fine new friends. Most of them were going on to the US, Canada and England. There were two I knew who would be leaving the boat in Panama: Frank, the Spaniard who shared my table, and an attractive but rather serious German girl named Rosie, whom Frank had befriended. They were both *en route* to Caracas.

Just before we docked in Panama, immigration officials came on board to interview the travellers about to disembark, setting up a table in the dance-hall for that purpose. Offering up a silent prayer, I presented my passport to the agents. There was a problem: I didn't have a visa to land in Panama. I explained my reason for leaving the ship in Panama and said that I was unaware that I needed a visa 'just to pass through'. I was granted a stay of seven days, but was obliged to pay a $200 bond which would be refunded when I could show the authorities an airline ticket out of Panama.

$200 was about all the money I had and I needed that to cover the cost of a flight to Rio. The official was adamant; he would have his bond. I was wondering how I was going to manage when there was an announcement over the Tannoy that Michael Haynes was wanted in the Purser's office. I dragged my feet. Had somebody recognized me? Was I about to be arrested, as Dr Crippen had been in 1910, after a radio message had been flashed across the ocean to Captain Kendal of the SS *Montrose*? There was a message, but it was from Charmian who had managed to radio to the *Ellinis* a further US$200 which was now at my disposal. The gods were smiling on Biggsy.

I picked up my battered suitcase and prepared to leave the ship at Panama. It was early evening and many passengers were going ashore just for a look around. There was much hustle and bustle of people coming and going. Suddenly I heard someone calling the name John several times. It was Mr Harrison, the polite Englishman.

'John Haynes?' he said, holding up an envelope. 'Here's a letter for you!'

Sure enough, the letter was addressed to Mr John Haynes, c/o SS *Ellinis*.

'I thought you said your name was Mike,' said Mr Harrison. 'You can't fool me! What are you up to, old lad – running away from a woman?'

'My name is Michael John Haynes,' I told him, 'and I'm not running away from a woman, I'm running away from her husband!'

The playful Englishman slapped his thigh with delight. 'You old rascal!' he chortled. 'Anyway, may God take care of you wherever you go – I like your spirit!'

We shook hands and wished each other luck. The letter wasn't for me; there was another Mr Haynes aboard the *Ellinis*!

Molly, Greg and Bill went ashore with me. After I had booked in to a ramshackle hotel and unburdened myself of my equally ramshackle suitcase, we went off to a bar for a few last jars together. We were not too impressed with Panama City.

Steel-helmeted police, armed to the teeth with machine guns and grenades, patrolled the streets in pairs, looking distinctly unfriendly.

After handshakes and back-slapping, my Aussie friends returned to the ship to give Molly and me a last chance to be alone. During those last few weeks, Molly had been feeling less and less like returning to the love of her life. She fancied the idea of going on to Rio with me.

At the hotel where I had booked in there was a problem: the *senhorita* could not be allowed to accompany me to my room. There are none so stupid as those who want to be. Molly and I didn't have a clue what all the fuss was about. We turned from the agitated hotel receptionist and went hand in hand straight up the creaking staircase.

In spite of Molly's insistence that she wanted to join me on my South American adventure, I managed to get her back to the boat before it sailed. She was young and pretty, I told her. She should go back to England, marry John and settle down to the kind of life that she was obviously cut out for. Like many of the people I have met on my journeys, I have often wondered whatever happened to her.

She and all the friends I had made on the crossing from Australia gathered at the stern of the liner, waving and shouting their goodbyes as the ship slowly inched away. The Pommy contingent was singing 'Maybe It's Because *He's* a Londoner'. The quay was quite deserted and suddenly I felt very alone.

I made my way back to the hotel, flopped out on the lumpy mattress and fell into a deep sleep. In the morning I was woken by the rattle of a snare-drum. Jesus! I thought, a public execution is about to take place! I jumped out of bed and peered out of the grimy windows which overlooked a square below. A detachment of soldiers was getting into line. Somebody blew a number of notes on a bugle and the soldiers snapped to attention. An officer took a couple of paces forward and saluted. Then the Panamanian flag was run up on a flagpole and everybody disappeared as quickly as they had arrived.

Later that same morning, I met Frank and Rosie at the KLM office where they were in the process of arranging their flight to Caracas. Frank invited me to stop off on the way to Rio and spend a week or two with him and his brother. So the ticket I bought was for Caracas, Rio and Montevideo. Montevideo was to serve as a red herring if and when the police traced me to the *Ellinis* and as far as Panama.

With the ticket in my hand, I went to the immigration office to collect the 200 bucks that I had left as a bond. The agent who had gone aboard the *Ellinis* attended to me, wishing me good luck on my trip south.

When I arrived at Caracas Airport the first thing I noticed was a lot of policemen. Many of them were wearing plain clothes, but it wasn't difficult to pick them out. They would have made perfect extras on any *Mission Impossible* set. However, I went through customs and the passport checkpoint without a hitch and joined Frank and Rosie, who had arrived a couple of days earlier and were at the airport to meet me. I found out later that the cops had been on the look-out for a Commie terrorist of some kind and had no interest in a mere British train robber.

I stayed in Caracas for two weeks, enjoying the hospitality of Frank and his brother Carlos. As Frank had started work, I found myself in Rosie's company a fair bit and we became fond of each other. She had split up with her husband in Australia and was seeking a new life in South America. She wanted me to stay in Caracas and I was tempted – I had even been offered a job, together with a work permit and other papers in the name of Michael Haynes. But nothing could change my mind: the plan was to go to Rio de Janeiro and to Rio de Janeiro I would go.

# 9. Mr Haynes Settles in Rio

On Sunday 11 March 1970, I landed at Rio de Janeiro's old Galeão Airport. It was early in the morning, sunny and already very hot. Once again I felt my heartbeat accelerating as I stood in line for my passport to be examined.

During the flight from Caracas I had struck up an acquaintance with an elderly American gentleman named Bill and now, trying to appear quite at ease, I was chatting away nineteen to the dozen with the old chap as we waited our turn behind a group of nuns. Subconsciously, I think, I hoped the nuns might bring some added heavenly protection. I need not have worried: my passport was stamped and returned with hardly a glance from the immigration official. I was in Brazil. I had done it again! I felt the same rush of adrenalin and euphoria that I had experienced when I escaped from Wandsworth and when I first arrived in Australia. It was the beginning of another new phase to my life.

Bill was only going to be in town for a couple of days. He was on his way to Argentina and had broken his trip to deliver a letter to a friend of his wife who lived in Rio. He was already booked into the Luxor Hotel on Avenida Atlantica, the Copacabana seafront, and suggested that I should find a room at the same place. In the taxi we drove along Botafogo Beach, which in places seemed within touching distance of the massive Sugar Loaf Mountain. It was that very same view that had first attracted me to Rio on the Varig Airline brochure I had seen in Melbourne and every bit as impressive. It was unbelievable.

The prices at the Luxor were equally unbelievable. I left my case with Bill and went off to find something more down-market and within my limited means. A couple of blocks back from the seafront I found exactly what I could afford: a flea-pit, the Hotel Santa Clara, at three dollars a night. The doorman-owner was a swarthy Portuguese who smelled of sweat. After we had laboured over a sign-language deal, a bulky black lady, also smelling of sweat, showed me to a room. The window looked out on to the wall of a neighbouring apartment building. The furniture was old, the washbasin was cracked and there was an unpleasant, sweaty-sock smell in the air. But it was all I could afford and I had known worse. It was to be 'home' for the next couple of months.

I lunched with Bill and afterwards went with him to deliver the letter to his wife's friend, who lived within walking distance of the hotel. Nadine Mitchell was her name, a beautiful American lady in her late fifties (I think she would settle for that). A Christian Scientist and an English teacher, Bill had described her as 'quite a gal'. Later she confided in me that she had been in show business, dancing with the Ziegfeld Follies at a time when gangsters regularly made passes at the girls. She had been 'married' to a Brazilian army colonel who had died and so she now considered herself to be a widow.

When she heard that I had spent some time in Australia she told me about a young Australian fellow, Rob, who had left Rio just before my arrival. Rob, she said, had come to Rio with a 'serious drinking problem' and she was happy to tell me that she had cured him. Now, no self-respecting Aussie I had ever met would let some sheila gal get between him and his grog, so I thought this bloke had to be a bit of a wimp. Nadine said that he was travelling in the north of Brazil but would soon be back and she wanted me to keep in touch so that she could introduce us.

When Bill left, apart from Nadine, I knew no other English-speaking person in Rio and it was no easy matter getting to grips with the Portuguese language. Asking for a beer, I was offered milk, wine and Coca-Cola. The taxi-drivers, it seemed, found it more difficult to understand my Portuguese than anyone else. If ever I wanted a grand tour of Rio I only had to ask to be taken from one end of Copacabana to the other. I was pleased, therefore, when I met Adauto Agallo, a clerk at the American

Express office in downtown Rio. He was a young Brazilian who could speak English fluently and we soon found that we had a mutual interest in jazz.

I had gone to the Amex office to see if I could receive mail there. The smiling, helpful Mr Agallo told me there was 'no problem, man'. By a happy coincidence, he lived only a stone's throw from the flea factory where I was staying. Sunday afternoons, Adauto told me, were dedicated to serious drinking and jazz, so I took him up on his offer to visit him at his home.

I met and liked his family and friends, particularly a young medical student called Mauricio, who laughed a lot and could also speak fairly good English. He called me 'Gringo'. One evening, following an afternoon of slugging back a goodly number of gin and tonics, I agreed to go with Mauricio and a couple of his friends to a 'special' night club. We roared off into the night in Mauricio's Karman Ghia coupé. The club was way out in the sticks and I didn't have a clue where we were, but it appeared to be a popular place. The 'Gringo' was introduced to the young proprietor, who spoke a little English, and a table near the raised dance floor was quickly arranged. The music pounded, the strobe lights flickered and the booze flowed. I was enjoying myself immensely. Mauricio drew my attention to a slender young girl dancing alone and smiling in our direction.

'Hey, Gringo,' he shouted, 'I think that girl wants you to dance with her.'

When I awoke the next morning, I found myself lying on the floor of a hotel bathroom. I remembered the smiling girl and dancing with her. I remembered taking a couple of drags at the cigarette she was smoking and telling myself that it was marijuana . . . Never again, I vowed.

Nadine contacted me a few days later to tell me that Rob was back in town and invited me to meet him over dinner at her apartment. Rob was from Adelaide and seemed like a decent sort of a bloke. After a superb dinner, washed down with water, Nadine said that she would like to read to us from the Bible. Hours later Rob and I left the apartment together.

'Christ!' he said when we were out of earshot. 'I need a bloody drink after that!'

'I thought you had stopped drinking,' I said. 'Nadine told me that she had cured you of a serious wine-drinking problem.'

'Cured me of drinking wine, my arse,' scoffed the Aussie. 'I gave up drinking wine because I discovered cachaça!'

Cachaça, I knew, was a cheap, potent white spirit produced from sugar cane. The original elixir of life.

'Speaking of cachaça,' Rob went on, 'I'm going to take you to the Bip-Bip bar. You are going to love it!'

The Bip-Bip bar was in nearby Ipanema, specializing in drinks made from fruit juices and cachaça. The choice was wide and exotic to a newcomer to the tropics. We started with tangerine and then went on to passionfruit, followed by strawberry, lemon and tamarind.

Around midnight, and now back in Copacabana, we decided to go for a swim. The surf was up! Quite pissed and completely starkers we threw ourselves into the foaming breakers. We sobered up a bit when we came out of the water as we couldn't find our clothes. During the time we had been frolicking in the sea, the current had taken us further down the beach and away from where we had left our stuff. We eventually found it untouched and went dripping back to my hotel. Rob hoped that he would be able to crash out in my room, but the Portuguese doorman-owner, who never seemed to leave his post, even to sleep, wouldn't hear of it. I was already in his 'black book' for being a couple of weeks in arrears with my rent, so there was no point in arguing with him.

Nadine had got us to promise that we would go with her to church the following Sunday morning.

'Fuck that!' said Rob when I phoned him at his hotel to remind him of our obligation. 'I'm going to the beach.'

So I went alone and was rewarded with a warm smile from Nadine. After the service she introduced me to a number of the congregation, including Werner and Joyce Blumer, a Swiss stockbroker and his wife, leading lights in Rio's Christian Science community.

Everyone was very friendly, especially the Blumers. When Werner learned that I knew a thing or two about carpentry he immediately invited me to his house to take care of a number of things that needed repairing. He had a fully equipped workshop, he told me, so tools would not be a problem. I jumped at the chance to earn some extra cash. Apparently satisfied with my work, Werner suggested that I should move in with them and be part of the family. There were only two rules, said my new boss: no girlfriends and no alcoholic beverages on the premises.

It was about this time that I met an attractive mulatta named Edith. She was Adauto's sister-in-law and worked for General Electric as a bilingual secretary. She was twenty-seven. We started out as 'just good friends', but when our relationship developed into an intimate one I told her my story, including the fact that I had a wife and children in Australia. We became closer friends than ever, Edith wanting, above all, to see me reunited with my family.

Six months after I arrived in Brazil, when I was still living with the Blumer family, the time came for me to renew my visa. I did not want to attract the attention of the Brazilian authorities by overstaying my welcome and that meant that I would have to leave the country, if only for a couple of hours. After consulting a map, I decided to take a bus trip to Argentina – I thought it would be a nice little jaunt. Werner provided me with an advance against my salary which enabled me to buy the bus ticket and still have money over for other expenses.

I got off to a bad start on the trip, finding that my seat on the 1000-mile journey to Porto Alegre was next to a very fat Brazilian lady. During the night, when she stretched out to sleep, she overflowed into my seat, making it impossible for me to get any shut-eye. I spent the night sitting on the steps by the door of the bus. At Porto Alegre, in the south of Brazil, I had to change buses and I was grateful to find myself on a much less crowded one. It was still many hours and over 650 miles to Buenos Aires, but at least I would be able to get some sleep.

It started to pour with rain as we left Porto Alegre. The bus lurched and shimmied on the muddy highway, finally slipping off the road altogether and into a ditch. All the *hombres* were called upon to get the bus on the road again, even the sleeping gringo in his suede shoes.

Treading warily, I made my way to the rear of the bus and joined in the heaving and shoving. We were winning!

Push!

Suddenly and without any warning the driver hit the gas and the bus slewed back towards the ditch. I leapt aside to avoid being knocked over and landed up to my knees in soft, wet red mud. Soaked and muddy, I returned to my seat in the hope of catching an extra forty winks while I dried off.

By my calculations, we should arrive at the Argentine border about five o'clock in the morning, an hour, I told myself, when frontier guards could be caught napping. Leaving Brazil presented no problem. The bus driver collected our passports and other documents and took them away to have '*saída*' stamped into them. I relaxed – it was going to be easier than I thought. The driver soon returned and the bus proceeded across a bridge into Argentina, stopping at the Argentinian checkpoint. Here we were all taken off the bus and herded into a large, well-lit office where we stood in line waiting to be attended by a solitary official behind a small desk.

The line moved quickly as the official appeared to give only a cursory glance at the documents before stamping them. When I reached the table and held out my passport, however, he gave me a long, hard stare. He took Michael Haynes' passport and began going through it slowly, page by page. He returned to the page with the photograph, looking from the picture to me. He did this several times. He then picked up a paper-knife and attempted to raise the corners of the photo. Still not satisfied, he went through the passport a second time, stopping at a page where there was an entry written in red ink. At one time, the real Michael Haynes had crossed from India into Pakistan and had been suspected of trying to smuggle in a Land-Rover, hence the entry in red. The official pointed to the page, said something in Spanish, and looked at me enquiringly. I shook my head.

'I'm sorry,' I said, 'I don't speak Spanish.' Then, with a flourish, he stamped the passport with an '*entrada*' and scribbled his initials beside it. He fixed me one last time with a long, hard stare, tapping the passport against his hand for what seemed like an eternity before handing it back to me without further comment.

Leaving the office I looked around for a toilet; the incident had given me an urgent desire to relieve my bowels!

The trip continued without further drama and I arrived in Buenos Aires looking a picture, with my by now dry pants pink from the knees down with shoes to match.

One of Nadine's friends in Rio, an Argentine lady by the name of Fanny, had kindly suggested that I could stay with her relatives in BA, and had given me some small presents to deliver to them. I found the address without much trouble and received a warm welcome from Fanny's sister and her husband. They took me around to places of interest and various bars and restaurants, but there was a serious language barrier as neither one of them spoke any language other than Spanish and my Portuguese was still not up to much. My funds were low and the weather had turned cold, so I didn't stay much longer than a week in BA, returning to Rio by a bus that was taking a different route to the one that I had arrived on. I didn't fancy a second encounter with the border official who had literally scared the shit out of me!

Back in Rio and the bosom of the Blumers, I picked up from where I had been before my excursion. I wrote to Charmian, describing my 'near thing' in Argentina and its laxative effect. At that time, Charm and I were kicking around a few ideas and making uncertain plans to reunite at some stage. We had written about the possibility of me sneaking back into Australia and for that reason it was necessary for me to keep my passport ready for action.

One of Werner's partners in the stock market was a middle-aged American named Scott Johnson. He was also in need of a carpenter and I started working for him at weekends. We became good friends and frequently went to the samba clubs that abound in Rio. Scott was pretty well off, drove a Ford Cutlass and was extremely popular with the dusky young girls who flocked to the *escolas de samba*, as the clubs were called. I really enjoyed these evenings at the samba schools. The beer was cold and the prices were as friendly as the girls. I also happened to like the samba.

I spent most of Christmas 1970 with Edith and some of her friends, one of whom was a detective who went around with a gun tucked down the front of his trousers. Like many of his kind, he believed that all thieves – with the exception, of course, of detectives – should not be allowed to live. Despite his presence and views we still managed to have a jolly time and celebrated Christmas Day by eating *feijoada* – a traditional Brazilian stew of black beans and hunks of fat salted pork and other meats, served with rice, kale, pork crackling and slices of fresh orange. A truly superb dish which remains one of my all-time favourites.

Everything seemed to be going well. With the extra money I had been earning by working for Scott I was able to buy myself some new clothes and other small luxuries. Although I was quite happy with the Blumers, I was keen to rent a place of my own and regain my personal freedom. Scott had told me about an apartment in Copacabana which belonged to one of his friends. He was confident that he could get it for me at a really low rental.

Then, one sunny morning in February 1971, I received a phone call from Adauto Agallo. A letter had arrived for me at the American Express office and he had taken it home for me to collect. His wife would be there if I wanted to go by his apartment and pick it up. I told the Blumers I had something important to take care of and took the bus to Adauto's home. His wife, Olga, all smiles as usual, handed me a fat envelope bearing Charmian's unmistakable handwriting. Not wanting to be away from my job for too long I thanked Olga and left, happily tearing the letter open as I went. The opening line of the letter stopped me in my tracks: 'Wherever you are and whatever you are doing, sit down . . . our darling son Nicky has been killed in a road accident . . .'

I felt physically sick and faint, completely stunned by the terrible news. I don't know why but I felt I had to talk to somebody about it. Like someone in a trance, I got to a bar and sat down. I tried to read the rest of Charmian's letter, but it was impossible. I could only cry silently. I saw a pay-phone on the wall of the bar and got up to call somebody – anybody. I dialled a number and heard Adauto's voice. 'Hello – hello? American Express – hello?' I did all I could to force myself to speak, to say Adauto's name, but I was unable to utter a sound. I hung up and stumbled out of the bar. Still in a trance I wandered aimlessly down the road. Then, through the haze, I knew what I was going to do. I would go to the British Consulate and give myself up.

A fifteen-minute bus-ride later, I found myself standing outside the British Consulate in Flamengo. The journey, however short, had been time enough for me to get over the initial shock and regain part of my composure. I went to a bar close to the Consulate and quickly gulped down two large brandies. From where I stood, I could see the Union Jack hanging in front of the Consulate building. All I had to do was walk in through the door and announce who I was. Instead, I crossed the road, sat down on a bench in Flamengo Park and read Charmian's letter from beginning to end. She gave details of the accident, which had occurred on 2 January, and said she felt heavily responsible because she had been driving when the tragedy occurred. The crash had happened less than thirty yards from the Haynes' front door. Charmian had just dropped Mike and Jessie off after the New Year break when the car was hit by another vehicle going straight across a junction which was Charmian's right of way. Farley had been badly cut in the crash, but would be okay, and Charmian and Chris were badly shaken. I sat in the park for a long time thinking things over and came to the conclusion that the last thing I should do was to give myself up. I felt it was not what Nicky would have wanted.

The Blumer family had no idea that I had a wife and three children on the other side of the world and I had never given them any reason to believe that I was anyone but Michael Haynes. When I returned to the house they could see that I was very unhappy and naturally wanted to know why. I thanked them for their concern and invented some lie.

Life continued, but Nicky's death at the age of ten had left me devastated. I found it hard to garner any enthusiasm for anything. When Carnival came around, my first in Rio, Edith got tickets for us to see the parade of the samba schools. I was not really in the mood to watch a Carnival parade but Edith and her chums insisted that I needed something to lift me out of the doldrums. I'm glad I went. It was – and is – a wonderful and moving experience.

Each day, however, I thought more and more about getting back to Australia, which meant I had to keep 'my' passport up to date. To do that, and not attract unnecessary attention, I had to make a second trip out of Brazil.

I had been in Brazil for almost a year. Loth to return to Argentina, I decided in March 1971 to take a bus to Corumba, a town on the Bolivian border.

During the long, dusty journey, the bus was stopped by the military and civil police at least half-a-dozen times. The police either boarded the bus or took us all off for a more thorough search; whichever method they chose they always demanded to see every passenger's identity and travel documents. When I chose Brazil as a refuge, I had been quite unaware of the fact that the country was under a strict military dictatorship. A Communist witch-hunt was on and anyone found without some kind of identification was hustled off to the nearest *delegacia* for some heavy questioning or worse.

One evening in Rio when waiting for a friend, I was approached by a couple of Colombian hippies who showed me a piece of paper and made it clear that they needed money. As they were going through their routine, two cops appeared out of the shadows with guns in their hands. '*Documentos!*' said one in an unfriendly fashion. I froze. I didn't have my precious passport or any other identification with me. The hippies showed the cops the piece of paper they had shown to me, but the policemen were clearly far from satisfied and the Colombians were marched off at gunpoint, leaving me standing holding my breath. The police had obviously thought the hippies were trying to shake down a British tourist. Even though I had been in Brazil a year, I was still very much the innocent abroad. It was to be one of many close calls.

It was only when I got to the police post in Corumba and saw the photographs on the walls of the cocaine busts that had recently been made that I realized that I was using a well-trodden South American drug trail. This at least explained the number of searches, but I still had to return the same way!

At the Brazilian–Bolivian border a friendly Brazilian police-man stamped the '*saída*' into my passport and advised me to stay on the other side of the border for a couple of days before re-entering Brazil. He was clearly used to 'tourists' who needed to revalidate their visas.

A bus took me over a bridge into Puerto Saurez on the Bolivian side of the border. It was very different from my arrival in Argentina – I was in Bolivia and I had not even been asked to show my passport. I found a cheap hotel and booked in. With great difficulty, I asked the proprietor of the humble establishment where I should go to get an '*entrada*' stamped into my passport. Every evening, he told me, the man responsible for the border could be found at a nearby bar where he had his dinner. This was the *hombre* to speak to.

I had no trouble spotting my man, another *Mission Impossible* type. I soon discovered that he was running a nice little scam shaking down 'tourists' like myself who required his initials in their passport so that they could return to Brazil for another six months. He started out at $100 for the '*entrada*' and '*salida*' stamps plus his initials, but grudgingly settled for twenty when he found I was not kidding about my worldly wealth.

Two nights at the Mosquito Motel were two nights too many; I was glad when I got back to Corumba and caught the bus back to Rio, even if Rio was over 1200 miles and a number of police searches away.

Soon after my return from the Bolivian trip, thanks to Scott's diligent work, I moved into a twelfth-floor, fully furnished apartment in Rua Prado Junior in Copacabana, a short walk from the beach. I was still unhappy, but gradually the pain of losing Nicky eased and I picked up the pieces of my life. I worked long hours during the week and relaxed on the beach at the weekends with Edith and her friends.

About the middle of 1971, Edith went off on a long vacation to England and the US, so I started frequenting Adauto's Sunday afternoon jazz sessions again. On one of these visits I was introduced to a lively, friendly Brazilian fellow called Paulo. He spoke English quite well, having lived in the US for a couple of years, and I found him interesting company. He was also a samba enthusiast and we made an arrangement to go to his favourite club, the Bola Preta (the Black Ball), the following Friday.

The Bola Preta is situated in downtown Rio, the business

heart of the city, next to the Municipal Theatre. It has a reputation for 'hot' samba and is very popular with people of all ages, colours and creeds. We got there early so that we could be sure of getting a prime table near the dance floor and ordered a couple of beers. Among the dancers I noticed a small young woman with long black hair and an enchanting smile. She was accompanied by a young Brazilian guy, but before the evening was over I had a chance to exchange a few words with her. Her name was Raimunda Nascimento de Castro, she said with the same wide smile, and she would be happy to meet me at the club the following week.

It was a fine romance until the day that Edith was due back from the US. Raimunda had left her baby-doll nightdress on the bed and I suggested that she might like to take it with her in case Edith, who had a key to my apartment, turned up without warning. Raimunda exploded, giving me the ultimatum that I had to make a choice between her and Edith. I chose Edith and the fiery Raimunda stormed out of my life in a huff.

While I had been dallying in Rio, Edith had not been wasting much time in New York: she had met and become fond of a hotel manager, something she made no mention of on her return. I noticed, however, a distinct change in her. She spoke enthusiastically about New York and said that she would be going there again for her next vacation.

Unwilling to make another trip out of Brazil after my experiences in Argentina and Bolivia, I allowed the validity of my passport to expire in September 1971. Charmian was still nursing the hope that I would be able to get back to Australia, but the more I thought about it the less likely it seemed to be a good idea. My return to Australia, even if it were possible, could only be disruptive as far as Chris and Farley were concerned. They were both at school and leading reasonably orderly lives; my presence was sure to create complications. I outlined these misgivings in a letter to Charmian, who wrote back saying that she saw my reluctance to go back to Australia as an attack of cold feet.

Edith's holiday was coming up and she was going off to the States again, but promised to be back in time for my birthday on 8 August. I took her to the airport with a number of her cronies, one of whom jokingly teascd her that she was going to take 'good' care of me while she was away. But Edith hugged me and told her friend to back off – she would be back soon, she said, to claim 'her man'.

Another of Edith's friends, who was always referred to as 'crazy', was a Brazilian airline steward by the name of Magalhães. He was crazy because he smoked marijuana, something that Edith strongly disapproved of. Magalhães was enthusiastic about his vice and on more than one occasion he invited me to share a joint with him. But I remembered my first and only experience and turned down his repeated offers.

A few days after Edith's departure Scott gave me a call and, discovering that Edith was away, suggested a night out at one of the samba clubs. I was all for it and we made arrangements to meet at the Bola Preta at the weekend. As always, the club was full but Scott bribed one of the waiters and a good table was soon made available. A couple of pretty mulatta girls at a neighbouring table were showing obvious interest in the two big gringos and at Scott's invitation they came across and joined us. The one that I took a fancy to was called Ana Paula. She was very attractive with high cheek bones, white teeth and a good figure. We drank and we danced and eventually went back to my apartment to get to know each other better!

August 8 came and went and there was still no sign of Edith. I telephoned her home and her sister Zelia answered. Zelia was Edith's eldest sister and it was obvious from the start of our affair that she didn't approve of Edith being involved with a married man. She had even resorted to *macumba*, the Brazilian voodoo, to try to stop us seeing one another. I asked Zelia if she had any news of Edith.

'Haven't you heard?' she asked, in a more friendly manner than I was accustomed to.

'I haven't heard anything,' I replied. 'Edith said she would be back before 8 August but I haven't heard anything. What's going on?'

Zelia could hardly wait to tell me. 'But Ronnie, Edith got married last week. Didn't you know?'

'What! Who to?'

'A German, someone she met when she was in New York last year.'

I was amazed by the news. Edith had mentioned meeting a German and it had crossed my mind that she might have had a fling with him, but I found it unbelievable that she had actually gone and got married. Zelia must be lying, I thought.

But Zelia wasn't lying. Edith flew back to Brazil a week later to collect her clothes and to quit her job. She phoned me before returning to New York and said tearfully that she had made the decision to marry on the spur of the moment. She hoped that I would understand. I said I did and wished her good luck and much happiness. She had been a fine friend and I was going to miss her.

It was a Saturday and although we were well into winter it was a warm, sunny day. I had just finished tidying up the apartment when someone rang the bell. I opened the door to three young hippies, one of them sporting a large Afro hairstyle. He had heard that I was looking for a carpenter and was applying for the job. Some time before I had been needing some help with some work and I had spoken to various people in the building trade about a carpenter. At the moment I had little work on, but I invited the group in so that I could write down Afro's name and address in case I needed someone in the future. I opened a couple of beers and asked him about his experience as a carpenter. If it had rested solely on the look of the chap I doubt very much if I would have hired him. Out of the blue he asked me if I had any objection to him rolling a joint and I told him to do his own thing, no problem. He rolled a long, thin *cigarrinho*. He told me that his name was Marcelo and he lived in Ipanema. The joint finished, he lit up and took a couple of long tokes before passing the cigarette on to me. I hesitated for a second, then took the joint from him and took a drag on it. I passed it on to Marcelo's pals; it duly came around again and I had another puff, wondering if I was doing the right thing. The joint was smoked down to the end and the hippies got up to leave. I thought they looked a bit unsteady on their feet and asked myself why anyone bothered to smoke the stuff. All I felt was a slight nausea. When they had gone I cleared away the beer bottles and glasses and put on a record. It was *Jazz Samba* with Stan Getz, Charlie Byrd and Luis Bonfá, a record I particularly liked and often played. Then I stretched out on the settee to relax.

What followed defies description. I've been told that I went on an 'astral voyage'. Whatever it was, it was no ordinary trip. I was omnipotent – until it was time to turn the record over. The floor had turned to cotton wool.

The experience was so extraordinary, if that's the word, that the next morning found me knocking on Marcelo's door for more of the shit. I was hooked.

It was Ana Paula's birthday on 8 September. I was going to take her to dinner and we had arranged for her to arrive at my place around seven o'clock. About six the doorbell rang and I presumed that Ana Paula had arrived early, but it wasn't Ana Paula, it was Raimunda with her wide smile.

'*Como vai, seu vagabundo?* (How are you, you bum?)' she asked.

In no time we were on the bed and talking about old times. I was really getting carried away when I remembered Ana Paula. It was ten to seven. Hastily I explained the situation to Raimunda and asked her to come back the next day. She called me a son of a bitch, but promised to return. Through the spyhole in the front door I watched her walk down the corridor to the lift. Almost as soon as she got there the door opened and out stepped Ana Paula.

She entered the apartment sniffing the air like a pointer. 'I can smell a whore,' she said. 'You've had a whore in here. I just saw her getting into the elevator.' I tried to talk my way out of it, but Ana Paula was a bright girl and she knew very well what the score was. We talked about our relationship over dinner and decided quite amicably to go our separate ways. Two days later Raimunda moved into my apartment and my life.

Until her arrival, the apartment was – to say the least – untidy. In one day, while I was at work, Xuxu (pronounced 'shoo-shoo', a small green vegetable), as I called her, had the apartment clean, polished and in apple-pie order. As I looked around admiring her handiwork, she appeared with a glass of cold beer, invited me to sit down and switched on a table lamp. I was surprised to see that the white bulb had been replaced by a blue one. Then she put on a lazy samba record and began to dance to the music, letting down her long black hair. Artistically, she stepped on to the marble coffee table and slowly started to strip off her clothes. We got on very well together and she was fun to be with. At what I thought was an appropriate moment, I told her my true name, the reason I was in Brazil and that I had a wife and children in Australia. Raimunda took this piece of news in her stride and it appeared to make little difference to our relationship. She showed a lot of interest in my children and told me that she herself had a young son who was living with his father, a doctor, in Maranhão, in the north of Brazil.

Around the end of 1972 I received word from Mike Haynes that he needed his passport back: he was planning to return to England with his family the following year. He had applied for a new passport, claiming that he had lost his old one, but for some reason his application had been turned down. He would have to find the old one, he was told.

I was wondering how I could get the passport back to Mike, as it's not often you meet people travelling between Brazil and Australia, when at a party I was introduced to a Brazilian girl called Dilse who worked in tourism. She told me that she would be taking a group of Brazilians to Australia in February 1973. I explained to her that I knew the country quite well and had friends there – perhaps she would be kind enough to take some small presents to them for me. She agreed readily and when she went she took a small package with her which among other things contained Mike's well-travelled passport – minus the pages relating to my exit from Australia and the subsequent trips around South America. When Mike received it he mutilated it further and scribbled in it with coloured pencils before presenting it for renewal. It had fallen into the hands of his young son, he explained, and was believed!

The months passed, bringing financial ups and downs. More than once the power was cut off when I failed to pay the light bill on time, so I was very pleased when the Blumers called me in to work on an art gallery they were in the process of setting up. It was during this period that I met Joyce Blumer's sister-in-law, Phyllis Huber, an attractive and intelligent lady in her late twenties. She had been well educated and spoke English with an American accent.

'Hi,' she said when we met. 'You must be Mike Haynes – I've heard a lot about you.' She invited me to dinner where I was introduced to her hippy friends, Brazilians and Americans, who of course were all 'heads'. After the meal we sat around talking, drinking cheap wine and smoking grass. I enjoyed the company and I became a frequent visitor to Phyllis's apartment. It was there that I met a young Englishman of White Russian extraction by the name of Constantine Benckendorff – 'Conti' to his friends. Over a joint or two we became quite pally and started going around together. He became interested in a stoned-out idea that Phyllis and I had to set up an interior decorating business we planned to call Planet Venus.

I had told Phyllis my real name and why I was in Brazil, but she didn't believe me! 'Don't freak me out, Mike,' she had said. I also trusted Conti enough to reveal my identity to him. It blew his mind, but he said that he was ready to help me in any way possible.

A little less than a year after she had moved in, Raimunda asked me if I minded if her mother came to stay with us for a while. There was only one bedroom in the apartment but Raimunda said that her mother would be quite comfortable on the settee. We wouldn't even notice she was there, she promised. So I agreed.

A couple of weeks later Dona Maria arrived in Rio after close to three days on a bus, accompanied by Rosangela, Raimunda's fifteen-year-old adopted daughter, who would also be quite happy to sleep on the floor of the living room and go 'unnoticed'. It soon became clear that all three of the ladies had the same insatiable thirst for Brazilian television soap operas, which further induced me to seek the company of my grass-smoking friends. The 'blue lamp' cabaret had sadly closed.

One evening I returned home to find Raimunda, her mother, Rosangela and two other females I didn't even know all soaking their feet in bowls in preparation for a manicure session. The air was a mixture of cigarette smoke and nail-varnish-remover fumes and the telly was going full blast. The next morning I had a bit of a showdown with Xuxu and ended up by saying that the time had come for Dona Maria and Rosangela to return to Maranhão. Raimunda's reply was along the lines that if her mother and her adopted daughter had to go, then she would go with them. A few days later I took all three of them to the bus station and waved a sad goodbye as they set out on the long journey north.

Scott Johnson had just bought a roof-top apartment and planned to make extensive changes, so I was invited to take charge of the job. We started going to the samba clubs again at the weekends and it was on one of these jaunts that I met a nineteen-year-old bank clerk named Lucia. Pretty, long-legged and sex mad. It was something of a whirlwind romance and we spent as much time as possible together, mostly in bed. She didn't move in with me, but she did bring some clothes to the apartment and left them hanging in the wardrobe.

Around this time I received a desperately unhappy tape from Charmian telling me how much she and the boys were missing and needing me. There was further mention of somehow me getting back to Australia. The content of the tape left me very depressed and thoughts of giving myself up began to enter my head again. Charmian and my children were unhappy and so was I. The only way to put our lives in order, I thought, was to go back to prison.

I talked the matter over with Conti, who thought I had to be potty to be thinking of going back to the nick. But he knew I was serious. During the time I had been free the long-awaited parole system had become a reality in Her Majesty's Prisons. In theory, certain cons would be considered for release on parole after completing one third of their sentence. By this time the members of the gang who had been sentenced to thirty years were already eligible for parole and their cases were no doubt being 'considered'. Had I not done a bunk in 1965 I would have been standing alongside my colleagues, also cap in hand. Now, if I went back to jail voluntarily, I decided, it could weigh heavily in my favour in front of some future parole committee. Roy James, by the way, was the first of those who had received a thirty-year sentence to be paroled. He was released in August 1975 having spent nearly twelve years in prison.

Conti was going back to spend the Christmas of 1973 in England. I asked him to do me a favour.

'When you get back to London,' I said, 'I'd like you to make a few discreet enquiries to see if you can find a paper interested in buying the story of my return to HMP Wandsworth.'

'If that's what you want, I'll do the best I can,' said Conti, 'but I still think you're mad.'

One evening, after a not very happy Christmas, I arrived home to find Raimunda sitting in the living room. She said she had decided to come back to me, she was 'my woman'. However, she wanted to know what was the 'shit' hanging up in the wardrobe. Inadvertently I had left the front door open, and almost on cue, Lucia came into the apartment with her best friend, Ana. I sensed that an ugly situation was about to develop and herded Lucia and her friend out of the apartment. I apologized to Lucia about the unexpected turn of events and told her that I would explain everything the following day. Then, while she waited in the corridor, I put her clothes into a suitcase and took it out to her. Raimunda's anger had subsided and I found her weeping when I went back into the living room. A long conversation followed, during which I told her of my decision to give myself up, outlining my reasons. She said that she knew that I was unhappy and that I had to do what I thought was best. But she wanted to be with me until I left Brazil, she loved me.

Xuxu was back in my life!

# 10. Caught – Slipper Drops His Catch

In January 1974 I received an excited phone call from Conti. He had met a *Daily Express* reporter named Colin Mackenzie at a cocktail party in London and it was almost certain that his paper would be interested in buying my story. He handed me over to Mackenzie, who asked certain questions to verify that it was the real Ronald Biggs on the line. Satisfied with my answers, he said that the *Express* was ready to send him to Brazil as soon as he presented some written evidence. The paper wanted some concrete proof that I really was who I said I was because it had recently been left with egg over its face over another hunt for a fugitive in South America. The fugitive in question had been, or rather had turned out not to be, Hitler's number two, Martin Bormann.

I sent Mackenzie a letter bearing my signature and a copy of my fingerprints. The letter read: 'Hi, Colin, Perhaps not the best set [of fingerprints] that have been taken, but certainly as good as those found on the Monopoly box and the sauce bottle! Convinced?! R.A. Biggs.'

I was somewhat uneasy about dealing with the *Daily Express*, as I was well aware that it had been responsible for the capture of gang member Jimmy White. But I was going to give myself up, so I ruled out the possibility that anything could go wrong with the business in hand.

My letter having been received, Mackenzie sounded ecstatic on the phone. It was a great story, he enthused, and there would be no problem with regard to the 'bread'. Everything was being kept top secret, he assured me, as did the *Express* News Editor,

150

Brian Hitchen, who also came on the line. Only Colin and Conti would be travelling to Rio, Hitchen assured me, while only the very top brass on the paper were in on the story.

Early on the morning of Wednesday 30 January there was a phone call from Conti informing me that he and Mackenzie had arrived safely in Rio and were comfortably installed in room 909 at the Trocadero Hotel on Copacabana beachfront – a stone's throw from where I was living.

I had made an arrangement with Lucia, with whom I had still remained friendly despite the presence of Raimunda in the apartment, to meet her at the beach that morning. I picked her up at her flat, told her what was happening and took her with me to meet the man from the *Express*.

When the door to room 909 opened, I saw that there were two men besides Conti in the room. They were introduced to me as Colin Mackenzie and Bill Lovelace. I reminded Mackenzie that I had been assured that only he and Conti would meet me in Rio. I wasn't very pleased to see a third person.

'Don't worry about Bill,' Mackenzie said disarmingly, 'you can trust him with your life. We must have photographs for the story and Bill is the best.'

Lovelace was already taking pictures, suggesting poses that I should take with Lucia, murmuring his appreciation of her charms all the while.

'By God, Ron, she's beautiful! Where did you find her?'

When Lovelace stopped for a breather, I asked Mackenzie how much I was being offered for my story.

'How much do you want?' he asked.

'£50,000,' I suggested.

'My office has only authorized me to go as high as thirty-five,' Mackenzie said, looking me straight in the eye. I reached out to shake hands with the representative of the *Daily Express*.

'It's a deal,' I said. 'I'll settle for that.'

I went on to explain to Mackenzie exactly how I wanted the *Express* to handle the money. Part of it was to go direct to Charmian and part to Raimunda. I asked if there was any way of avoiding paying tax on the sum and Mackenzie assured me that it would all be taken care of.

I had imagined that the *Express* 'team' would want to rest

after their overnight flight from London, but Mackenzie was all for getting started on the story immediately.

'Let's get the work out the way, Ron. Then we can relax,' he suggested.

Lovelace went off to get some shots of the local scenery and Conti was volunteered to take Lucia to the beach, a chore he jumped at. Mackenzie and I worked on my story for the rest of the day, only taking a short break for lunch. Early the next morning, Thursday, I was back at the Trocadero with a new round of revelations for Mackenzie. Again we worked through the day and into the evening. I felt like a little light-hearted entertainment after all this work and suggested to Mackenzie that we should go out to a nightclub or something of that nature. But the reporter made a face and said that he must have eaten something that had disagreed with him, he had an attack of 'tourist tummy' and would prefer to retire for the evening.

The following morning, as I was getting ready for day three in front of Mackenzie's tape-recorder, Raimunda announced that she thought she might be pregnant. She had been pregnant a couple of times before and a friend of hers, who is a nurse, had been called upon to take care of the problem. I saw it as a complication I could well do without and suggested that she should visit her friend and take whatever steps were necessary to terminate the pregnancy, should her suspicions be confirmed.

When I arrived that Friday at the Trocadero, Lovelace was already taking photographs of Lucia, who was wearing a tiny bikini, the type known in Brazil as *fio dental* (dental floss). Conti and Mackenzie were watching and drooling, the latter showing no signs of his malady of the previous evening. Lovelace wanted some shots of me in beachwear and so I changed into a pair of striped bathing trunks which belonged to Conti.

Not long after the end of the photo session there was a knock at the door which I took to be room service. Conti went to open the door. He was propelled back into the room by a much taller person whom I recognized immediately as Old Bill. I was sitting on the floor, still wearing Conti's swimming trunks and, regardless of what has been written or reported in the past, I simply said, 'Oh, fuck!'

To give him his full title, it was Detective Chief Superintendent Jack Slipper, head of Scotland Yard's so-called Flying Squad, who had stalked into the room.

'Hello, Ronnie,' he said, 'I think you know who I am? I certainly know who you are and I'm arresting you.'

He swung around on Mackenzie and continued, 'You've overstepped the mark this time, my lad. You're in trouble.' He turned back to me. 'Where are your clothes?'

'In the bathroom.'

'Right, let's go there.'

In the bathroom as I was getting into my clothes, there was a conversation between Slipper and me that went something like this: 'Now look, Ronnie, I've been working fucking hard on this for a long time. I've nicked you fair and square and I'm taking you back to England. I want you to come back without giving me any trouble because later on, when you come up for parole, I'll be asked to speak in your favour, or otherwise. You help me, and I'll help you – have we got a deal?'

It reminded me of a conversation I had had many years earlier with Inspector Basil Morris in Reigate.

'You're not going to believe this,' I said, 'but I was trying to give myself up. It would mean a lot to me not to go back wearing handcuffs.'

'I don't know about that,' Slipper said doubtfully. 'If I was to go back to England without you I'd be looking for a new job next week.'

'I'll go back without giving you any trouble,' I promised Slipper, 'but if I go handcuffed it will look as if I have been nicked and I've already told you that I was going to give myself up. Ask the reporter in the other room if you don't believe me.'

'I can't promise anything just yet,' said Slipper. 'We'll have to see.'

When Slipper had marched into room 909 of the Trocadero to 'nick' me (acting without any official power in Brazil whatsoever), he had been accompanied by a fellow policeman from Scotland Yard, Detective Inspector Peter Jones; the British Consul General, Henry Neil; his Brazilian Vice-Consul, Costa; and the Rio Police Commissioner and his assistant.

Back in the bedroom Slipper gave Jones, who had been taking down the particulars of everyone else in the room, some orders with regard to our exit from the hotel, then he produced his handcuffs.

'If you don't want me to give you any trouble,' I threatened, 'don't even think about putting those cuffs on me.'

A short argument followed. It was interrupted by the Police Commissioner, who opened his gabardine jacket to reveal the handle of a gun tucked down the front of his trousers.

'Oh, great,' said Slipper. 'That's great.'

'What's so great?' I demanded. 'This son of a bitch might shoot me and you think that's great? I don't think it's all that great.'

Up until that point the commissioner had not uttered a single word. I was unaware that he could speak English and certainly had no idea that he was a commissioner.

The commissioner looked mean and took a step towards me. 'Did you call me a son of a bitch?' he hissed.

'Yeah, I called you a *filho da puta*. I'm unarmed and you might just shoot me. Sure you're a son of a bitch!'

Slipper stepped into the arena. 'Calm down, Ronnie. No one is going to get shot.' He put his handcuffs away and took a firm hold of my belt. 'All right, we'll go down to the car like this. Peter, get the lift.'

With Slipper hanging on to my belt we left Mackenzie, Conti and Lucia in the room and departed the hotel in silence. On the way down in the lift I was trying to work out exactly how the police had arrived on the scene. When Slipper entered the hotel room Mackenzie had appeared to be as surprised as I was, so I had not suspected foul play as far as he was concerned. He swore later that he had no idea his superiors at the *Daily Express* had contacted the Yard.

The vice-consul's car, a chocolate-coloured Austin Maxi, was parked in front of the Trocadero and as we approached it Bill Lovelace ran up and began shooting pictures of my 'arrest'. I glared angrily in his direction; the evening before we had been drinking and chatting together like old chums. I was put into the back of the car between Jones and the commissioner's number two; Slipper got into the front with the commissioner and the vice-consul who was driving. Henry Neil was to follow in his car with his driver.

As we pulled away, Slipper turned to face me. 'We're going first to your flat, Ronnie, so that you can pick up some warm clothes,' he said. 'It's bloody cold in England at the moment, so you'll need a jacket or a sweater – and you can also collect any personal stuff that you may want to take back with you.'

At that moment I resigned myself to the fact that I had been nicked and there was little point in not co-operating. During the journey to my apartment the commissioner apologized for threatening me with his gun and I in turn apologized for calling him a son of a bitch. With Slipper once again holding on to my belt we went up to my twelfth-floor apartment in Avenida Prado Junior. There was no sign of Raimunda.

Keeping a close watch on me, Slipper made small talk while I got together the things I wanted to take back with me to Britain. He indicated that he was not keen on Brazilian food and was looking forward to getting home to some 'decent grub'. With one last look around my Brazilian home we headed back down to the car.

We proceeded from Copacabana to a grand old building known as the Catete Palace in Flamengo. At the time, part of the palace was being used by the federal police as their headquarters in Rio. Between 1896 and 1954 the palace had been the official residence of the Brazilian President: that was until President Getulio Vargas shot himself to death on 24 August 1954.

The police chief, or *delegado*, was Inspector Carlos Alberto Garcia, a flashy character with a pearl-handled gun showing above the waistband of his pants. Puffing on a cigar, he received Slipper and his party, listening intently to the details of my capture and identity from the British Vice-Consul, Costa. Leaving me in the care of Peter Jones, Slipper, Costa and Garcia retired to the *delegado*'s office to discuss the matter further. Jones appeared to be as anxious as his superior to get back to London; he and Jack, he confided, had plans to take their wives out for dinner the following evening. It was only later that I discovered that the night out was to celebrate my return to prison!

A federal agent, probably acting on Garcia's orders, appeared from nowhere and slapped a pair of handcuffs on my wrists. Moments later, Henry Neil arrived in the charge room puffing and panting. Having witnessed my reaction to handcuffs when Slipper wanted to put them on me, he protested on my behalf, speaking to the agent in Portuguese.

'Take these things off this poor boy. He's not a common criminal!' He explained who he was and the handcuffs were removed.

Neil sat down beside me and told me what he thought would be the best way to treat my present situation. 'I'm most anxious,' he said, 'that you should do everything to avoid spending any time in a Brazilian prison. I have visited one and I can assure you that it would horrify me to see you pass even one night in such a place.'

He explained that I would have to make a statement to the Brazilian authorities, but to be certain that I could leave the country without a hitch I would have to be careful what I said. If I was asked how I arrived in Brazil, said the British Consul General, it would be better if I didn't mention the fact that I had entered Brazil on a forged passport; such an admission might well result in up to six months in a filthy Brazilian prison before I was sent back to England to serve my time there. The best thing, he advised, was to say that I had entered the country from Paraguay, having crossed the border without a passport. It sounded like good advice, and when I was called to make my statement I explained my arrival in Brazil along these lines and signed my statement.

From that moment on, I was considered by Brazil to be in the country illegally – I was no longer 'on the run' – and, as a result, it was necessary to take my fingerprints forty times. I asked the cop why he needed to make so many copies and he simply said that it was normal in cases of 'expulsion'. That didn't sound so good.

Raised voices came from the *delegado*'s office and a little later a disgusted Jack Slipper came out to say that nothing was going to happen until after lunch. I was left in the care of two Brazilian cops who promptly put me back into handcuffs as soon as Henry Neil was off the premises. The afternoon session was very much like the morning one: another shouting match.

Jones was pacing up and down, glumly looking to his watch as the hours ticked by.

'It doesn't look as if we're going to catch our plane,' Jones said with a worried frown at one point, 'and there isn't another one until tomorrow morning.'

Finally Slipper emerged from the *delegado*'s office looking distinctly miserable. 'We won't be flying back tonight,' he said dejectedly. 'The chief has got to wait for instructions from Brasilia.' I sensed a slender ray of hope. The *delegado* came to speak with me, telling me that I would have to spend the night locked up. He seemed quite friendly and shook hands with me as he was leaving.

Late that evening I was taken under a heavy armed escort to a tiny prison in Praça Quinze, close to the docks. It wasn't really a prison, it was a very old police station that had half-a-dozen cells in its basement. But it served as a 'special' prison where, it was said, political prisoners had been taken for interrogation. 'The Presidential Suite', as one cell was called, was under several inches of water. Henry Neil had not exaggerated when he described a Brazilian prison earlier that day.

I was put into a cell which already housed three other prisoners, all awaiting trial. One of them, Mario, a middle-aged taxi driver, was a friendly fellow who wanted to know how and why a gringo had landed in their midst.

There were no beds or mattresses in the cell and the prisoners were expected to make do with newspaper and cardboard to lie on. While I told them the outline of my story Mario prepared a place for me to sleep, taking paper and cardboard from the three existing makeshift pallets. The Brazilians listened carefully to what I had to say, finding it difficult to believe that anyone involved in the robbery of the *trem pagador* (pay train, as it's called in Brazil) should be sharing their cell. Mario had an immediate answer to my problem.

'You've got to arrange a Brazilian child,' he said emphatically. 'Buy, borrow or steal one if necessary, any colour, any age – the only way to get out of the fix you are in is to get a kid and say it's yours. Do you have a girlfriend? Would she help you?'

I told them about Raimunda and mentioned that only that morning she had told me she might be pregnant.

'*Que beleza!* (How beautiful!)' said the taxi driver. 'You lucky son of a bitch! If you've got a Brazilian girl who's expecting your child you've got it made. *Puta que pariu!* If you father a child in Brazil you will never be made to leave.'

Mario's words were cheering and the slender ray of hope broadened, but I was still a long way from being 'home and hosed'. It occurred to me that Raimunda might not be pregnant, or might not want to have the child even if she was. Perhaps Slipper would get me on a plane the next morning before I could get to see Raimunda.

The following morning, with my predicament in mind, I filched the razor blade I was given to shave with and hid it under the lining of one of my shoes. I had read an article in a magazine about an American con who had avoided a number of court appearances by swallowing razor blades wrapped in bread – I, for one, was ready to give it a try if it kept me off the plane. If I declared that I had had a razor blade for breakfast there was a good chance I would be rushed to the hospital and not to the airport.

By the time I was transferred back to the Federal Police Headquarters, Slipper, Neil and the *delegado* were already involved in yet another heated discussion and it soon became clear that it would be impossible to get me to the airport in time to catch the morning plane. The session ended with Slipper and Jones being told that, as it was Saturday, nothing more could be done until the following Monday or Tuesday. Even though I was sitting handcuffed I was delighted with this piece of news.

Not long after they left the *delegacia* Raimunda was escorted into the room where I was being held. When she saw that I was handcuffed she broke into sobs and began protesting in a loud voice. The chief came out of his office, no doubt wanting to know what all the noise was about. He managed to calm Raimunda down, giving her his handkerchief to dry her eyes.

'Now, you come into my office and tell me everything you know about your boyfriend. Stop crying, and I promise to help you all I can.' Garcia put his arm around Raimunda and led her into his office, talking to her like some kindly uncle.

I could hear some of the conversation between Raimunda and Garcia from where I was sitting and Raimunda was clearly doing her best to let the *delegado* know what a wonderful and kind person I had been to her and her family. Garcia now wanted to hear what I had to say, from the time I had arrived in Brazil until today. I began by telling him that the statement I had made the previous day was not true, mentioning the fact that the British Consul General had advised against telling the true story to avoid complicating my return to Great Britain. After I had told my tale the *delegado* repeated his desire to help us in any way he could, indicating that he had not exactly fallen in love with his visitors from Scotland Yard.

After a fresh and lengthy statement, I was given time to have a private conversation with Raimunda. She was pregnant and she was certain that she wanted to have the baby whether I went back to England or not. At that time, I assessed my chances of staying in Brazil as close to zero but, even so, I also wanted Raimunda to have my child.

All the time our little drama was going on inside the *delegacia*, a horde of reporters and photographers, many of whom had flown in overnight from England when word of my arrest had got out, were struggling to get to see us. But the good Dr Garcia had given strict orders to keep them at bay – he had a special presentation of his own in mind.

At the time of my arrest the most popular television programme in Brazil was a Sunday evening series called *Fantastico!* (*It's Fantastic!*) on TV Globo. The programme combined news, current affairs and entertainment with a weird and wonderful mix of events from around the world. Dr Garcia had come up with the idea of putting Raimunda and me on the programme with a view to letting the Brazilian public see us 'in the flesh' – and, at the same time, collecting a few cruzeiros for his trouble. The filming took place in the *delegado*'s office, Raimunda and I sitting side by side on an ancient settee. As the camera rolled Dr Garcia stood to one side assuming the role of director, making signs for us to snuggle up together, to hold hands and kiss.

'Let the Brazilian people see that you love each other!' he said. 'Smile! Look happy!'

When I got back to the dirty little prison, my cellmates were delighted when I told them what had transpired during the day. Mario, the taxi driver, kept repeating his favourite oath,

'*Puta que pariu!*' It's an oath that is certainly more poetic in Portuguese than in English, as it roughly translates as 'Whore that gave birth to you!'

Dr Garcia's production was shown on television the following evening and although I didn't get to see it, I heard that the programme created a lot of public sympathy. The *delegado*'s superiors were not as impressed, however, and Garcia was later demoted for allowing the filming to take place in the *delegacia*.

On the Monday morning, with the razor blade still in my shoe, I was taken once again to the Catete Palace. A decision was expected with regard to my position and the mob of reporters and photographers were pushing and shoving at the front gate as we drove into the palace grounds. Raimunda was there, now a celebrity after her appearance on *Fantastico!* and a weekend of giving interviews to the press. So were Slipper and Jones, neither one of whom was looking particularly cheerful. Colin Mackenzie, I was told, was taking care of Raimunda and had given her some money to buy clothes. My friend Constantine was also being helpful by 'taking care' of Lucia.

At that time I was still unaware of the *Daily Express*'s double cross, believing that Mackenzie and Lovelace had been followed to Brazil. I had not seen the issues of that newspaper following my arrest and I was foolish enough to believe that the £35,000 'deal' I had made with Mackenzie was still on. The Brazilian newspapers I had managed to get hold of gave no indication that the *Express* had put the Yard on to me. There was, however, much criticism levelled at the British police for the manner in which they had arrived in Brazil unannounced and brought about my capture.

At six o'clock on Monday 4 February Garcia made an announcement. I was to be detained in Brazilian custody for ninety days pending further enquiries. Slipper and Jones, without their man, returned on that night's British Caledonian flight to Gatwick to a cruel reception from the newspapers who had not got the goodies. In Britain an enquiry was already under way as accusations and excuses began to fly between Scotland Yard, the Home Office, and the Foreign Office.

A few days later I was on a plane with a federal police

inspector as my escort and flying to Brasilia, where there was a special prison for foreigners. Apart from the inspector and me, the only other people on the flight besides the crew were a reporter and a photographer from the Brazilian newspaper, *O Globo*. That was the newspaper, one of the most influential in Brazil, which had run a front-page story on the day following my arrest, telling the population that the man who had been taken into custody had shot the train driver three times through the head at point-blank range.

Soon after we had taken off, the *Globo* reporter showed me a copy of the *Daily Express* with screaming headlines of my capture. Reading on, I soon discovered that I had been well and truly shafted and that the *Express* was not about to come up with any money for my story. These tidings plunged me into a black mood, but a little later I was cheered up somewhat by a conversation I had with the inspector. Back in 1974, he explained, there were quite a large number of left-wing Brazilians who had sought political asylum in Great Britain, some of whom were wanted for alleged acts of subversion. Even though there was no Treaty of Extradition between Britain and Brazil, the Brazilian authorities had approached the British government, seeking the extradition of certain individuals, but Britain had steadfastly refused. With that in mind, said the inspector, he found it hard to imagine that Brazil would hand me over to the Brits.

'Inspector Helio,' I told him, 'you have made my day!'

At Brasilia Airport the inspector and I parted company and I was handed over to another federal policeman named Vivaldo, who spoke with a stutter and who, I later discovered, was the jailer at the 'special' prison. Still handcuffed, I was put into the back of a closed police truck which must have been standing in the sun for hours before I arrived; it was like getting into an oven. On arrival at the steel and concrete jail where I was to pass the next three months, I was greeted by an educated voice coming from one of the cells.

'Good afternoon, Mr Biggs. How was your flight from Rio?' Before I had time to reply or see who it was who had spoken, Vivaldo had unlocked an empty cell and hustled me inside.

I was relieved of everything except my underpants, with

Vivaldo carefully inspecting each item and passing it to a trustie who stood holding a cardboard box. There was a wafer-thin mattress on one of the beds, which Vivaldo flung into the corridor with a '*Puta merda!*' A newspaper had been concealed under the mattress and when Vivaldo saw it he started shouting and stuttering at the trustie for not having removed 'everything' from the cell, as he had instructed.

'*Filho da puta!* Do I have to do everything myself!'

Well, I thought, Mr Vivaldo and I are going to get along just fine. He slammed the gate of the cell and locked it, then shook the gate to make sure it was locked.

'Welcome to Brasilia, Mr Biggs,' said the same refined voice when the jailer had left the area. 'Please don't let Vivaldo disturb you. He's really quite nice when you get to know him.'

There were eight cells all on the same side of the corridor, so it was impossible to see who was speaking to me. He introduced himself as Fernand Legros, a Frenchman and, according to what he told me, a wealthy art dealer, unjustly accused of selling paintings that 'turned out to be' forgeries. He was awaiting extradition to face charges in France.

There were five other prisoners besides myself, most of them also waiting to be 'repatriated'. Every evening, Monsieur Legros had dinner sent in from a nearby French restaurant, Le Paysan – for everybody. He would go from cell to cell with a menu from the restaurant, taking the orders.

'I am sorry that it is such a poor menu,' he said, when he first appeared at the gate of my cell. 'But we must remember that we are in Brasilia. How does steak and chips sound?'

My mattress had been returned and I was given a thin blanket that didn't smell too pleasant. But I stayed in my underpants for the first three days; no clothes, no comb, no toothbrush. And the food was served without knives, forks or spoons, obliging me to eat with my hands.

Late in the afternoon of the third day, Vivaldo appeared bearing the cardboard box containing my clothing and other items. He unlocked my cell and handed me the box.

'Get yourself ready quickly,' he ordered. 'Your wife is here to see you.' He went away and returned with a razor holder and blade. 'Here. You need this,' he said. 'You must make yourself look tidy.'

My wife had arrived! I almost felt friendly towards Vivaldo for bringing me such wonderful news. I shaved and got myself ready – without a mirror – in record time while my jailer waited poker-faced. Then he led me out of the cell block, across a yard where a number of police vehicles were parked, up a staircase and into another building.

Without knocking, Vivaldo opened an office door and nodded for me to enter. I found myself in a large room full of seated people with notebooks on their laps. Close to where I had entered the room, there was a desk and a chair . . . but no sign of Charmian. I had been conned into giving a press conference. Son of a bitch!

Most of the journalists were Brits, wanting to know how I was being treated and that kind of stuff. I was feeling more than a little hostile about the way I had been tricked, so I wasn't really in the mood to answer a bunch of dumb questions. When the interviews came to an end, Vivaldo made a sign for me to stay seated until all the journalists had left the room. One of the last to leave was a reporter dressed in a safari suit who came to the desk where I was sitting and said, 'I have a message for you from George: he asked me to tell you that he has moved from number 30 Grand Avenue to number 9.'

'Thanks,' I said. 'That's wonderful news!' The message let me know that the last £30,000 remaining from the train robbery money was now worth less than £9000. A great investment!

I was just thinking how gratifying it would be to see Vivaldo drop dead when another visitor came through the door. It was Charmian.

She was glad to see me, but she was unhappy. For me to be living with another woman was one thing; to be having a child with her was something entirely different. With Vivaldo and a federal police public relations officer, who could speak English, hovering within earshot, it was not easy to discuss our situation. But, said Charmian, what was more important than anything was for me to keep my freedom and she was prepared to divorce me if it would strengthen my case. If I should be sent back to England at the end of my spell in Brasilia she would also return to England so that we could live again as man and wife when I had 'paid my debt'. A week later, on 16 February, we were jointly interviewed by the press before Charmian returned to Australia.

I was allowed to keep my clothes and other possessions – and I was surprised to see that the razor blade was still concealed in my shoe! Life was much more pleasant now that I could eat my food with the handle of my toothbrush. I was allowed the 'privilege' of buying certain foodstuffs with my 'private cash' and I was permitted to join the rest of the prisoners for an hour or so in the sun each day.

Colin Mackenzie and Raimunda had taken rooms at a hotel in Brasilia and became frequent visitors at the prison. When I learned that the *Express* had called Scotland Yard to bring about my arrest I was reluctant to see Mackenzie, believing that he must have known I was being set up. He swore to the contrary and said that he had been 'devastated' when Slipper had entered the scene. Bill Lovelace, he went on, a case-hardened Fleet Street photographer who had captured many a heart-rending moment on film, had 'cried like a baby' when I went off as Slipper's prisoner.

Mackenzie was interested in writing a book with me. He felt that I had been treated unfairly; he, too, had been betrayed by his own newspaper. He also said that the proceeds of the book would ensure that Charmian and Raimunda could be taken care of financially if I eventually went back to do my time. In view of the fact that I had already given him a large part of my story before Slipper's arrival, I agreed to work with him in putting a book together. All he wanted for his labour, he said, was thirty per cent of whatever the book might net.

One day he turned up at the prison with a wide smile. Granada Publishing had advanced him £65,000 on his book.

'Colin,' I said, when I heard the news, 'I need a lawyer!'

A week later I was visited by Dr Paulo Sepulveda Pertence, a highly respected Brazilian attorney whom Mackenzie had engaged to fight against my possible deportation – for $10,000. I was not too impressed with him on his initial visit: he looked and acted bored, frequently examining his nails. He drove a red Porsche convertible. But after receiving half his fee he started to shape up and one of his first moves was to get me before a Family Court, where I duly swore that I was the father of Raimunda's expected child.

Raimunda was looking radiant in her pregnancy and was a familiar figure in the Brazilian newspapers. She made a lot of friends and won people over with her smile and her cheeky repartee. Fernand Legros, who met her during visiting hours, admired her and asked if he could 'have the honour' of becoming the godfather to our child. We accepted. In March he was deported to France where, although found guilty on some charges, he was set free because of the time he had already spent in prison in Brazil awaiting his deportation.

Back in the cells, the days and weeks dragged on. It was stinking hot, and just as Fernand had departed the much feared Dr Brito, the superintendent, had returned from his holidays and was back in charge. Radios and tape-recorders that had been permitted by Brito's stand-in were promptly removed. Visiting time was curtailed and cells were searched daily. Vivaldo was reduced to a stuttering mess, such was his fear of his boss. Most evenings, Dr Brito would visit us, going from cell to cell, tugging at the padlocks on the doors. He would often come to my cell and stand glaring at me. I would glare back, neither one of us saying a word. He gave me the impression that he wasn't all there.

It was coming to the end of my ninety days and I knew that Dr Pertence, my attorney, was standing by with a writ of *habeas corpus* to get me out of jail when my time was up. In April he had managed to get confirmation of paternity from the Family Court.

On the morning of 6 May Pertence arrived at the prison to visit me, but was not allowed to enter. I wondered if this could mean that my case was before the judges at the Supreme Court. An agent took me from my cell to the adjacent office block, where he took five copies of my fingerprints. I asked the man if he had any idea what was happening in my case, to which he said he knew nothing. I mentioned that when I was fingerprinted in Rio, forty sets had been taken.

'Forty sets are taken in the case of expulsion,' the agent told me.

'Well,' I said, 'as you've only taken five sets that must mean that I'm not going to be expelled from Brazil!' My case had been heard. I could feel it in my water!

During the afternoon, Vivaldo came to my cell and said mysteriously, 'Biggs. You should prepare your soul for a journey.'

'What do you mean by that?' I asked.

'Nothing. Just prepare yourself.'

'Vivaldo,' I said, 'you know something! What you mean is, that I am going to be released!' I was almost dancing around the cell by now.

'I don't know anything,' Vivaldo insisted. 'If Brito knew I was down here talking to you, I would lose my job.' Then, to my amazement, he put his hand out to shake mine, saying, 'Good luck, Biggs. Go with God.'

A short while later, the second-in-command, Barbosa, paid me a visit. 'Get yourself ready, Biggs. You're being taken to Rio de Janeiro in half an hour.'

'Has my case been heard?' I asked. Barbosa was a decent bloke and had often come down to the cells to shoot the breeze with us, so I knew he would tell me what had transpired.

'It has,' he told me. 'You're going back to Rio tonight and tomorrow morning you will be released on conditional liberty.'

'Are you taking me to Rio?' I asked hopefully.

'No,' said Barbosa. 'Your escort will be Dr Brito.'

Even though I was going to Rio to be released, Brito insisted that I should make the journey in handcuffs. When I protested he said that once we were on the plane he would remove them, but he never did.

The press had got word that I was travelling to Rio and a small army of reporters and photographers were already on the plane when I got on with my loony escort. Colin Mackenzie and Bill Lovelace were among them and immediately started talking to me.

'Ron, you're free!' said Mackenzie delightedly. 'Why the handcuffs?'

Before I had a chance to say anything, Brito shouted at the reporters, 'No talking! No pictures!'

'Who's the idiot?' someone asked. Brito had picked up a blanket and was holding it up in front of me.

'No pictures!' he repeated.

The press were as baffled as I was by Brito's attitude and I found myself thinking that some kind of trick must be being played. Perhaps I was being taken to Rio to be deported after all. The press, mostly Brits, were not intimidated by Brito's order for silence. Mackenzie began telling me that he had been present at the hearing of my case and that as of that moment I was free. Brito had had enough. He told me to get up and marched me to the back of the plane to sit in one of two jump seats normally used by the cabin crew during take-off and landing. I was sitting beside one of the rear doors of the plane, within easy reach of the door handle. Brito was still glaring in the direction of the mob of journalists when I drew his attention to the fact that I could easily open the door while we were in the air and have him sucked out along with Fleet Street's finest. Brito thought for a moment, then hurriedly called a stewardess, who confirmed what I had said.

'We are going back to where we were sitting,' Brito decided. 'You will not talk to anyone! If you don't respect this order your release can be cancelled. I want no conversation.'

Our return to our original seats brought a volley of piss-taking cheers from the press and rude remarks were made about the angry Dr Brito. When we finally touched down in Rio,Brito insisted on waiting until everybody had left the plane before taking me off. We went down the steps of the aircraft with Brito holding the blanket over my head and shoulders. But the Fleet Street pros knew all about taking pictures under these circumstances. One of them simply put his camera under the blanket and got the shot he wanted.

A car was waiting to take us to the federal police headquarters at the Catete Palace. When I entered the charge room where the drama had begun to unfold three months earlier, the first person I saw was Inspector Helio, the cop who had taken me to Brasilia. We exchanged greetings and then he asked me, 'Why are you handcuffed?'

I looked towards Brito. 'I don't know. Perhaps this gentleman can tell you.' Brito produced the key to the handcuffs and removed them. His mission was accomplished. With luck I would never see the arsehole again.

Inspector Helio told me that I was free to go but, he pointed out, there was a large crowd of newsmen waiting at the front gate and it was going to be virtually impossible for me to get away from them. He suggested that I pass the night in the *delegacia*, in a room that had no bars at the window so that I would not feel that I was still being detained. He would instruct an agent to wake me at 5 a.m., by which time, we hoped, the mob would have dispersed and I could be driven anywhere I wanted to go. I was given the night-watchman's room where there was a bed with a comfortable mattress and the windows were wide open. But I was too excited to sleep. I was free!

# 11. Celebrity Status – Life in the Spotlight

It was the beginning of a beautiful morning as I was driven out of a side gate of the Catete Palace on my way to Copacabana. It was a new day, a new dawn and I was feeling good! I was back in Rio and this time as Ronald Biggs. Michael Haynes had had his day in the sun. The date was 7 May 1974.

The *Daily Express*, still interested in getting every last little scrap of news on the 'Biggs story', had rented an apartment in Copacabana for their team of reporters, which consisted of Mackenzie, Lovelace and a friendly Irish fellow by the name of Michael O'Flaherty. Raimunda was also staying in the apartment, but when I got there she was out. The lads from the *Express* had been up late celebrating my release. After much back-slapping and hand-shaking, O'Flaherty, whom I was meeting for the first time, told me that he was 'indeed honoured' to make my acquaintance. He put a tumbler of whisky into my hand and we drank to 'freedom' – what else!

It soon became clear that the *Express* was still trying to keep the 'copy' I could provide as their exclusive property. My attitude at that moment was 'fuck the *Express*!' Mackenzie was now saying that he thought I should 'string along' with the *Express* for the time being. He was only staying on, he said, because he wanted to be in a position to take care of the 'little matter' of £35,000. I was hoping he could make the 'bastards' cough up.

I ran a bath. I felt like having a long relax in the tub to get the stink of prison and travelling off my body. Jesus! It was good to be out of that shit-hole in Brasilia.

I was stretched out in the warm sudsy water, probably humming 'The Good Life', when Mackenzie brought the telephone to the bathroom. Charmian was on the line, happy to know that I was a free man, but glum at the implications. She supposed it meant that I had gone back to my 'Indian whore'. She informed me that she would be arriving in Rio with Farley and Chris a week hence and that a booking had been made at a seafront hotel in Ipanema. While I was talking on the telephone, Lovelace pushed open the door and snapped a picture: another 'scoop' for the *Express*. The following week the picture appeared as a centrefold in the Brazilian magazine *Manchete* and apparently pissed off a lot of people in high places. The Feds advised me to adopt a lower profile.

Raimunda arrived, bringing with her an entourage of reporters and photographers, some of whom managed to push their way into the apartment. Lovelace and O'Flaherty went into action, physically ejecting their uninvited guests with a rich assortment of bad language. Xuxu looked a picture of health and happiness, laughing delightedly at the wild confusion she had caused. We were pleased to see each other, hugging and posing for Lovelace, who was still breathing heavily after his struggle with his brothers from Fleet Street.

During the morning, Dr Pertence paid us a visit and outlined the findings of the court. I had gained a victory disguised as a defeat, he explained. An order had been made for my deportation which gave me thirty days to look for a country that would accept me. But there was a rider to the effect that it had to be a country that did not have an extradition treaty with the United Kingdom. Pertence went on to explain that deportation would mean extradition and the letter of the law – which was also to help me later, in Barbados – clearly stated that the father of a Brazilian child could not be extradited. He advised me to comply with the order and go through the motions to see if I could find another country willing to receive me. This chore was taken off my hands by the *Daily Mirror*. There appeared to be only two countries in South America that did not have an extradition treaty with Britain – Venezuela and Costa Rica – and when approached by the *Mirror* they were swift to decline my company. The Venezuelan authorities had by now learned that I had passed through Caracas Airport on a false passport and would be happy to charge me with that offence should I choose to visit them again.

As the news of my arrival at the apartment in Copacabana spread, the press started to gather in the street in front of the apartment building and the commotion brought residents to their windows to see what was going on. Some photographers had talked their way into apartments across the road and waited with cameras at the ready. More than once Lovelace told me to keep away from the windows. But I'd had enough. I had just spent three months cooped up in a prison with rats and cockroaches for company and now I wanted to feel my freedom. I wanted to walk along the beach, see people, drink a beer at a bar and visit my friends. The *Express* men whined about losing their 'exclusive'. But I wasn't interested. I wanted out.

Outside was worse than I had imagined. Questions were thrown at me from all sides in Portuguese and English. Flash-bulbs blinded me. I tried to reason with the mob, which was a complete waste of time. I managed to get into a nearby bar, but it was immediately packed out with reporters and photographers, all desperate to buy me a drink. By now the *Express* gang had joined me in the confusion. Mackenzie suggested that we should get into a taxi to get away from the pack. But the pack took taxis too, and followed us in a wild chase down Copacabana. Finally I decided that I would have to talk to the journalists and let them get their precious copy and photographs. Then mercifully it was all over – or so I thought.

It was early evening when I got back to the apartment where Raimunda was preparing a meal. We were alone and had a chance to sit down and talk. She had been busy during the three months I had been away. She had knitted and crocheted a lot of baby clothes and had even found time to crochet a beautiful black and white poncho for Mackenzie's wife, Tina, who had visited Brazil soon after I was sent to Brasilia. Although Raimunda was only a little over three months pregnant, her belly was already quite distended. But she carried it well and was obviously happy with her 'lump'. By now Raimunda was well established in the hearts of the Brazilian people, many seeing her as a heroine who had saved the hapless gringo. That's certainly how I was beginning to see her!

There was a light tap at the front door and I went to investigate. It was yet another reporter, notebook in hand. His name was Harold Emert, he said, an American reporter for British newspapers resident in Rio, and he would like to ask me a few questions. I turned him away. I couldn't take any more punishment. I've seen Harold many times since that day and it's funny, he always calls on me when the other reporters have gone home.

During the early days following my release I met many journalists and found out a lot about them. The journalists' motto, one told me, was 'Never let the truth stand in the way of a good story'. The Brazilian press, never far behind their Fleet Street colleagues in terms of inventiveness, had declared that I was O Cerebro, the brain of the hold-up of the 'pay train', providing me with instant celebrity status in Rio.

It was a strange sensation meeting up with my old friends again, especially the ones who had only known me as 'Mike Haynes'. The Blumer family had said kind things about me to the press while I had been away and received me with open arms, offering me their home if I needed somewhere to stay. Fine people. Scott Johnson, whom I had at one time thought might be a CIA agent, found it hard to believe that his carefree friend was a fugitive. I looked up my hippy friends, of course, and broke the law with them, listening to Dylan and Pink Floyd. Far out, man!

Shortly before I met up with Constantine, Phyllis Huber had introduced me to one of her best friends, an attractive mother of three young children named Ursula – or Ulla – Sopher, and she and I had got to know each other. Ulla was also very surprised when she heard that I had been taken into custody for my involvement with the train robbery, but it didn't affect our friendship. We became closer.

Thankfully, the press interest in Raimunda and me began to taper off with time and most of the newsmen disappeared from the vicinity of the flat. Mackenzie and co. stayed on, awaiting Charmian's arrival.

Eager as I was to see Charmian and the boys, I had serious

misgivings about the pending encounter. When Charmian and I met in Brasilia, she had said that if I was allowed to stay in Brazil she would be ready to come there with the children and live with me. And even though she had spoken of divorcing me, she was not going to hand me over to Raimunda on a silver platter – my head, perhaps, but not the rest of me!

My wife and sons arrived on 16 May, the eve of Charmian's thirty-fifth birthday, and booked in at the Hotel Sol Ipanema on Ipanema Beach. Farley was now seven and Chris was a stocky eleven-year-old. Seeing my kids and being able to hug them for the first time in four years was a great treat, but there was a certain amount of uncertainty on their part when I met them. Although Farley was gabbling away excitedly, Chris was much less effusive, answering my questions in monosyllables. Charmian's attitude was friendly enough, but somewhat frosty. During the day, however, the initial stiffness wore off and we began to enjoy ourselves.

Within the terms of my Conditional Liberty I had to be 'home' by no later than 10 p.m. My plan, therefore, was to spend my days with Charmian and the boys, returning to the apartment in Copacabana each night in time to beat the curfew. Raimunda was not exactly enthusiastic about me passing my days in my wife's company. I asked Mackenzie to give Raimunda extra attention during Charmian's visit and he bore the brunt of Xuxu's displeasure until I got home.

As Charmian planned to spend at least two weeks in Brazil, Mackenzie arranged a two-bedroomed apartment in Copacabana for her and the boys within walking distance of the apartment I was sharing with Raimunda. He also hired a maid, explaining that these expenses would be coming 'off the top' of his book, which was nearing completion.

The weather was still hot and much of the time we went to the beach where Charmian and I would discuss our complicated situation at length while the kids played and swam. Charmian said again that she would give up everything in Australia and come to live with me in Brazil, but we both knew that this was not a practical solution or even a possibility. The more we talked about the subject, the more bitter Charmian became, until one evening when I was preparing to leave to meet my ten o'clock deadline she put her foot down.

'I've had enough of this,' she declared angrily. 'I'm your wife and I demand my rights! I'm going to that apartment with you and I'm going to sleep with you – whether your Indian is there or not!'

As good luck would have it, Raimunda was not at the apartment when Charmian entered the flat with her sleeves rolled up, ready for action. In the bedroom that Raimunda and I were using, Charmian noticed a baby-doll nightdress draped over a chair, together with the poncho that Raimunda had made for Tina Mackenzie. She picked it up between finger and thumb and dropped it instantly as if it was going to contaminate her.

'I suppose this is something you bought your Indian?' Charmian sneered.

'No,' I replied truthfully, 'that was a present from one of the *Express* reporters, Mike O'Flaherty.'

I could see that Charmian was in an ugly mood and offered to make tea, leaving her in the bedroom to cool down. While I waited for the kettle to boil I was praying that Raimunda wouldn't return to the apartment. I didn't fancy the idea of refereeing the fight of the year. I was pouring the tea when Charmian appeared in the kitchen doorway, almost snorting with rage.

'I'm not staying here another moment,' she announced belligerently. 'I can't stand the smell! Please have the decency to take me downstairs and find a taxi.'

Hiding a sigh of relief, I went to the bedroom to get my shirt. I noticed a piece of black and white material on the floor beside the bed, and I stooped down to pick it up. Then I saw more pieces of the same material under the bed, and some pieces of pink fabric as well. To my horror, I realized that Charmian had cut Raimunda's nightdress and Tina's poncho into small pieces. Jesus Christ! I put everything into a plastic bag and went back into the living-room where Charmian stood smiling maliciously.

'Charm,' I said. 'That was an insane thing to do.'

'Perhaps it was,' she said viciously, 'but it's only a small token of what I would like to do to that bitch!' I tried to calm her down as we went down to the street and stood waiting for a taxi. I knew that she was hurt and frustrated and I did everything I could to console her, but she was not to be mollified and left in tears.

Xuxu arrived the next morning, having spent the night in a small, first-floor kitchenette she had rented in one of Rio's busiest thoroughfares, Avenida Nossa Senhora da Copacabana. She had found the place a few weeks before I was released from Brasilia and had rented it principally for herself, knowing that she would not be able to afford the high rent of the *Daily Express* apartment when the pressmen left. With Mackenzie's help she had bought some second-hand furniture and a refrigerator. All the kitchenette needed, she said, was a coat of paint. Suddenly, she asked, 'Where is the poncho I made for Tina?'

'Oh, I forgot to tell you,' I began to lie. 'Bill Lovelace flew back to London last night and I asked him to take it to give to Tina.'

'You should not have done that,' Raimunda said, sounding put out. 'I wanted to send a letter with it . . . and where's my nightdress?'

'Isn't it hanging on the chair by the bed?' I asked, looking into the bedroom, playing out the charade, not over eager to tell her that I had thrown it down the rubbish chute the previous evening.

'I don't understand,' she said. 'I left it on the chair together with the poncho.'

'Do you know what must have happened?' I said speciously. 'Bill must have picked it up with the poncho without realizing it. But don't worry, we can go out and buy another one.'

My story wouldn't have convinced the sleepiest jury, but Xuxu accepted it without question.

Later that day, when I went to the apartment where Charmian and the kids were living, I was pleased to see that Charm had recovered her composure. Her vandalism of the previous evening was not mentioned and as it was sunny we decided to have another afternoon at the beach. There, Charmian told me that she had reluctantly resigned herself to the fact that she would be facing her future without me. It was not what she wanted, but she would divorce me, as she had said during our meeting in Brasilia, so that I would be free to marry Raimunda and give the child my name. And, she hoped, it would also enable me to keep my freedom. We loved each other – as we still do – but, under the circumstances, we could only be friends.

When Charmian and the boys left Brazil at the beginning of June, I moved into Raimunda's tiny apartment in Copacabana. There was a double and a single bed, a dining-room table, four chairs and the refrigerator in the principal room. There was a minute bathroom and an even smaller kitchen. The rent was $50 per month.

The front window looked out on to the roaring Copacabana traffic, seemingly within touching distance. There was a bus stop immediately in front of the building where buses would stop with a squealing of brakes and pull away again with high revs, leaving a wake of black smoke. When the window was raised, you could see the smoke and fumes creeping into the room. Cockroaches outnumbered the tenants in the building by at least a thousand to one and then there were the rats.

I set to with sandpaper, filler and paint and in a week or so I got the place looking bright and cheerful. One of my hippy friends, 'Stainless' Steve Able, painted a huge blue butterfly on the wall next to which we planned to install the baby, and one of the Blumer children, Linnie, did a beautiful job of painting a golden lion on a facing wall because she knew that the new arrival would be a Leo. Ulla's young daughter, Carla, also came and painted some animals on the wall of the 'nursery'. Raimunda had put herself into the hands of an obstetrician – a certain Dr Paulo – and he had estimated that the baby would arrive in the second week of August.

Although Raimunda seemed perfectly happy with the apart-ment and did her best to keep it clean, I started to look around for somewhere more salubrious. One afternoon, not long before Raimunda's confinement, I found myself in a lazy paced, picturesque fishing village called Sepetiba. It was about forty miles from Rio and could easily be reached by bus. I liked the place and made a mental note of the name.

It was about this time that I met John Stanley Pickston, a fellow Londoner a few years younger than myself. Highly entertaining and always ready for a laugh, he soon became a firm friend. He was – and is – married to a Portuguese lady named Maria Emilia (known as Lia) and lived only a couple of blocks from our apartment. We found we had a lot in common, both having the same working-class background. And, of course, we both liked a pint. We visited each other frequently, Raimunda always happy to entertain.

Raimunda and I had already agreed on names for our offspring and Michael Fernand Nascimento de Castro Biggs, to give him his full name, was born at 10 a.m. on 16 August, with Dr Paulo taking care of the Caesarean delivery.

Reporters had renewed their interest with the new twist in the Biggs story and were vying for the first picture of the new Baby Biggs with offers of a thousand dollars for an exclusive shot. But a wily nurse at the hospital beat us all to it and had her palm greased by a Brazilian freelance photographer who was let into Raimunda's room a few short minutes after the baby was delivered.

As we did not have a telephone, we had arranged for a neighbour – a lady by the name of Lena – to receive a call from the hospital the moment the baby was born. When Lena knocked at the door to tell me 'It's a boy!', I was as delighted as I had been when my other three sons were born. Our apartment was full of friends and reporters waiting for the news and, after 'wetting the baby's head' with beer and a bottle of champers, I grabbed a taxi to the hospital to visit Raimunda and our new little Brazilian. Newborn children are rarely up to their fathers' expectations, but Raimunda thought he was *lindo* (beautiful) and I had to agree. The old fortune-teller had been right again: I had had a child with a woman with long black hair.

Back at the flat, the booze was still flowing and the newsmen were waiting for my comments on fatherhood and my future plans with Raimunda. Was I going to marry her? At that time, the terms of my Conditional Liberty did not permit me to marry and it was to be eighteen years before this restriction was rescinded. As I was not allowed to work, either, it was difficult to say what my plans were for the future. I could only hope that Colin Mackenzie would come through with enough of the proceeds from his book to keep us going. He was still in Brazil, but once we moved into the kitchenette we saw little of him.

A couple of days later I picked Raimunda and Mike up at the hospital and brought them back to the flat. Neighbours and friends soon arrived with presents and congratulations, cooing and baby-talking. Mike was a great little kid with lusty lungs and a healthy appetite, slurping away at feeding time.

By Christmas, at four months, Mike –or 'Mikinho' as we all called him – appeared to be making good progress, but I was not altogether happy about bringing him up in the pollution that surrounded us in Copacabana. I decided to take another trip to sunny Sepetiba to see what I could find by way of alternative accommodation and discovered exactly what I wanted: a house with a big sandy garden, about fifty yards from the beach. The house had not been lived in for some time and was badly in need of decorating. But the rent was only slightly higher than the shoe-box in Copacabana, so I closed a deal with the Portuguese owner and returned to Rio delighted with my good luck. Raimunda was uncertain about making the change. I had done so much to our flat, she said, and we would be so far away from our friends.

'But, Xuxu,' I said, 'you'll love it when you see it!'

I took Ulla to see the place, driving to Sepetiba in her car. We took cleaning materials and cleaned the house from top to bottom between us. Afterwards we passed a couple of hours relaxing at a bar on the tree-lined seafront and, later, became lovers.

Fernand Legros, the fraudulent Frenchman, had made contact with us soon after Mike was born. He had read of the event in the newspaper, he told us, and wanted very much to keep his word about becoming Mike's godfather. Xuxu had been impressed with Legros' claims to fabulous wealth and liked the idea of having someone like him to look out for her son's spiritual requirements. Legros suggested that Mike should be baptized in France – at his expense, of course – and so it was agreed. About the same time a certain David Cohen became interested in Raimunda and Mike and approached her with regard to making some kind of a story for the *News of the World*. A deal was made to take them both to England with Mr Cohen acting as a chaperone. Raimunda was to be paid a thousand pounds. So, at the beginning of January, she, Mike and Cohen flew to London. Shortly afterwards, Xuxu, the little half-Indian girl from the interior of Brazil, showed her beautiful tits on the front page of the world's largest-selling Sunday newspaper.

Within a few days of Raimunda leaving for England, I hired a van and took our bits and pieces to Sepetiba; I moved in, glad to be away from the noise and grime of Copacabana. Once again, I got busy with tools and paint and set about fixing the place up, calling in a good friend, Valmir, to give me a hand. I made a giant playpen and a cot with built-in coloured lights and a lift-out wicket fence at the front. Harrison Ford could not have done better. I renovated our furniture and shaped up the garden, enjoying the hard work. Twice each week I had to take the bus into Rio to sign a register at the federal police headquarters. And twice a week I spent the night with Ulla with whom I was now becoming deeply involved. Although Raimunda and I lived and slept together following my release from Brasilia, we had not resumed an intimate relationship. Furthermore, she knew of my affair with Ulla.

From England, Raimunda and co. moved on to France for the much publicized baptism of Mikinho. Fernand Legros spared no expense to turn the event into an unforgettable experience for Raimunda and introduced her to artists and show-business friends. Champagne! Bright lights! And phoney promises. Xuxu was enchanted. The godfather bestowed heavenly protection upon his godchild in the form of a diamond-studded gold cross, which turned out to be as snide as the canvases he was dealing in. But Raimunda would not have a bad word said about Monsieur Legros. She saw him and his friends as people who would enable her to become an artiste. They could open her *caminho* (or road) to stardom.

I met the party at the airport on their return to Brazil. David Cohen was smiling, Raimunda was using French perfume and Mike was just beautiful! Raimunda was also looking beautiful and elegantly dressed in expensive-looking clothes. We parted company with Cohen and went by taxi to Sepetiba. I had hired my friend Valmir's sister as a maid and when we got to the house it was clean and polished as well as being freshly painted. Xuxu was pleasantly surprised. Mike's room was ready, with a white mosquito net hanging in place over the 'dream bed' I had built.

So Raimunda was back and we continued to live together. With the ease with which she always made friends, Raimunda was soon mixing with the neighbours, inviting them in for a *cafezinho* and a spot of gossip.

Dona Maria José was our immediate neighbour and very *simpatica*. She had a gang of kids of her own to take care of but she was always ready to look after Mike if ever Raimunda and I had to go out. Her youngest – adopted – daughter, Renata, was about Mike's age and as they grew up they became sweethearts and sparring partners. Raimunda also made friends with a very fat couple named Borges, who ran a small general store around the corner from where we lived.

Borges and his wife were involved in a religion known as Candomble, often described as *macumba*. Candomble, which was brought to Brazil by the African slaves, is widely followed in the country and involves many weird and wonderful rites which, it is claimed, can bring about good fortune, good health and spiritual fulfilment. It is Brazil's voodoo, if you like, but more established.

Mr Borges said he thought that Raimunda and I should submit to one of these Candomble ceremonies and 'seek out our true destinies'. Raimunda was all for it and I – after my experience with the fortune-teller – agreed to go along, more out of curiosity than anything else.

The first part of the ceremony took place in the front room of a house close to where we were living in Sepetiba. We had been told to arrive at the house wearing old white clothing, bringing with us a clean set of clothes, also white, to change into later. After Raimunda and I had been introduced to the *mae-de-santo* (spiritual mother), decked out in her traditional voluminous white clothing, she asked us what it was that we were looking for in our lives. What were we asking of our saints? Raimunda had answered that she was looking for the road that would lead her to a career as a professional entertainer. My request was to receive a 'document' that would enable me to stay in Brazil legally. We were instructed to kneel on two rush mats which were placed side by side. A *pai-de-santo* (spiritual father), also taking part in the ceremony, and a female acolyte, a form of Candomble altar girl, began chanting while the *mae-de-santo* 'sprinkled' Raimunda and me over our heads and shoulders with a mixture of cubed fruit and vegetables which she took from two earthenware dishes. Any pieces that fell outside the area of the mats were gathered up by the altar girl and put back into the dishes. Then two live black chickens were produced and the assistant held them while the *mae-de-santo* cut their throats, letting the blood flow over the fruit and vegetables in the two dishes. This part was an offering to Exu, the devil, and was put into a locked chamber at the side of the room where the ceremony was taking place.

Then, with Mr and Mrs Borges, who were going to be our 'witnesses', plus the *mae-* and *pai-de-santo*, we were taken in a van to a secluded, wooded area where there was a waterfall. Here all four of us took off our clothes down to our underwear and threw them into the fast-flowing water which, we were told, would take all our worldly problems out to sea. It was all I could do not to laugh as Mr and Mrs Borges floundered around in the water, looking like a pair of beached whales. With no apparent warning, Mrs Borges went into a trance and threw herself shrieking into the torrent of the waterfall, falling down with the impact of the water. After 'cleansing our bodies' in the icy water we were instructed to get dressed in our clean, dry clothing. Then we were led to a flat rock where the assistant, who was also by now in a trance, was preparing for us plates of sliced apple covered with honey.

On the way home in the van, Raimunda's eyes were shining. As far as she was concerned it had been $100 well invested: within a year she became a striptease artist and, I imagine, a good one.

A month after Mike's first birthday, Raimunda took off for her second trip to Europe, this time alone. She said she would be away for three months. I was left holding the baby. But I didn't mind in the least: Mike and I got along fine. The only blot on the horizon was the fact that funds were running low and Mackenzie had not responded to an SOS for more cash which I assumed would still be forthcoming from our deal. I started buying goods on credit from the Borges' store, running up a hefty debt. Then, when I had a number of bills to pay, I borrowed money from Ulla to get by.

Things were tough from a financial point of view and I reluctantly dismissed the maid, Lucia, when I could no longer afford that luxury. I took on the housework, washing clothes and nappies and doing all those other interesting domestic tasks. Mike got accustomed to seeing me do the housework and started to call me *mae* – almost pronounced 'mine' – meaning mother! After a fall, he would pick himself up, bawling, '*Mae-eh!*' Patiently I would wipe the sand out of his mouth and tell him that I was his *pai*.

Living in Sepetiba without a telephone, I was somewhat cut off from the outside world, but I was thoroughly enjoying rural life and my anonymity out of the spotlight. I liked the people in the area, who were simple but friendly, and I got on very well with them. Everybody, it seemed, had a kindly word for 'Biggies' (as I was known) and Mikinho. At weekends, a small group of musicians would gather at a nearby bar and play samba music, with everyone singing along and having a good time. There was always someone having a barbecue or a *feijoada*, a stew of black beans and salted pork, traditionally served on Saturdays, and I was frequently invited to these informal parties. Most days, when the weather permitted, I would take Mike to the beach for a couple of hours. I especially liked its peaceful atmosphere early in the morning. Friends often came down for the day. Johnny Pickston was a regular visitor – and so was Ulla, now that I was unaccompanied by Raimunda. She would sometimes bring her children, Alex, Felipe and Carla, and stay for the weekend, enjoying the relaxed lifestyle that was Sepetiba, on-the-rocks.

Over the next few years there were many financial ups and downs. There were numerous offers of 'big money'. Merv Goldfinger – for want of his real name – invited me to join him for dinner at the Copacabana Palace Hotel to put to me a deal for the film rights to the story of my life. It looked good: $100,000 at the signing of 'the contract', $100,000 at the beginning of the filming and the rest when the film was in the can. But Merv was only one of a string of people who wanted to make some kind of a deal with me in the hope of a quick buck.

I was facing a fairly bleak Christmas in 1975 as Roy James, Jim Hussey and Gordon Goody looked forward to their first taste of freedom after thirteen Christmases in the nick. I was wondering how I was going to put a turkey on the table, when a television crew from Argentina turned up at the front gate wanting to interview me. I told the producer a story of Yuletide hardship and charged $200 for the interview. The word must have been passed around that I was tucked away in Sepetiba, as I was quickly sought out by TV networks from Germany, Japan, Belgium and Australia. Now I had raised my price to $2000 an interview, and soon I was able to hire another maid and pay Ulla back the money I had borrowed from her.

There were other visitors to our house besides the newsmen. Total strangers, some from abroad, would manage to find their way to Sepetiba and the home of 'Biggies'. Often they would just be looking for a chat and the chance to pose beside me for a photograph; others had a more professional interest. One such person was a lady named Maria Ippen who had escaped from custody in Vienna and come to Brazil to 'consult' with the person whom she considered to be the 'leading authority on escaping and staying free'. A young runaway from Scotland turned up on my doorstep with a 'wee present' of twenty-odd paperback books about famous criminals and crimes. He also wanted to know how to stay 'one step ahead of the law'.

One visitor, who came uninvited to a birthday party at my house, was a Rio resident and tour guide, Clive Wilson, a pompous young fellow with a face set in a permanent sneer. I took an instant dislike to him. I did not know at the time that he would later give me ample opportunity to continue to dislike him and for rather better reasons.

During the early part of 1976 most of the gang were released from prison. Only Bruce Reynolds and Charlie Wilson were still inside. Then, one morning in July 1976, I received a visit from a smooth-tongued South African named Gary van Dyk. He told me that he had been sent over by the gang and had a letter for me from Bobby Welch. Bob's letter was to introduce van Dyk and went on to say that the gang were in the process of putting a book together with a writer called Piers Paul Read, who had done well with a book called *Alive*, about a disaster in the Andes. I had read the book and I knew that Mr Read was a very competent author indeed. Bob suggested that I should throw my lot in with the 'boys', most of whom had come out of prison hard up, as their 'minders' had scarpered with the dough they had been left taking care of. Gary van Dyk was 'one of us', Bob wrote, and I could put my trust in him. I agreed to join forces with my colleagues and van Dyk, so I found a lawyer and signed the contract which van Dyk had brought with him.

I didn't like van Dyk, especially when he told me that he had killed eighteen men when he had been a mercenary in Angola. He had a dangerous look about him that didn't go with his glib tongue.

He told me that various members of the gang had tried unsuccessfully to get the story of the train robbery published and he, van Dyk, had come up with the idea that had got W.H. Allen, the publishing company, to do business. There was going to be a new angle introduced into the story; the robbery had been financed by a group of Germans, one of them being a man called Sigi, who was said to have been with us at Leatherslade Farm. For their investment the Germans, supposedly led by one Otto Skorzeny, an officer in the Waffen-SS who had rescued Mussolini from the Marshal Badoglio government, had 'creamed off' a million pounds from the haul and the gang had divided the rest. I thought it sounded a pretty stupid idea and said as much to van Dyk, arguing that someone with Piers Paul Read's ability could write a sensational book by simply sticking to the facts. But van Dyk's plan had been approved by the gang, and just as with the votes taken before the robbery, that was the way it was going to be done.

Soon, van Dyk told me, I would be visited by the author with a view to substantiating the German angle and I would have to be 'letter perfect' with what I told him. He would write, he promised, giving me the full details of the plot. He left, leaving me with $1000 which the gang had 'scraped together' for me. With regard to the proceeds from the book, I would be in for a 'full whack' of £14,000.

I heard nothing more from van Dyk, Read or the gang for over three months, then I was called to attend the telephone in the neighbour's house. It was van Dyk. He hadn't been in touch

Detective Chief Superintendent Jack Slipper and Inspector Peter Jones, who arrested me in Brazil, return home empty-handed.

Raimunda and I enjoy my new-found freedom.

With my nemesis, John Miller, the man who tried to kidnap me twice and failed miserably on both occasions.

Roda Viva, the site of my 1981 kidnapping.

My triumphant return to Rio de Janeiro from Barbados on 24 April 1981. Mike – by then a celebrity in his own right – and the world's press were there to greet me.

John Stanley Pickston: he and his wife Lia proved extraordinarily good friends before, during and after my kidnapping ordeal.

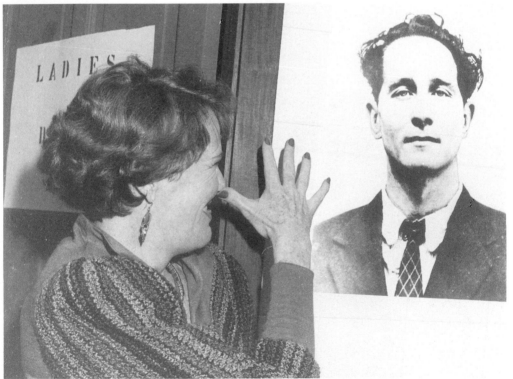

Ulla Sopher shows what she thinks of that dashing young man from Lambeth. I can't remember who my tailor was, but it is more likely to have been HM Prisons than Man at C & A.

A picture is often worth a thousand words. Father and son.

Brazilian singer-songwriter Djavan presents Mike (left), Simony and Toby of A Turma do Balão Magico with another collection of gold discs.

A reunion in Rio. Charmian joins me for lunch with photographer Russell McPhedran and his wife.

My family reveal their alter egos at a fancy-dress party in Australia in March 1984. Chris appeared as Errol Flynn, Farley as outlaw Josey Wales and Charmian as Madame Binnie of Brighton Pier fame.

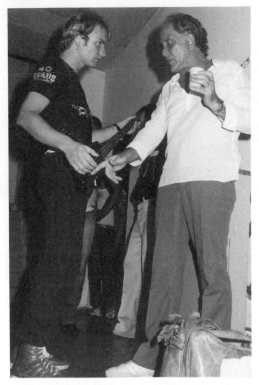

I give Sting a few tips on how to play the bass during one of his early visits to Brazil with his band the Police.

The cover of the sales kit used by the producers of *Prisoners of Rio* – a disappointing film, despite the presence of Steven Berkoff, Paul Freeman, Peter Firth and the Brazilians Florinda Bolkan, José Wilker and Zezé Motta.

It's not surprising that German actress Dolly Dollar and I look happy. Earlier in the day we nearly drowned when shooting a scene in the surf for a German TV special.

Friends through thick and thin. After a gap of twenty-nine years, Bruce
Reynolds and his son Nick join me and Mike in Rio.

No party at my house would be complete without a barbecue – or the presence
of the media, in this case BBC TV.

The Brazilians are probably the friendliest people in the world. The kindness and warmth they show me as a visitor in their midst never cease to amaze me.

Father and son in 1993.

Just a few of the letters addressed to 'Ronald Biggs – Rio de Janeiro' I receive each month.

for various reasons, but now the 'business' was very much on and he would probably be arriving with Read within a couple of weeks. I protested that I had no idea of what I was supposed to say, but van Dyk promised yet again that he would write, filling me in with all the details, before the arrival of the author.

Another three months went by without further contact from van Dyk. Then, sometime in January 1977, I received a telegram from a certain Jeffrey Simmons, representing W.H. Allen, inviting me to telephone him to discuss the book business and the pending visit from Piers Paul Read. I was wondering what I should do when van Dyk contacted me out of the blue. I told him about the telegram and reminded him that I still didn't know what I was expected to say. He told me not to worry, he would be back in Brazil before the author got there. Under no circumstances should I phone W.H. Allen. But I did phone and I got hold of Jeffrey Simmons.

During our conversation, Mr Simmons asked me if I had received the £2000 from Mr van Dyk. I assured him that the only money I had received up until that moment had been $1000 – and that had been a hand-out from my old pals. Mr Simmons insisted that I must have received £2000. He had personally handed that amount to Mr van Dyk with instructions to pass it on to me in Brazil.

'Our intention,' Simmons said, 'was to pay you between £4000 and £10,000, depending on what you are prepared to tell us. We understand that there are certain things that only you and Buster Edwards know about and we will pay you the full £10,000 if you can confirm what he has told us.'

I wasn't surprised to hear of van Dyk's little deceit and I suddenly lost interest in the whole business and told Mr Simmons I would be pulling out of the deal. He pleaded with me not to.

'Just meet our author at the airport,' he said. 'Have a few words with him and if you still want to forget the matter, put our man on the next plane back to London. If you will do just that, we will pay you a further £2000 – do we have a deal?'

I reluctantly agreed, and a couple of weeks later Ulla drove me to the airport to meet Piers Paul Read. We went to his hotel, the Castro Alves in Copacabana, where, without preamble, I told him he was being hoaxed and that there was no truth in the German connection. Up until that moment he had been the essence of self-confidence, chatting away about the 'fine bunch of lads' he was working with.

'What do you mean, no German connection?' he asked. 'Wasn't the whole thing financed with German money?'

'There was no German involvement whatsoever,' I told him. Read looked and sounded disconcerted.

'No Sigi at the farm?'

I shook my head. 'No Sigi at the farm.'

He dropped his head into his hands. 'Oh, those bastards! Those dirty bastards!'

I could see that he didn't want to believe me and later, when his book, *The Train Robbers*, was published in 1978, he went so far as to say that he thought the 'German connection' had paid me a visit and told me to say that the whole thing was a hoax. Ulla's Germanic looks seemed to have strengthened his suspicions. He wrote to the effect that he didn't feel safe in Brazil and could imagine himself being flown over the Mato Grosso in a light aircraft and thrown out.

Read paid me my £2000, packed his bag and lost no time in returning to London. Later he sent me a copy of his book and wrote in it that he hoped it was the better book that we had both talked about. Unfortunately, it wasn't.

The federal police HQ had moved from the Catete Palace and was now in a dockland area of Rio known as Praça Maua. It was here that a squadron of British warships docked in April 1977. I had been to sign in at the *delegacia* and was on my way to a bar to have a beer when I noticed a couple of uniformed British sailors standing around a newspaper kiosk. They appeared to be buying postcards and were having a bit of a problem with the Brazilian currency. Mr Nice Guy stepped in.

'Can I be of any help to you fellows?' I offered. The sailors looked at me.

'You speak English?'

'Yes. I am English.'

The sailors looked harder. 'You wouldn't be Ronnie Biggs by any chance, would you?' one of them asked.

I confirmed that I was.

'Blimey! We only came off our ship not ten minutes ago and I said to my mate here – joking like – we might run into Ronnie Biggs, and we've done it!'

We got the postcard business out of the way and stepped into one of the numerous bars in the area. The sailors, Harry, a signaller, and George, a cook, told me that they were off a ship named the HMS *Danae* and that the squadron was in Rio for naval exercises with the Brazilian fleet. George mentioned another cook on the *Danae*, known as 'Slinger' Woods, who was on duty and unable to get ashore. George described him as a 'great fan' of mine and said that he was going to be pissed off if he didn't get to meet me. Harry suggested that I go aboard the *Danae* with them to 'meet the lads'.

'I can't go on board,' I said. 'I wouldn't be allowed in the dock without an identity document.'

'You don't have to worry about that,' Harry insisted. 'You're dressed in civvies. If you walk in with us, the blokes on the gate will think that you're one of our officers. Come on – me and George will take care of you.'

I allowed myself to be persuaded, even though I realized that I was taking a bit of a risk.

We went through the dock gate without being challenged, then on to the flagship, the HMS *Tiger*, which we had to cross to get aboard the *Danae*, anchored alongside. As we boarded the *Danae*, the lowering of the flag ceremony was in progress, so we stood waiting silently until it was over. The officer in charge of the proceedings then turned to me and said, 'I know you. You're that fellow Biggs, aren't you?'

'Yes, sir,' I replied.

'Well, welcome aboard, lad, but if anyone should ask you how you got on the ship – I don't know anything!'

I went down a steel companionway, with Harry and George leading the way, until we arrived at a room where a number of sailors were sitting around writing letters and so forth. Harry spoke.

'We would like you all to meet our friend – Ronnie Biggs!' The sailors all looked up, registering surprise and pleasure. A lad with an unmistakable Liverpool accent put a can of warm beer in my hand.

'Nice to meet ya, Ronnie. Here, have a can of Her Majesty's duty-free beer – I'm sure she would approve!'

I was talking to the lads, drinking the duty-free booze and signing autographs, when George reappeared at the cabin door.

'Sorry to have to tell you this, Ron, but the word has gone around that you are on board and the Top Brass are in a bit of a panic. Perhaps you had better go ashore. Me and Harry are coming with you – and if anyone wants to join us I'm sure Ronnie won't mind.'

About a dozen of us invaded one of the clip-joints in Praça Maua, grogging on until it was time for me to meet my curfew. I still hadn't met 'Slinger' Woods so, at Harry's insistence, I agreed to come to the same bar the following morning when 'Slinger' would be off duty.

I spent the night with Ulla and when I got to the bar the next morning, there was a whole mob of sailors waiting to meet me. The beer began to flow. Harry told me that he had been up the best part of the night sending and receiving messages to and from the Admiralty.

'They've gone potty about you being aboard one of our ships,' he told me. 'They want to know why you were not arrested and put in irons! What seems to have pissed them off more than anything is the fact that you were drinking our duty-free beer! But fuck 'em, that's what I say!' I was inclined to agree.

'Slinger' Woods turned up at the bar – and he didn't care who knew it; I was his bloody hero. Another round was called, then another.

I had planned to get back to Sepetiba during the afternoon to spend some time with Mike. Ever the genial host, I invited some of the ratings to come with me and five of them agreed, including 'Slinger'. We went by bus.

Smothered in tattoos, the boys off the *Danae* were quite a hit in sleepy-time-down-South Sepetiba with their rousing sea shanties. They were having a lot of fun and a lot to drink. It was a great party, but the next morning they had to be at their posts. I called on a local taxi-driver, Agusto, to take them back to Praça Maua, in Rio. A price had to be agreed. With the driver there would be six of them in the vehicle, the roads were bad, the passengers were drunk – and they had passed the best part of their money over to Mr Borges at the bar.

Predictably, perhaps, the taxi broke down and the HMS *Danae* sailed off on manoeuvres without the help of 'Slinger' Woods and his mates. They had to be flown out to their ship by helicopter and were no doubt up before the Old Man. Back in the old days they would have been flogged.

When the ships returned to port to let the jolly jack tars have one final fling in Rio before heading for calmer waters, they were issued with a notice: 'All personnel are advised against making contact with Ronald Biggs.'

The incident was blown up by the press, of course, and much talked about. Stories in the papers included one about a rating making a citizen's arrest and the Brazilian Navy threatening to blow the British ships out of the water if they tried to leave Rio with me on board. Pure fantasy, as were tales that the incident caused a major diplomatic incident between Britain and Brazil. Today the British Navy still comes calling and when they do you can normally find a group of ratings and officers enjoying the hospitality of the Biggs household. My snooker table is, in fact, proudly covered by a Union Jack which was presented to me by members of the crew of the HMS *Campbeltown*.

Mike, who was going on for three years of age, had heard reporters talking to me about the *Danae* incident and had some idea of what had been going on. By now he was a cute little chap and not a bit shy, opening conversations with perfect strangers. He made a point of telling everyone who I was.

'This is my dad,' he would announce in a loud voice. 'Ronald Biggs. He stole a British ship! Isn't that right, Dad?'

As far as Mike knew, quite a few of my friends smoked 'English tobacco' and from time to time he would see me smoking the same stuff. One day, when I took him with me to sign in with the federal police, a cop offered me a cigarette. Ever ready to help, Mike put up his hand, refusing for me. 'No! My dad only smokes English tobacco.' Such a dear little boy! By the time Mike was five, he was already correcting my Portuguese – something he does until today.

Raimunda returned to Brazil. She had been away for two and a half years rather than three months, thrilling European audiences with her 'exotic dancing', and had plans to return. She now appeared to be very worldly wise and could speak French well, but she was still a country girl and obviously happy to be back in her own country. She had arrived with presents for everyone, including Mr and Mrs Borges, whom she saw as instrumental in her success abroad. Raimunda and I were still 'the best of friends' and she lived with us in Sepetiba until she went back to France to continue her artistic career.

In January 1978 the punk rock group the Sex Pistols had fallen out during a tour of the US. Johnny Rotten, the singer, and Sid Vicious, the bassist, decided to pull out of the group. The Pistols' manager, Malcolm McLaren, took their desertion in his stride and in February headed for Brazil with the two remaining members of the group, guitarist Steve Jones and drummer Paul Cook.

McLaren, always one with an eye for publicity, planned to reform the Pistols in Brazil with two of the world's most wanted men: Nazi war criminal Martin Bormann and little ol' me. Realizing that it might be difficult to make contact with Herr Bormann, McLaren hired the services of a Hollywood bit-player, dressed in uniform and jackboots, as a stand-in. Once more the gentlefolk of Sepetiba had reason to raise their eyebrows when the punks arrived with their clothes held together with safety pins. Even the poorest locals looked well dressed alongside the tatty lads from London.

Over drinks at the bar, McLaren invited me to 'join in the fun' with the boys, outlining what he had in mind. They had been filming their antics during their trip to the US and McLaren's plan was to turn the footage into a film, which was subsequently released under the title *The Great Rock'n'Roll Swindle*. If I participated in the film, said McLaren, I would be paid a fee of $2000 and if I sang on record with them a further $1000 would be coming my way. I pointed out that although I came from a talented family, I was not much of a singer.

'So much the better,' he declared. 'That's what punk is all about!'

Well, $3000 was an offer that I couldn't refuse and I didn't dilly-dally in signing a contract with them.

Having listened to the Pistols' *Never Mind The Bollocks,*

*Here's The Sex Pistols,* I felt that I could write something in a similar vein and suggested as much to McLaren. I wrote a piece which I called 'A Punk Prayer' and recorded it with Steve Jones and Paul Cook in a studio in Rio. It was later released under the title 'No One Is Innocent' and sold over seven million copies worldwide. What happened to the royalties I should have received is something that I would dearly love to talk to Mr McLaren about some day.

# 12. Kidnapped

'Ronnie! Long time – no see!'

The cliché came from Clive Wilson, the Englishman to whom I'd taken a dislike when I first met him. He had lived in Rio for many years working off and on as a tour guide. Until Clive's appearance I had been enjoying a Saturday afternoon barbecue in Rio.

'Ronnie, look. I've got this journalist chap with me and he'd like to do an interview with you and perhaps take a few pictures.' Clive had sat himself down at my table and was warming to his subject. 'It's for *National Geographic* and the fellow can pay $200. What do you say, Ronnie – a hundred for you, a hundred for me?'

'You piece of shit,' I wanted to say, but I needed the money so I let it pass. 'Okay,' I told Clive, 'invite your friend over in the morning around eleven.'

I had met many reporters and photo-journalists over the years before observing this one at work and I had a feeling, right from the start, that something was wrong. He didn't have a tape-recorder or a note-pad. Neither did he have the brash line of bullshit particular to newsmen. He was not at all professional with a camera – and he only had the one. But for the amount of time the 'interview' took, a hundred bucks was money for old rope even if he wasn't a reporter from *National Geographic*.

The reporter, who went by the name of Patrick Richardson King, paid me. Smiling and looking a good deal more relaxed than before the interview, he told me that his wife would be joining him in Rio the next day. He asked me to suggest a restaurant and a show he could take her to and then asked if I would care to join them.

The following day would be Monday 16 March 1981, the eve of St Patrick's Day. As I had nothing else planned, except for my weekly signing on with the federal police, I thought why not?

The Sugar Loaf Mountain is one of Rio's most magnificent and best known attractions. The peak is reached by a two-stage cable-car trip, a trip that was made internationally famous by James Bond's struggle with Jaws on top of the cable car in *Moonraker*. The first leg of the journey takes visitors to the top of a neighbouring rock, Urca Mountain. Both summits have the usual souvenir shops and ice-cream kiosks, while on Urca there is also a restaurant and a semi-open-air amphitheatre where samba shows were, at the time, a weekly attraction. This was my suggestion for Patrick and his wife. I arranged to meet them at 9 p.m. at Roda Viva, a barbecue restaurant at the foot of Urca Mountain. I was also expecting John Pickston and some of his guests from London to put in an appearance, if not at the restaurant then at the show afterwards.

I arrived ten minutes early and took up a place a few tables away from the entrance to the restaurant, so that I would be easy to spot when Patrick and his wife arrived. I need not have worried, as apart from one couple at a nearby table the place was quite empty. I ordered a beer.

A few minutes after I had got myself settled the couple were joined by a fair-haired young man who I noticed had his right leg in a plaster cast. He spoke briefly to the couple, looked around the restaurant and left. I ordered a second beer and looked at my watch. It was 9.10 p.m.

Suddenly and without warning, I was grabbed from behind in a choking necklock. I reacted and struggled for air. A second person ran at me and started punching me in the pit of my stomach. I kicked out and managed to break free from the person who was holding me around the neck.

Instinctively I ran for the exit. Thoughts raced through my head, and they told me that I was being attacked by the Brazilian police. But why?

As I flew, half falling, through the door of the restaurant I was grabbed by strong hands, overpowered and forced into a Kombi van parked close to the entrance. I was pushed, struggling, into the van and a hand appeared in front of my face. I bit the person's thumb and bit it hard. I tasted blood. They had me pinned face down on the floor of the van. It was then that I heard a Scots voice I could never forget:

'It's us again, Ronnie! This time we got you bang t'rights – an' if you don't do everythin' I tell you to the letter there is every chance that you won't ever see your wee kid again – so just fucking behave.'

The voice belonged to the man who had tried to kidnap me two years earlier, ex-Scots Guardsman John Miller, sometimes known as John McKillop.

The van pulled away from the restaurant under the noses of some armed sentries guarding a nearby naval establishment. Miller gave an order.

'Driver, keep the speed down. We've got plenty of time.'

While Miller was talking and giving orders he was taping my hands behind my back. It was obvious that he knew what he was doing. I was then gagged and blindfolded and bundled into a sack which I later discovered had been tailor-made for the operation and was equipped with four handles to facilitate carrying. Miller continued talking.

'Your old friend Fred is with me, Ronnie. You remember Fred, don't you, Ronnie? You've given him quite a nasty bite on the thumb an' he doesn't seem very pleased about it. He's right here beside you an' he's holding a nice big cosh which he'll be very happy to use if you try and give us any trouble. Give Ronnie a tap with the cosh, Fred, to let him know I'm telling the truth.' Fred dutifully gave me a whack across the legs. 'Now listen up, Ronnie. We are going to drive around for a wee while, then we are going to transfer you to another vehicle. Don't try and make any noise – I don't want to have to give you an injection to knock you out – and let's not forget that we have got wee Michael.'

It had been two years since I first met Miller. At that time, March 1979, I was still living in Sepetiba. Miller had arrived there in a small yellow Volkswagen with two hefty friends whom he had introduced to me as Fred Prime and Norman

('Norrie') Boyle. Miller was well over six feet tall, powerfully built and sported a small diamond earring in the lobe of his left ear. They were all ex-Scots Guards, he told me, and they were in Rio as a second-unit film crew doing fill-in shots for Lewis Gilbert's *Moonraker*, which had recently been filming there. Miller presented himself as the cameraman. Norrie, who was about Miller's size, was the sound technician and Fred, a shorter, smiling, fat man with a huge, curved, beak-like nose, the boom operator. They had read about my exploits over the years, they said, and admired my deeds of derring-do. Fred presented me with a bottle of Johnnie Walker Black Label, telling me as he squeezed the life out of my hand that there was plenty more to come as long as they were around.

Although Fred had been a regular in the Scots Guards like his two mates, he was clearly a Londoner. He said he had been a boxer and a physical training instructor during his years in the army. Norrie, like Miller, was a Scot. He told me he had held the rank of Company Sergeant Major before being demobbed. He appeared less boisterous than his friends and said very little. The quiet type, he enjoyed playing with Mike – who was four at the time – declaring that he loved kids and had two of his own.

Miller was quite clearly the leader of the little band, exhibiting brash self-confidence. Towards the end of his army service, he said, he had been a plain-clothes undercover agent in Northern Ireland, posing as an IRA sympathizer. The earring had been installed to provide him with a more devil-may-care appearance.

A little later, at a nearby bar, a curious local asked me why the big gringo was using an earring. I relayed the question to Miller.

'Och!' explained the brawny Scot. 'Tell him I'm queer and that Fred here is my husband.' With that he grabbed Fred and kissed him full on the mouth. 'You great sexy thing! Ronnie, just look at Fred's nose. Have you ever seen anything like it? It's not a nose, it's a sail. With a nose like Fred's you could sit in a boat and sail around the fucking world.' Fred took it in good spirits and laughed, obviously accustomed to his friend's rather ribald sense of humour.

'He's like this all the time, Ronnie, never serious.'

Over a lunch of giant prawns, Miller told me that their work on the film would be taking them down to Argentina the next day, but they would be returning to Rio soon. They wanted to be back in Brazil to celebrate Norrie's birthday on Wednesday 4 April.

'We'll get you nice and pissed that night,' Norrie promised.

Not even a week had gone by and Miller was on the phone to say they were back. 'Fred hasn't stopped talking about you. I reckon you've got a friend for life there. So when are you coming into town next, Ronnie?' Miller asked. 'We're staying at the Copacabana Palace and we would like to invite you and wee Michael to come and have a spot of lunch around the pool. Would Friday at one be okay?' It was, so I signed off, agreeing to meet them at the hotel at the end of the week.

Something bothered me, however. Miller was being just a bit too friendly for comfort. I already had a feeling he was up to something, but I needed to find out exactly what. I telephoned Armin Heim, a German friend of mine and a respected photographer. I outlined recent events and expressed my suspicions. Finally I asked him if he would come along and meet the friendly 'film crew'. Armin, good friend that he was, was all for it.

When I arrived with Mike at the Copacabana Palace, Miller and co. were already holding a small but somewhat noisy party around the hotel's pool. The group's behaviour was certainly not what would normally be associated with a hotel of such old world charm. Besides my three new friends, there was a young English couple, a blonde Canadian lady of ample proportions and the tour guide, Clive. Now it became clear how Miller had got my address in Sepetiba. The big Scot pumped my hand and put his arm around my shoulders.

'Glad you could make it, Ronnie. Let me first introduce you to these fine people. Are you ready for a drink? I've got some great news for you. I've got you a part in the film – you big handsome brute. I'll tell you the details later.'

It was clear that Miller was in fine form. The wording of his T-shirt said it all: 'I'm So Happy, I Could Shit.' I sat next to Fred, who was effin' and blindin' away, his voice echoing off the granite walls of the normally sedate hotel.

'You should have been 'ere last night, Ron,' he said. 'We was all nice and pissed. I was fuckin' paralytic. Norrie here chucked the fuckin' night porter in the pool!'

'He slipped,' Norrie corrected. 'I was just trying to save him.'

Fred chuckled and, lowering his voice as if to reveal some terrible conspiracy, went on: 'The Canadian bird sitting next to 'im was all dolled up t'go to some fuckin' samba party an' when she had a go at Norrie about chuckin' the porter in the pool 'e chucked 'er in as well. What a fuckin' laugh.'

I noticed that Norrie and the Canadian lady were holding hands, so she was obviously not bearing a grudge for her unexpected bath. Armin arrived at this point with his cameras – I had told him I wanted to get some shots of the Miller gang – and he was soon enjoying the high jinks and free-flowing grog.

Over lunch Miller told me about the part he had arranged for me. In Argentina he had told his boss, the film's director, Lewis Gilbert, that he had had the 'privilege' of meeting me. He had mentioned that I was on Conditional Liberty and not allowed to work and was badly in need of a 'few bucks'. Apart from being something of a fan of mine, Miller said, Gilbert was apparently quite sympathetic with regard to my impoverished situation and had come up with the 'great idea' of giving me a part in his next film, which was also scheduled to be shot in Brazil. It would only be a small cameo role, a chase scene in which I would escape my pursuers by jumping into a row boat and rowing out to a yacht.

'Shouldn't be too difficult for you,' Miller said. 'I have also taken the liberty of telling Mr Gilbert that you would require $10,000 for participating in the film. I hope that will be enough.'

Work was to begin on the film soon, in Porto Alegre in the south of Brazil. I pointed out to Miller yet again that under the terms of my Conditional Liberty I could not leave the State of Rio de Janeiro.

'Och, I don't think we need worry too much about that wee detail,' said Miller. 'One way or another we'll get you on location.'

The Canadian lady rose from the table. She was leaving Rio

that evening and had a number of things she needed to do before she left. Norrie escorted her to her room. Suddenly Miller was on his feet.

'Grab your cameras, Armin. Let's get ourselves a few candid snaps of Norrie humping the Incredible Hulk.'

On the second floor, where the boys had taken two adjoining suites, Miller discovered that the doors had been locked from the inside. The large Scot backed down the corridor and then came flying at the nearest door, executing a near perfect double drop-kick. The door, the door frame and the architraves burst into the room, taking the plaster with it and ripping the wallpaper from the walls. I was getting a close look at the Scots Guards in action! Norrie and the lady were caught in the act as Armin clicked away through the rising dust.

Miller later apologized to the hotel's management for the 'dreadful accident' on the second floor. People in show business, he explained, were inclined to get a wee bit rowdy from time to time. He would, of course, pay for all the necessary repairs.

I went back to the Copa the following morning with Mike. He wanted to see the 'crazy men' again. Miller asked me to be at the hotel around ten o'clock, as he was expecting a call from Gilbert. I invited Armin to come along for the ride.

On arrival we found the gang had been moved to rooms on the third floor. Drinks were poured by Norrie, who was showing no apparent sign of resentment towards his friends for the previous day's invasion. He laughed when I mentioned the subject.

'John's fuckin' shell-shocked. We're accustomed to that kind of thing,' he said by way of an explanation.

At 10.30 a.m. the phone rang. Miller picked up the receiver. 'Is that you, Lewis? . . . Aye, Ronnie's sitting right here in front of me . . . Aye, he's quite willing to take part in the film but there's a wee problem. He's not allowed to leave Rio . . . you can't change the location? Och! that's too bad . . . aye, I understand. I'll talk to him, Lewis, and get back to you later. Bye for now.'

Miller replaced the receiver. 'Ronnie, there is no way that Lewis can change the location for the shoot. He just explained that it would cost far too much to bring the cast and crew back up to Rio – we've just got to get you down to Porto Alegre.'

'Forget it,' I said. 'There's no way I'm leaving Rio. I'm just not willing to take the chance. I can't afford to.'

'Listen, Ronnie,' Miller insisted. 'You could get a short haircut, put on a pair of shades and nobody would recognize you. Christ, look at me! I don't have to tell you of all people how to nip in and out of places. We could get you a plane and fly you down to Porto Alegre. You don't need any documentation for a private plane. You do your piece of acting and you're back in Rio in three days with ten grand in your pocket. Think about it, old son. You can even bring Armin if you want.'

'I don't have to think about it,' I replied firmly. 'I'm not leaving Rio – not even for a hundred grand – no way in the world.'

'Is that your final decision, Ronnie?'

'Yes, that's my final decision.'

Miller broke the building tension with a new idea which had nothing to do with the film. Clive had told him about Paradise Island, also known as Jaguanum, and a boat trip offered to tourists where they could see crystal-clear water, white sandy beaches, tropical birds and exotic plants.

'I'd like to take you, wee Mike and your pal Armin to the island tomorrow. Let's have some fun. Fuck the film deal! What do you say?'

Mike said yes!

That night I took the boys off to the local British pub, the Lord Jim. While John set about hooking up with one of the many young ladies there, Fred and I stood at the bar and talked about London.

'Don't let me ever see you wiv yer 'and in yer pocket,' Fred said as he organized yet another round of drinks.

Miller had picked up a cute blonde called Lucia and suggested, at the girl's instigation, that we move on to Dancin' Days, a popular disco on Urca Mountain. As we emerged from the cable car the lights were flashing, the Bee Gees were belting it out and the young Brazilians were getting it together.

While Miller took Lucia off to the dance floor I continued my chat with fat Fred.

'Ronnie,' he said, 'I just want to tell you that you've got a friend for life. That's no bollocks – I fink of you as a bruvver and if you ever want anyone taken care of over in London you only have to give me a call.'

Our conversation was interrupted by a rather sweaty Miller. 'Och!' he said. 'Are you two going to stand there all night making love? Come on, Biggsy, let's boogie a wee bit.' And boogie we did. Miller, in fact, probably boogied rather harder than he should have done, which ended in a scene: we left after Miller had been accused by one of the other Brazilian customers of being a 'bad man' for the way he was treating young Lucia on the dance floor. In true Miller style, the Scot laid his critic out, splitting his knuckles in the process.

Despite the late night we all met outside the Copacabana Palace the next morning, Sunday, and took the bus tour to the coastal town of Itacuraça. The sun was shining and there was a clear blue sky. Everyone was in high spirits. Fred had arranged a case of cold beers from the hotel for the journey and Mike was sitting on Norrie's lap, chatting away. Miller explained that the hotel had been far from happy in letting Lucia up to his room, but he had simply slung her over his shoulder and told the night porter that she was a registered nurse who had come to dress his damaged hand. At Itacuruça, we boarded a traditional saveiro, a type of schooner, which would take us out to the island.

All in all it was a jolly day, swimming and playing football on the beach, the visiting gringos against the locals. We ate well and drank many a caipirinha, a drink made from limes, sugar and cachaça. Ulla's brother was at the island when we got there and he fell in with our group. He shared my opinion that Miller and co. were 'up to no good' and suggested that I should be on my toes. They are too good to be true, he said.

During one of the drinking sessions, Norrie asked me if I had ever taken Valium. I told him that I hadn't. Fred offered the information that Valium, when mixed with alcohol, had a 'fuckin' devastating' effect. He knew, he said, because he had 'fuckin' tried it'.

Miller's physical strength was obvious. During the fun and games in the sea, he grabbed me around the waist and stripped me of my bathing trunks in just a few seconds. At a later date somebody sent me the front page of a Scottish newspaper, the *Sunday Mail*, with a picture of John Miller in training for my kidnapping. He was photographed jogging in a park while carrying somebody across his shoulders.

That evening Mike and I returned to the relative peace and calm of Sepetiba, close to Itacuraça. Although I trusted the gang less and less, I was now even more curious to find out exactly what they were up to. With his arm around my shoulder, Miller had told me what 'a great guy' I was. He didn't want to be a nuisance, but could he and the boys see me again before they left Brazil – they would be leaving at the end of the week. I said that I would see them again on Tuesday, two days later.

I arrived at Ulla's apartment in Santa Teresa (about twenty minutes by car from Copacabana) at around seven o'clock on Monday evening.

'Hey!' said Ulla when she saw me. 'Guess what? You are supposed to have been kidnapped and on your way back to England on a chartered boat!

'I have just had a call from some man called Chris Buckland who said he was a reporter with the *Daily Mirror*,' Ulla went on to explain. 'He told me that you had been grabbed by a group of ex-Scots Guardsmen and were now on your way back to England in an ocean-going yacht. He called from New York and I told him I was expecting you, so he said he was going to ring back later. For God's sake, Ron, what's going on?'

I brought Ulla up to date with the activities of my Guardsmen 'buddies', the film offer and the conversation Miller had supposedly had with Lewis Gilbert. We discussed the whole thing at length. Why would they want to kidnap me? Why the cock-and-bull story about a movie deal? Why Porto Alegre – which was way down south – when Rio had a port and numerous places where a yacht could be moored?

As promised, Buckland called again, confirming everything that Ulla had told me. The ex-Scots Guardsmen had indeed been highly trained for the job, he said, and their plan was to get me aboard a yacht and return to England with me as their prisoner. He wanted to know if this information coincided with anything that was going on in Rio at that moment. I gave

him a brief account of recent happenings and he said he would
speak to his editor in London to see if he could fly down to
Rio from New York to cover the story, possibly booking in at
the Copacabana Palace to see if he could befriend the would-be
kidnappers. He didn't make it.

A little later Ulla's sixteen-year-old son came home. He told
me that earlier in the day he had answered the telephone to
somebody by the name of Kenny Lynch, who was staying at
the Inter-Continental and had left his room number so that I
could call him. I wondered if it could be the English entertainer
Kenny Lynch, so I rang the hotel. Sure enough, it was. He was in
Rio with his friend Bobby Moore, the great England footballer.
This, at least, was a pleasant surprise. Lynch said that he and
Bobby were both fans of mine and would like to get together
with me while they were in Rio for a 'meal and a chat'. He
suggested the following Saturday, as he and Bobby were in Rio
for a pro-am golf tournament and had to be on the course every
day till then. So we agreed to meet at their hotel for lunch.

Ulla thought I was crazy, but I decided to go to Copacabana
the next day to meet Miller and co. as arranged. In a strange
way I was starting to enjoy our little game of 'cat and mouse'.

When I got to the Copacabana Palace on the Tuesday the
boys were already around the pool, grogging on. Big John told
me that he had just got back from Fortaleza, a city in the north
of Brazil that is nearly twice as far from Rio as Porto Alegre,
having flown there the previous day.

'Aye, it was a hell of a journey, Ronnie, but Lewis was up
there and wanted me to look over a new location for the film.'
Miller had even found time during the past two days of travel
to check out Rio's domestic airport, Santos Dumont.

'The film offer is still open, Ronnie. I went down to Santos
Dumont and looked it over. It would be dead easy to get you
on a plane and fly you to the shoot. Don't say "no" just yet.
Just come down to the airport and see for yourself — would you
do that? I would just love to see you score the ten grand.'

Before leaving Ulla's apartment I had phoned Johnny Pickston.
I had not seen him for some time and as he lived only a couple
of blocks back from the Copacabana Palace, I invited him to
join me for a drink. I told him about Miller and co. and

that I was due to have lunch with Kenny Lynch and Bobby Moore at the weekend. John expressed envy as he was and is a fervent West Ham supporter and a great fan of Bobby Moore. Next I called Armin and filled him in on the information I had received from the *Daily Mirror* reporter. I asked him to appear at the hotel as well.

Soon after I got to the hotel, John and Armin arrived together. We sat around and had a couple of beers and then Norrie suggested going up to his suite on the third floor for 'some serious drinkin''. There were still a couple of bottles of Johnnie Walker Black Label remaining. As Norrie poured generous measures of whisky into six tumblers, I enquired if it wouldn't be a better idea to keep the booze until the following day, reminding him that it would be Wednesday and his birthday.

'My birthday is on Thursday, Ronnie. The 5th. Don't you remember?'

'I remember,' I said, as Norrie passed me a full tumbler of whisky.

I finished my drink, now feeling quite drunk, and decided to go down and sit by the pool again. Armin and John joined me. Suddenly, I made a decision.

'I'm going out to the Inter-Continental! I'm going to go and see if I can give Kenny and Bobby a nice surprise.'

Miller came hurrying up as John, Armin and I were staggering into a taxi. 'Where are you lot off to at this time of night?' he wanted to know. When we told him, he wanted to come too, making out that he was a big fan of Bobby Moore.

The gang followed us out to the Inter-Continental in a second taxi. By the time we reached the hotel it was just past midnight. As luck would have it we found Moore and Lynch sitting alone in the hotel's night club, the Jakui Bar. Most of the lights had been turned down and it was quite gloomy. We all shook hands and then my two friends and I joined them at a table. John soon made it known that he was a football buff and launched into a conversation with Moore while Armin and I talked 'show business' with Lynch. Miller and co. sort of hovered around the table saying little, if anything.

The visiting VIPs were still a little jet-lagged, but said they looked forward to our lunch on Saturday. It was time to say goodnight as they were expected early at Gavea Golf Club for the pro-am.

Outside the Inter-Continental, Miller drew me aside from the others and had yet another go at getting me interested in the 'film deal'.

The boys and me think the world of you and wee Michael,' Miller went on. 'Go for the bread, old son – ten grand is ten fuckin' grand.'

'Okay,' I said. Years of criminal cunning coming to the fore. 'Five grand up front here in Rio and five grand at the end of the shoot.'

'I won't promise, Ronnie.' Miller said, 'but I'll do my best.'

I got a cab and headed over to Ulla's place in Santa Teresa to spend the night.

Miller phoned early the next morning. 'Ronnie, it's fuckin' heartbreaking, but we've only got a day or two left in Rio,' he began. 'Look, come by the hotel for lunch and bring wee Michael. Norrie's got a present for him, the walkie-talkies we've been playing with. We're covered. Norrie will just say they were stolen when we get back. Better still, he'll say you nicked 'em!'

I told him that I had to go and sign in with the federal police, but Miller was most insistent that I come over and have lunch first.

'Look, Ronnie, I'll even drop you off after lunch and as we are in the area you might as well get a look at Santos Dumont. See you at noon.'

I had left Mike with my neighbour in Sepetiba, so I went over to the hotel alone. I wasn't really interested in having lunch or seeing the 'boys'. My main interest was to see if I could make Miller part with some money up front. A sort of reward for all the trouble they had put me to.

After lunch we took a taxi to Praça Maua, where the federal police are located. The gang went into one of the local clip joints to wait and I went into the *delegacia* to sign in. At that time it was a ritual that had to be followed every Wednesday and Friday. Then I joined them at the clip joint. Again Miller broached the subject of the filming, urging me to go with them to Santos Dumont.

'The only place I am going,' I told Miller, 'is on a bus back to Sepetiba. There is absolutely no point going to the airport, because I'm not going to go ahead until I get paid something up front. At least two grand, because before I start putting my liberty at risk there are a few debts I want to clear up first.'

'Ronnie, old son,' Miller interrupted earnestly, 'I promise I'll ring Lewis as soon as I get back to the Copa and I'll have your bread by Friday. You have my word on that.'

I rose early the following morning in Sepetiba and took Mike to the beach. While he played in the sand I sat thinking. It was not very likely that Miller would come up with the money – but he just might. If he did I could try and grab the money and run. Soon after we got home from the beach there was a call from Ulla. She had just received a call from an editor on a Manchester newspaper. A Scotsman called McGovern, he had given Ulla much the same information as the *Mirror*'s Buckland had provided, emphasizing the fact that I should avoid contact with the Guardsmen at all costs. He described them as 'extremely dangerous' and wanted me to call him just as soon as I could.

I called Manchester, I think it was the *Daily Star*, and got straight through to McGovern. I told him I was calling in regard to some 'dangerous' Guardsmen.

'I'm sorry,' he said to my surprise, 'I'm unable to help you.'

'But didn't you just call and speak to my girlfriend and tell her that I should avoid some ex-Scots Guardsmen at all costs?' I asked.

'I'm sorry,' he repeated. 'I know nothing about the matter.'

To say the least, I was baffled. I decided to ring Ulla back and tell her what had happened.

'Come back to Rio,' she urged. 'In Sepetiba you are a sitting duck.'

I knew she was right, so I started to prepare to head for Rio that very night with Mike.

Minutes later, as if he had been listening on the line, John Miller called. 'Ronnie! How are you this morning, you old reprobate? Did you get a good night's rest? . . . That's magic, Ronnie. Look, I rang Lewis as I promised and he is sending down the two grand. That okay for you? . . . You'll be coming

into Rio tonight for Norrie's birthday party, won't you? . . .
Och, don't say you can't, you've got to come to Rio tomorrow
anyway to sign in, right? . . . If you can't make it for Norrie
you'll have to come and have a spot of lunch at the hotel. About
one then? . . . And listen, Ronnie, what I'd like to do is for you
to come straight up to my room when you arrive. We've got to
have a serious talk about all those bastards that have ripped you
off over the years. I want you to give me a list of everything that
is owing and I'll go and get the bread for you. You've got my
word on that, Ronnie . . . See you tomorrow, old son – oh, and
by the way it might be as well if you were to leave wee Mike at
home, as we do have business to discuss.'

I had a feeling that Mr Miller was preparing to pounce. But
why did he now want to get me to Fortaleza?

I was still far from happy about the conversation I had had
with the editor in Manchester, so I decided to call him again.
The same Scottish voice came on the line. He was glad that I
had called back. He explained that when I called earlier there
had been someone in his office and he had been unable to speak
freely. He endorsed all the things he had told Ulla and went on
to say that Miller and co. were being financed by a wealthy
jet-setter, an Englishman who spent most of his time abroad.
He knew the identity of this person, but he was afraid to name
names. He was not a brave man, he said. He was also unable
to tell me why Miller wanted to abduct me.

If I hadn't been confused before, I certainly was now. Who
was the mysterious Mr Moneybags? What was his interest in
having me kidnapped? Why did an editor on a Manchester-
based newspaper, and a Scot to boot, want to play Mr Nice
Guy to Ronald Biggs? One thing was for certain, it was time
to stop putting my head in the lion's mouth.

I phoned my mates, Armin and John Pickston, and brought
them up to date with the latest twists to the 'plot'. I suggested
that they might like to go to the hotel the next day for yet
another free lunch – but not to be surprised if I didn't put in
an appearance. I called Big Ziggy, a heavyweight all-in wrestler
whom the boys had met at the Lord Jim, and invited him to join
me for lunch. Then Rick, the 'rock-wrestler', a landscape artist
who was a friend of mine and who had a formidable appetite.

'And take your friends,' I told them. 'Mr Miller is a big-time spender.' With that organized I packed my bag, grabbed Mike and headed for Rio.

As 'my gang' gathered poolside at the Cop Palace with Miller's gang, I was having a quiet lunch with Ulla. The pieces were beginning to fall into place. A friend had called from London to say that he had been in touch with Lewis Gilbert's office and they were quite certain they had no film crew operating in South America nor had Gilbert ever heard of John Miller. I had made a decision that was quite foreign to my nature – I was going to call the cops!

Before doing anything I had to go to the police to sign in. If I saw a certain friendly cop – Barradas – I would tell him the story and ask for his advice. As I went into the *delegacia* about an hour later, the very same Mr Barradas was standing in front of me.

'Hello, Biggs! How's the shrimp in Sepetiba?'

'You,' I said, pointing at the smiling cop, 'are just the man I'm looking for. Can we step across the road for a *cafezinho* or something stronger?'

I told Barradas about my big 'friend' John Miller, giving him a detailed description which included the diamond ear-ring.

'And now, you – the thief of the century – are asking the Brazilian Federal Police to protect you? I don't believe it,' laughed Barradas. 'But let's go back to the *delegacia* and you can tell the very same story to my boss – give him all the details and he'll decide what needs to be done.'

Dr Bizzo, a dapper fellow in a pale blue gabardine suit, was the chief or *delegado*, as they are known in Brazil. I told him how Miller had been trying to lure me out of Rio, mentioning an offer of $10,000. Bizzo listened intently to my story, making notes on a pad on his desk and occasionally asking questions for clarification.

'Find these clowns and bring them in,' he instructed as I finished my story. 'Biggs, you stay here, I might want you to make a statement.'

Barradas left the room and was back within five minutes. 'You're not going to believe it, but we've got the big son of a bitch with the earring,' he announced. 'He was standing across the road from the *delegacia*.'

Bizzo asked me where I was staying and at what number I could be reached. I told him I would be with Ulla.

'Go there now and stay there,' Bizzo said. 'I'm going to ask this fellow some questions and it will be better if he doesn't see you.'

I left the *delegacia* a happier man knowing that Miller was out of circulation. I made contact with John and Armin, who recounted the lunchtime episode at the Copacabana Palace. Seven of my friends had turned up for lunch at Mr Miller's expense. Their host had been as genial as could be until it became clear that I was not going to put in an appearance.

'Where the hell is Ronnie?' he had asked the boozy congregation with obvious agitation. He had then gone into a huddle with Norrie and Fred before excusing himself, saying that he had to make some important phone calls. John, on the pretext of going to the gents, followed him out of the hotel and saw him hail a taxi.

Ulla also had her own story. Shortly after I left her flat to head down to the federal police, Norrie had called. He wanted to know if Mike or I was there. When Ulla said I wasn't, he was most insistent that he wanted to drop around with Mike's walkie-talkies. Ulla told him to leave them at the desk but he kept wanting to know where Ulla lived. Miller, Norrie and Fred had, in fact, dropped me off at Ulla's but thankfully they had forgotten to make a note of the address. In Santa Teresa, where Ulla lived and where I now live, if you don't know where you are going you can spend weeks looking for the right road.

Later, after Miller and his friends had left Brazil, we also discovered that the gang had checked out of the Copacabana Palace at midday on that same Friday and booked rooms in the Gloria Hotel, just a stone's throw from the Santos Dumont airfield.

A federal agent, aptly named Cobra, worked as a clerk at the same *delegacia* as Dr Bizzo. He spoke English quite well and had been the interpreter when the *delegado* interrogated Miller. Cobra was in charge of the file which I had to sign twice weekly and frequently had a number of questions to ask as he was eager to perfect his English. I had recently explained to him what 'a piece of cake' signified.

When I went to sign in the following Wednesday, he told me what had happened to Mr Miller and his two friends. Fred and Norrie had been tracked down to the Gloria Hotel and had also been brought in for questioning. All three of them had denied all knowledge of a film deal involving me. They went further and said that they had obviously heard a lot about me and their only intention was to meet me and have a good time. They had been due to leave Rio that same evening and had hired a Lear jet to take them up to Belem in the far north of Brazil, where they had a yacht waiting for them to sail back to Britain. They had been cleared and released and Cobra had personally escorted them to Santos Dumont to catch their plane.

'Tell me something,' I asked Cobra. 'Would it have been easy for them to get me on the plane?'

'It would have been a piece of cake, Mr Biggs,' he winked.

Miller and co. were probably saved by their passports which, because they had only recently left the Scots Guards, still showed their occupation to be 'government service'. Given the manner in which Slipper and Scotland Yard had tried to grab me in 1974, the federal police probably thought it was just another bungled attempt by the British government to get hold of me. Rather than start another diplomatic incident they simply sent Miller packing without taking any further measures.

Shortly after Miller and the boys left Brazil I ran into Clive Wilson in Copacabana and put it to him that he knew exactly what the ex-Guardsmen were up to and that he had given them my address in Sepetiba. He was offended. The last thing he wanted, he assured me, was to see me come to any harm.

I never did get to have my lunch with Kenny Lynch and Bobby Moore. When I rang their hotel on the day we had arranged I was told they had gone travelling. Happily, I had not.

# 13. Barbados and Back

Nemo Me Impune Lacessit
(Nobody messes with me and gets away with it.)
                    Scots Guards' Motto (John Miller's translation)

That had all been two years ago. Now they seemed to have
pulled it off. Inside the bag I was seething. Clive Wilson had
obviously set me up for the phoney interview with Patrick King,
by arrangement with John Miller. My guess was that I was being
driven to Santos Dumont to take the trip I should have made
two years earlier. I tried to control my rage. Miller could well
be bluffing about having grabbed Mike, but I could not afford
to take that gamble.

'You're probably wondering what this is all about, Ronnie,'
Miller said, breaking into my thoughts. 'Well, I'll explain
everything to you in good time. First we're going to transfer
you to another vehicle.'

The other vehicle, as expected, turned out to be a plane. The
gang unceremoniously bundled me into the back of it as if I
were a piece of luggage.

The jet engines started up and in a very short time we
were airborne. The air pressure rose rapidly as we climbed,
causing my ears to pop painfully in the process. I was in a
very uncomfortable position and squirmed around in the bag
trying to stretch out. My movements alerted Miller and brought
him back to the bag. He spoke in a low voice.

'Just take it easy, Ronnie. Keep yourself quiet and still. I don't
want to have to give you an injection, but I will if I have to.' He
gave the bag a couple of light taps and moved away.

210

Exerting all my strength in the confined space, I tried to get my hands free. I clenched my fingers, forcing my wrists apart. Suddenly there was a sharp snap. I had managed to break one of the tapes which secured my wrists behind my back. I rested, hoping that no one but myself had heard the sound above the roar of the plane's motors. I could feel more movement in my hands now. I made a further mighty effort and the other tape snapped. My hands were free! Now, when we arrived at wherever the gang was taking me, I would tear the gag off and start screaming bloody blue murder.

Unbeknownst to me, one of Miller's men had been sitting close enough to hear the tape snapping. Miller must have been given some sign as to what was going on. He came to the bag and loosened the rope that held the side laces together. I could guess what he was going to do, so I clasped my hands together. His hands probed into the bag, taking no time to discover that I had freed mine. His face was close to mine, so close that I could smell his breath.

'You're being very stupid for someone with a reputation for being so smart,' he said softly. 'Another stunt like this and I'm going to have to give you a little jab of sodium pentathol. If I do, there's a very good chance you'll vomit into your gag and fuckin' choke to death. Think about it, Ronnie!'

As Miller talked he pulled my hands from behind my back and roped them to my belt. He gave my bonds a tug. Satisfied, he laced the bag up again. If there was a consolation it was that my new position was marginally more comfortable than the previous one.

In all my life I had never ever felt the urge to kill somebody. But with Miller, I decided to make an exception. I fell to planning his death. It would have to be slow, perhaps through daily injections of his own sodium pentathol.

After several hours the plane landed and taxied across an airfield before coming to a stop. I could hear Miller giving orders, then talking to someone I assumed must have been our pilot. He was thanking the person and congratulating him on a 'smooth and pleasant' flight. Then, with Miller supervising, the canvas bag and its contents were dragged and heaved from the plane. I was being carried again. I heard someone speaking

Portuguese, so I figured that at least for the time being I was still in Brazil, perhaps in Fortaleza.

From what I could tell from within the confines of my bag, the gang met with little or no resistance in getting me out of the airport and into a waiting car. I was lying on my back, stretched out along the seat. Someone placed a heavy bag of some kind on my face, making it almost impossible for me to breathe. I struggled desperately for air, trying to shake the weight from my face. Someone patted the bag. As the driver started the car, the radio came to life:

'*Rádio Belém. Uma hora da manhà . . .*'

The radio was turned off abruptly, I imagine by one of the gang, but at least I now knew where I was. We had come further than I had realized. Belem, Brazil's northernmost seaport, is just south of the equator, 975 miles north west of Fortaleza and over 2000 miles north of Rio. I calculated that I was already a third of my way back to Blighty.

The gang made no conversation between the airport and what I later learnt to be our destination, the Belem Yacht Club. On arrival at the club I was dragged from the vehicle in my bag and put on the ground. I heard the car drive off. I discovered later that the gang had left a car at the airport, but could not find it and had to use a taxi instead. These boys were a class act!

Miller and a voice I did not think I had heard before started bawling the name Greg. They shouted several times before I heard any response. After a short time there was the unmistakable splash of oars and I was dragged into what I imagine must have been a dinghy. Miller, still giving the orders, told everyone to take care not to overturn the boat. When we reached their yacht, Miller unlaced the bag.

'Ho-ly sh-it!' a voice exclaimed in a rather stupid hillbilly accent. My gag and blindfold were unceremoniously removed.

'From here on in, Ronnie,' said Miller as he stood over me, 'you can have it hard or you can have it easy. It's going to be entirely up to you. We're going aboard the boat now and then I'm going to tell you all about our little operation. Trust me.'

The 62-foot motor yacht *Nowcani II* (Now-Can-I-Too) had been hired by Miller and co. in Antigua in the Caribbean. It was roomy, comfortable and fully equipped with up-to-date sea-going devices. There was a saloon with a U-shaped seating arrangement around a dining table, at the end of which was a drawer containing cutlery. I was sitting at this table facing my kidnappers. Besides Miller and Fred Prime, there was the fair-haired guy with his leg in plaster who had made such a brief appearance at the steak house just before the gang struck. His name was Thorfin McIvor – another Scot, this time from Hawick – and he was the skipper of the yacht. There were two other men in the team, both in their mid-twenties. Anthony 'Tone' Marriage, of medium but wiry build, and Mark Aldgate, a tough-looking character who was quite obviously into body-building. On one of his arms was tattooed 'I have only loved one woman in my life and that was another man's wife. My mother.'

Miller was the essence of good humour by now, thanks to the apparent success of his operation. He was standing drinking from a can of beer. He offered me one.

'You look as if you could do with a wee dram, Ronnie.'

I ignored him.

'Perhaps a drop of brandy or whisky? You can have anything you like, you know. We have your best intentions at heart.'

'Where's Mike?' I asked sharply.

'Wee Michael? Och, as far as I know he's with your babysitter where you left him. That was all cobblers about having grabbed him. I knew you wouldn't dare call my bluff. But don't worry about the kid, we haven't laid a finger on him. However, I expect you are still a little pissed off with me, Ronnie, and I have to tell you, you have every right to be. But let me at least tell you what this business is all about and hopefully you'll see I'm not the total asshole you think I am.

'As I told you, it is not our intention to hand you over to the cops. There wouldn't be any point in that as there is no longer any reward for your capture. Simply, we're going to sell this story to the highest bidder – after all, we did the job that Scotland Yard failed to do. We're going to make a shit load of bread, Ronnie, and if you play your part and co-operate then you're in for a share of the proceeds. Fred only came along this time on that understanding. Isn't that right, Fred?'

Fred, his thumb now bandaged in a handkerchief, nodded. 'That's the gospel truth, Ronnie, I promise.' There was no

213

mention of Norrie Boyle and why he had decided to forgo the pleasure of coming back to get me.

Miller ran through his plan. Unfortunately, he said, he wouldn't be making the trip with us, but Fred would be taking care of my every need. He was not able to tell me where our next port of call would be, but I figured that his plans included as my final destination a branch of HM Prisons.

Before he left he promised that we would not land anywhere for the present. 'Any deal that's made will be on this boat,' he said, 'and outside territorial waters.' He elaborated, talking of flying a film crew out to the yacht to prove to the world that he really did have me. 'One thing is for certain, Ronnie, you're going to come out of this little drama as the hero. We're going to be seen as the villains. Mark my words.'

Miller got some more beers from the refrigerator and passed them around. I waved him away. Then, almost casually, Thorfin, the skipper, tossed a clear plastic bag on to the table in front of me. 'Perhaps you would prefer to roll yourself a joint?' he suggested. 'It's pretty good weed.'

Well, this was a different matter – if ever I needed a joint it was now. 'Go ahead,' prompted Miller, 'you're in good company. We're all heads, except for Fred.'

Just as Popeye can take on overwhelming odds with the help of a can of spinach, I felt that I could face my situation better after a few puffs of the proven panacea. I rolled a fat one and lit up. The gang sat quietly as I silently dragged away on my joint. The captain was not wrong, it really was good weed. Miller, who was standing some feet away, held up a sheet of foolscap. All I could see on it was an emblem of some kind in the form of a circle about three inches in diameter.

'You see this piece of paper, Ronnie?' Miller said as he waved it in the air. 'With this in my hands we sailed through Santos Dumont. The boys were carrying the bag, with me walking in front of them holding up the paper. Doors opened like magic!'

The doors of my mind, with a little help from the weed, were also beginning to open. We were still in Brazil and while I was in Brazil there was hope.

'I'll tell you something else, Ronnie.' Miller went on. 'Before

we came to Brazil I had a good heart-to-heart chat with your
old friend, Jack Slipper.'

'Really? Why did you do that?' I inquired.

'I wanted to find out what our position might be in the event
of getting caught during this operation.'

Since the kidnapping, I have been involved in several interviews with Jack Slipper. I have tried to approach him about
Miller's statement on more than one occasion. He has always
been evasive but he has never denied knowing Miller, who
thanks him for his help in his book.

'The most I will ever tell you, Ronnie,' Slipper said on one
occasion, 'is that shortly before you were kidnapped, I did
meet a group of likely lads — more than that I'm not prepared
to say.'

Obviously, the 'likely lads' were Miller and co. and I feel
certain that Mr Slipper had knowledge of my kidnapping
before it took place. And if Jack Slipper knew I was going
to be kidnapped, who else did? That is a question the media,
over the years, have chosen to ignore.

'Have you got any questions before I leave?' asked Miller.

I looked at my captors. 'Which one of you grabbed me from
behind in the restaurant?'

The muscular fellow gave a sheepish grin. 'That was me,
Ronnie. I hope I didn't hurt you too much.'

During the voyage, 'Muscles', as I took to calling him,
informed me that he had been sent to prison for three years for
blinding somebody. He had poked his fingers into the person's
eyes during a fight. He had been released on parole after serving
one year and, he claimed, he went to bed with his parole officer
after their first meeting.

Miller was leaving, shaking hands with the rest of the gang.
He whispered a few words to Fred, then, in a louder voice, said,
'Show Ronnie to his quarters — and don't take your eyes off him!
That's an order!' To me he said, 'Use your head, Ronnie, don't
try anything heroic — and before you think of jumping over
the side of the boat, remember that you'll be in shark-infested
waters!'

My cabin was equipped with two bunks, small but comfortable. Fred fastened the door open and stood 'at ease' on the

threshold, very guardsman-like, with his hands behind his back. 'Why don't you sit down?' I suggested. 'Or do you plan to stand there all night?'

'That's right, Ronnie. I'm on duty.'

'How's your thumb?'

'A bit sore, Ronnie.'

'I wish it had been your fucking nose!'

Fred smiled. 'I bet you do, Ronnie.' Nothing more was said for a while, then Fred broke the silence. 'I'll tell you what, Ronnie, that bloke Bizzo sold you right down the river – him and Cobra, the one who can speak English.'

'What do you mean?' I asked, pretending to be only vaguely interested. Fred opened up.

'When we tried to get you two years ago, Bizzo told John that if he really wanted to get you out of Brazil, he should come back and do it with his help.'

'So what did Bizzo do to help?'

'He gave John the paper he showed you. But it nearly didn't happen – he wanted more money than we could afford. He's a right greedy fucker.'

'So how much did he settle for?'

'I won't tell you how much, Ronnie, but it knocked a hole in our expenses!'

With the knowledge that Mike was not in any kind of danger I started to calm down and the gentle rocking movement of the boat plus the soporific effect of the grass finally lulled me to sleep. When I awoke, I found myself being guarded by Muscles, who gave me a friendly 'Good morning'. He hoped I had slept well. I was invited to use the toilet, but I was 'under orders' to keep the door open.

At the breakfast table I saw a slim, blond youth whom I hadn't noticed at the gathering the previous evening. It turned out that he was the Greg whom the gang had been calling to pick them up. Later Greg Nelson was to tell me that he was not one of the kidnappers, but a deck-hand from North Carolina who had been hired with the yacht.

Preparations were made to sail on the afternoon tide. There was some speculation that the Brazilian customs and immigration officials might come aboard and Muscles informed me that if that happened I would have to be tied up and gagged again. But perhaps, he said, it wouldn't be necessary, as they had 'made friends' with the port officials on their arrival in Belem, handing out bottles of whisky. They were hoping to make an exit in similar fashion. This, unfortunately for me, turned out to be what happened.

Soon we were chugging towards the mouth of the Amazon and the open sea. If I had had any ideas about jumping over the side of the boat, once we were sailing it would have been difficult. Fred had returned to duty and stayed close to me at all times.

'Once we're out of Brazilian waters,' he said, 'you'll have the run of the boat – until then you won't be allowed to show your face on deck.'

I thought it was best to give the impression that I had resigned myself to the situation. I conversed with my captors in a civilized manner, drank a few beers and smoked a joint or two.

There was a moment later in the voyage when I found myself alone with Greg, who was also fond of a smoke. As he was rolling one he said, 'Mr Biggs, the other night when I saw you smoke a joint in front of your kidnappers, I just knew that you were a cool dude, and,' he lowered his voice, 'if I can help you in any way, I will.' Sadly he never could.

My minder, Fred, was always anxious to have a chat. Out of the blue, during a conversation one day, he said, 'Major Ferguson is going to be pleased to see that we've been successful in grabbing you this time.'

'Who's Major Ferguson?' I asked.

'Major Ferguson is one of my old officers,' Fred said proudly. 'Two years ago, when we went back empty-handed, I saw the major, and he said, "Sorry to see you back in Britain, Fred, without your prisoner, Ronald Biggs." '

'Did this "old officer" know that you and Miller planned to kidnap me from Brazil?' I asked.

'A lot of people knew, Ronnie. John went to half a dozen newspapers, trying to find one to finance us.'

My thoughts returned to the phone conversations I had had with newspaper reporters two years earlier. 'So who did finance you – then, and now?'

Fred smiled. 'Ronnie, if I was to tell you, you wouldn't believe me!'

He never did tell me, and nor did any of the other members of the gang, but I still started mulling over what Fred had been saying as I lay in my bunk.

What was it to his 'old officer' Major Ferguson if I returned to Blighty or otherwise, I asked myself. From what Fred had said, it would appear that the major had known what Miller and his army chums were up to in Brazil. But who had told him, and why? As one of Fred's old officers, I assumed that he also must have been a Guardsman. Then I remembered having read somewhere that a number of prominent MPs had served in the Scots Guards and I wondered if they had an inkling of what had been going on. If Major Ferguson, 'half a dozen newspapers' and assorted MPs knew about the plot to kidnap me, who else could have been in on it?

Whatever thoughts I was having on the second morning out of Belem were broken by the noise of a Brazilian Air Fore spotter plane as it flew low over the *Now Can I Too* several times. The gang rushed on deck, waving and pretending to take photographs. Fred stationed his bulky frame in front of the companionway, warning me not to 'try anything'. I had got a glimpse of the plane from a porthole in the galley and felt a sudden surge of hope. Perhaps the game was up for my kidnappers and the Brazilian cavalry was on the way. When the plane flew off, Muscles descended into the main cabin with a worried look on his face.

'It was a Brazilian spotter,' he announced.

'Hooray!' I joked. 'I'm saved! And you lot are nicked.'

Tony Marriage joined us. He was also looking worried. 'What do you think?' he asked Muscles.

'I think there's a good chance they're on to us,' his friend answered, 'and if they are, they'll probably send a fast patrol boat after us.'

He addressed me. 'Now, if we are intercepted, there are three options open to you. One: we can tie you up, gag you and hide you. Two: you can hide yourself. And three: you can meet whoever comes aboard and declare that you want to continue the voyage with us and return to England.'

'There's a fourth option,' I interjected. 'Meet whoever comes aboard and declare that I want to go back to Brazil!'

I had started to write a log in my notebook and I read aloud my latest entry: 'A Brazilian Air Force plane has just flown over the yacht. My kidnappers are in a state of panic!' Muscles didn't seem to find it funny. He told Marriage to get together all the stuff they wouldn't want to be found so that it would be ready to be thrown over the side if anyone approached. The 'stuff', as far as I could see, consisted of several canisters of army-issue mace; passports, probably false; and at least one rifle.

'What do you think the penalty would be in Brazil for kidnapping?' Muscles inquired.

'Anything from thirty to fifty years,' I said sincerely.

My kidnappers were most certainly in a panic and the order was given for 'full speed ahead' to get out of Brazilian territorial waters as fast as possible. Thorfin McIvor, the skipper, calculated that we could be clear as early as the following morning if the engine was kept at full throttle.

During my stay with the Blumer family, I had learned the meaning of 'metaphysical work', applying the power of the mind to any given situation, so I began to think like a Christian Scientist in order to beat my abductors, calling upon the supernatural for help!

The following morning was sunny and there was a stiff breeze, favouring the course of the *Nowcani II*. The gang were all smiles as it became clear that we would soon be out of reach of the Brazilian authorities. To be on the safe side, the land-lubbers-turned-sailors tried to hoist the spinnaker to make even better speed, but they were unsuccessful. In fact, their efforts turned into something of a pantomime, prompting the clearly irritated skipper to say, 'Never, in all my time at sea, have I ever seen anything quite like it!'

A few hours later Thorfin calculated we were now safely out of Brazilian waters and so I was allowed on deck. As Miller had promised, I now had the complete 'freedom' of the boat. I could make my own meals and do my own thing, although Fred warned me that he would still be keeping a close eye on me.

Ripping across the water, with Brazil now far behind us, my shipmates were becoming more liberal in their behaviour and attitude, especially with their intake of booze. During their days of high-jinks in Rio, the gang had been turned on to *caipirinhas* and what could be more suitable to serve on deck? The skipper, I noticed, was quite fond of the potion. And so was I. He was also a 'head,' as I was, and wasn't averse to having a wee drag.

The party livened up, with the usual horseplay among young men. Tony Marriage and his bosom pal Muscles locked in 'deadly combat' and wrestled on the deck. Marriage lost and got up breathless. He saw that I had been watching.

'You have a go at him, Biggsy,' he suggested, 'you're bigger than I am!' A friendly wrestle? Why not? Moments later, well remembering an earlier encounter with Muscles, I had him in a necklock, giving him stick. The more he struggled, the more I choked the shit out of him!

'Do him!' spluttered Muscles. 'Do him, somebody! He's doing me!'

When I let go, Muscles sprang up, rubbing his neck. 'You cunt!' he threatened. 'If you try anythin' like that again I'll fuckin' swing for you!' He addressed the others: 'He's not old and fucked-up like the rest of the gang – he's strong! Tie the fucker up, he's a dangerous bastard!'

However, the incident blew over with the breeze and I went back to the afterdeck to sunbathe.

Now that I was beyond help from Brazil, I thought it was only a matter of time before I got to England. I would probably never set foot in Brazil again. I worried about Mike, hoping that Raimunda would be able to get to Brazil to take care of him. For myself I was not concerned; I was trying to work out a way to sink the yacht. I was still doing my metaphysical work and that evening the refrigerator packed up! Muscles and Tone tried to fix it, but without success. A lot of beer was going to get warm and a lot of food was going to spoil, so the order went up to eat, drink and be merry!

With nothing better to do that evening, I picked up a pack of Tarot cards I found and began looking idly through them. I had heard of Tarot cards but I had never handled a pack until that moment. I soon found the card that I thought suited me down to the ground: the Fool. Thorfin McIvor, 'the youngest skipper at sea', saw me going through the cards. He told me that he had studied Tarot at length and was convinced that it was an infallible 'science'. If I wanted him to, he said, he would 'read the cards' for me before the end of our voyage. I held up the card depicting the Fool.

'This must surely be me,' I suggested.

'That's a better card than you might think,' McIvor explained. 'The Fool, in a manner of speaking, has God's protection.'

On the fourth morning at sea I woke up early and immediately noticed that the boat was strangely silent. The engine was not running and we were becalmed. Suddenly, the skipper shouted, 'All hands on deck. We're sinking!' I was probably the only person on board who was pleased to hear McIvor's urgent cry. And we really were sinking. My only regret was that Miller was not with us to go down with his mates! I was almost rubbing my hands with glee.

Overnight a lot of water had flooded into the *Nowcani II* and I went on deck to watch the crew feverishly baling out with pails and saucepans. Fred looked up from his labours at one point and said, 'I reckon you're doing a bloody Uri Geller on us, Ronnie!'

'I'm working on it!' I replied.

To this day the people who were on board the *Nowcani II* probably think I did something to stop the engine and sink the boat. If I did, it is all credit to positive thinking.

By late afternoon, the 'engineers' had made the necessary repairs and got the engine going again. The voyage continued. By now the beer in the refrigerator was quite warm and eventually all the meat and poultry had to be thrown to the sharks. During a relaxed moment on the fifth day, Thorfin offered to read the Tarot cards for me and I agreed. While I was shuffling and cutting as he instructed, he repeated his conviction that the Tarot cards did not lie and I could believe what they were about to reveal.

I had no idea what McIvor was seeing in the cards as he turned them over one by one, but whatever it was, he was quite obviously puzzled.

'It's amazing,' he said incredulously, 'here we are just one day from our destination and it would appear that you have already got one foot in Great Britain. Yet the cards clearly show that you are going to come out of this situation as the winner.' He sat looking at the cards, shaking his head. I don't know if he knew it, but his prophecies had certainly given my flagging morale a much needed boost. It was also good to know that we were only a day away from our destination – wherever it might be.

There was excitement in the air on the morning of our last day at sea, 23 March, and everyone seemed extra friendly, even though the engine was again playing up and what headway we managed was mainly under sail. The skipper made radio contact with someone, somewhere, but I was not permitted to hear what was said. I assume the conversation was with Miller, who was planning to rendezvous with us.

As it might well be my last meal aboard the *Nowcani II*, I decided to prepare my own lunch. While I was searching in a cupboard for some condiments I came across a full bottle of Grand Marnier, a liqueur that I am particularly partial to. I opened the bottle and started pouring myself healthy nips. After lunch, without being told why, I was confined to my cabin, so I took with me the book I was reading, the grass and rolling papers and the Grand Marnier. I could see no reason why I shouldn't enjoy my last hours aboard; after all, they might be my last hours of 'freedom' for some time.

Fred Prime came to my cabin for a little chat, perhaps to offload his conscience. We were going to be parting company soon, he offered by way of explanation, and he just wanted to say that he hoped I wouldn't have any hard feelings towards him. He really liked me and he was going to make sure that I got my whack out of 'John's bit of business'. I was rather drunk by this time and I only vaguely remember the events that followed. I fell asleep, but awoke to hear raised voices and shouting. Tony Marriage was shaking me:

'Biggsy! You're needed on deck! Right now!'

As I lurched on deck I saw, to my surprise, a huge grey gunboat close by, bristling with armaments and people.

'Who's the man in the red cap?' called someone from the gunboat with a loud-hailer.

'It's Ronald Biggs!' shouted Muscles. 'A fugitive from Great Britain.'

The voice from the gunboat announced that we were going to be towed into port. The *Nowcani II* was put under tow by a Barbados coast guard vessel.

The next thing that I remember clearly was being in the middle of a sea of perspiring black faces, all gabbling away excitedly. A tall man wearing a light-coloured uniform and a cap with a lot of 'scrambled egg' on the peak was holding me firmly by the arm and saying, 'This way, Mr Biggs.' Later I discovered it was a gentleman by the name of Hudson, who was the Chief of Immigration. The rest of the events of that evening are far from clear in my mind, but I remember being fingerprinted and examined by a black doctor who announced to whoever that I was in a 'state of shock'.

I woke up in a single bed in a small room. There was a table and chair, where a middle-aged black man sat reading a newspaper, and a window with six vertical bars. It brought back memories. I was in a cell of some kind. The man put down his newspaper and we exchanged polite morning pleasantries. I discovered that I was in the Bridgetown police station in Barbados. I was feeling a little bit hung over and asked my guard if there was any chance of a wash and brush-up. There was 'no problem'.

Breakfast of coffee and croissants was brought to me in my 'cell' and this was followed by a visit from Mr Hudson, who asked me politely how I had passed the night and if there was anything I needed. Mr Hudson was a very pleasant individual with impeccable manners. He explained to me that, for the time being, I was his responsibility, having landed on the island without a passport. But every effort would be made to ensure a pleasurable stay on the island. He promised to have me removed to more comfortable quarters as soon as I was officially handed into his care.

I was taken to the office of the Chief of Police, another very dark person. His name was Whittaker, which he pronounced 'Widdiger'. He was more business-like than the affable Mr Hudson and very much a policeman. Early on in the piece it was evident that he wanted to see me returned to Great Britain.

He made some enquiries about the kidnappers and explained that in due course I would be appearing before a magistrate, who would decide my fate.

My kidnappers, who had been held in the same police station, had been released to take the yacht on to Antigua, Whittaker told me. It was not considered necessary for them to be in town for the hearing with the magistrate.

Miller's original plan, I was later told, had been to rendezvous with the yacht off Barbados so that he could have his moment of glory by sailing into English Harbour in Antigua with me on board. The *Nowcani II* sailed into English Harbour all right, only Miller and I were not on board. Before leaving, however, Mr Prime had thoughtfully left a hundred-dollar bill with Whittaker, to take care of whatever needs I might have.

As soon as I was back in my room from seeing Whittaker, another visitor was announced. This was a certain Mr Ezra Alleyne, a lawyer, bespectacled and also very dark skinned. I began to wonder if there were any other white people on the island. He presented his credentials, adding that on the island he was known as the 'Perry Mason of Barbados', having never lost a case.

'You sound just like the man I need,' I said, not really interested in the services of a lawyer at that moment. 'But I have to tell you that I have arrived on the island penniless.'

'Let us not think about money,' said Mr Alleyne in a most un-lawyerlike manner. 'Let us just think about getting you back to Brazil!' He saw my smile. 'You don't know me from Adam,' he went on, 'but I know you very well. When the train robbery trial was in progress I was in London, studying law with Mr Ellis Lincoln – does that name ring a bell?'

I knew the name very well. Mr Lincoln was the solicitor who had handled the defences of Wisbey, Welch and Hussey.

'Mr Lincoln taught me something that I will never forget,' continued Mr Alleyne. 'It doesn't matter how difficult a case may appear to be – there is always a loophole. And, if you will allow me, I would like to find the loophole that will enable you to return to Brazil.' I shook hands with him for the second time and accepted his offer.

While I was still talking to Mr Alleyne, a man whom the

*Jornal do Brasil* was to describe as a mixture of Sidney Poitier and Gilberto Gil, yet another visitor was announced. A Mr David Neufeld was waiting to see me. Neufeld turned out to be a smartly attired lawyer from New York. He had been retained by David Levy, a writer with whom I had collaborated on a book called *Ronnie Biggs: His Own Story* shortly before I was grabbed in Rio. The book was being serialized in the *Sun* in London and, at the time I was grabbed, many people, including the Brazilian authorities, thought my disappearance was all part of an elaborate plan to hype the launch. It was not, although even Miller gave this as an explanation once the media had tracked him down: he had flown to Miami from Belem to build himself an alibi in the days after I had been grabbed.

Mr Neufeld explained that he was in Barbados to secure the services of Mr Frederick Smith QC, who would take care of my case. He showed little interest in the fact that I had just engaged Barbados' Perry Mason. He had his 'instructions' from Mr Levy and he wasn't about to settle for anyone other than Frederick Smith. We were facing something of an impasse until I made the suggestion that Mr Alleyne and Mr Smith might possibly like to work together. Ezra Alleyne was instantly agreeable. Frederick Smith, he said, was an extremely competent counsel. But Neufeld grumbled that he wasn't keen on the idea.

But Alleyne and Smith it was – with the very able assistance of Mr Alleyne's partner, Alan Shepherd. The hearing before the magistrate was set for 5 April, giving my team just a few days to prepare the defence. In the meantime, the immigration chief had me moved into a dormitory that housed about twenty of his agents, all nice lads who stood in line for autographs!

Every morning, propped up in bed with pillows, reading the paper, I was visited by the police chief, Whittaker, and Mr Hudson. The latter was always anxious to know if I had any complaints. Did I need more books? Writing paper? Anything from the supermarket?

'And what would you like for lunch today, Mr Biggs?'

'Flying fish?'

'Of course we have flying fish, Mr Biggs!'

I could order breakfast – anything I fancied – and have it

served to me on a tray in bed, together with a copy of the local daily newspaper.

There was a PA system in the dormitory and during the day music and Bajan-language comedy programmes were played. One afternoon, I found myself listening to the country and western tune 'Lucille' and remembered my German friend in Rio, Armin, who played and sang that particular song often and well. I was singing along in my mind, 'You picked a fine time to leave me, Lucille . . .' when one of the cops came into the dormitory holding a piece of paper.

'Do you know a person by the name of Armin Heim?' he asked. 'He's here to visit you.'

Armin had convinced a German newspaper that he could get a photograph of me in custody in return for his expenses to Barbados plus a nice few marks on top. He had also convinced Whittaker that as my close friend he was on some kind of 'mercy mission' in Barbados, to get 'just one' photograph of me for my son Mike, who was asking for a picture of his daddy. Armin would have sworn on a stack of Bibles that it was not for publication. As he said, he had to get to see me somehow.

It was a real tonic to see the big kraut. The great news was to know that Mike was safe and sound and had been delivered into the tender care of my friends, John and Lia Pickston. Mike was missing me, said Armin, but the Pickstons were doing a top job of keeping him happy. John had sent me a kind, humorous letter, allaying my worries. He also enclosed a copy of *Ronnie Biggs: His Own Story*.

Armin casually got his Nikon out of his camera bag and had shot half-a-dozen frames of me before Whittaker could get a protest together. A true pro.

On the day of my first appearance before Mr Frank King, the magistrate, a great crowd assembled around the courthouse and a cheer went up as I stepped handcuffed out of a police car. My 'hand-picked' escort hustled me towards the court, one of them stumbling in the process and losing his gun from a shoulder holster.

The confusion was much like it had been on the evening of my arrival in Barbados. There seemed to be the same sea of black faces around me. A fat lady with few teeth and a hat full of imitation fruit was calling to me in a loud voice, 'Mr Biggs! I'm praying for you! I'm praying for you to go back to Brazil and your son! You're going back because it's God's will!' At every subsequent court appearance I made, that fat lady was there to tell me that she was still praying for me.

The courtroom was divided by an aisle with rows of benches on either side. To the left, facing the magistrate, sat the prosecution and the big noises of the police and immigration departments. To the right the goodies, plus two of Whittaker's armed cops who were a bit too close to me for comfort. My legal team sat at a table behind me with a fine array of law books. The prosecution brought one.

Every day the courtroom was crowded to capacity. The international press pack, enjoying this winter break in Barbados, were standing by, notebooks at the ready. Many of them had already been in the West Indies to cover the English cricket tour.

Shortly after my arrival in the courtroom on the second morning, I heard someone behind me making hissing noises, trying to get my attention. I turned around to look straight into the smiling face of one Ronnie Leslie. There was no mistaking those pissholes in the snow. It was the same Ronnie Leslie who had helped Paul Seabourne to spring me from Wandsworth!

In town at the expense of the *News of the World*, Ronnie was allowed to exchange a few words with me before the cops stepped in and put the block on further conversation. Needless to say, the *News of the World* was hoping that Leslie would be allowed in to visit me so that they could put together some kind of an 'exclusive' story. I would have been only too happy to help my good friend. God knows he had helped me – and had served a three-year prison sentence for taking part in my escape. But the headline in the local newspaper the following morning ruined whatever chance he might have had of being allowed to visit me. 'What is Ronald Leslie Doing in Barbados?' it screamed.

The prosecution, which was led by Eliot Belgrave, an ex-student of Frederick Smith's, opposed my application for bail, stating: 'If Mr Biggs is released on bail, I'm quite certain that he will make a beeline for the Brazilian Diplomatic Mission and then we'll never be able to get him out.' Once again I called upon my ability for 'specious and facile lying' and swore that the idea had never entered my head. But it was to no avail – I had to remain locked up.

Whittaker, the police chief, gave evidence describing my arrival on the island and pertinent facts relating to my story. He made it quite clear to the magistrate that the police were seeking my return to Great Britain.

'Brazil!' boomed Mr Frederick Smith for the defence. 'This poor man must be returned to Brazil! He was kidnapped from that country! Taken forcibly, against his will!' How sweet it sounded – especially in Bajan. 'Mr Biggs should be put on a plane and sent back to Brazil today!'

The court adjourned. Mr Frank King wanted time to think.

During the hearing, Mr Alleyne and his partner discovered an omission on the part of the police. A document relative to my presence on and possible exit from the island should have been prepared by the police and handed to a certain parliamentary official. The official was then responsible for passing the document on to whatever department of the government required it. The police, however, had neglected this small chore. Mr Alleyne tracked down the parliamentary official and brought him to the hearing. The official went to the stand and took the oath, going on to describe his job and his duties. With regard to a document concerning me he said that he had received nothing. Yes, he was quite sure. And yes, it was customary to receive such a document.

'Thank you very much, sir. Your witness!'

The next day the police prepared and submitted the missing document. I asked 'Smithy' why so much importance had been given to the oversight on the part of the police if they had been able to prepare the document and hand it in a day later.

'The police are just wasting their time,' he reassured me. 'It's not retroactive.'

Towards the end of the hearing, Scotland Yard sent a couple of beefy coppers over to Barbados in the hope that they would be returning to England with me. It looked as if they were going to get their way. The magistrate's findings were that I should be handed over to the British authorities and returned to prison in

Great Britain. I was given time to appeal against his decision. Without loss of time, the cops took me off to the cells at the back of the courtroom. Whittaker paid me a brief visit while I sat waiting for a car to take me back to the police station. He was all but smiling when he asked, 'Well, Ron, and how you feeling?'

I was in a mental slump, but I was not about to let Whittaker see it. 'I'm okay, Mr Whittaker,' I replied, 'it's only the end of the first round.'

The police chief laughed indulgently. 'You're right, Ron. It's only the end of the first round.'

Hudson was at the police station when I got there, looking more serious than usual.

'Mr Biggs,' he said, 'I am sorry to say that you are no longer in my care. As far as I'm concerned you are free to go, but I don't think Mr Whittaker is going to let you go very far.' We shook hands. It was nice knowing you, Mr Hudson.

Hudson was right. Glendairy Prison was not very far at all. From the clang of the front gate to the stink of 'receptions' I was thinking, I've seen this film before. The same old screws with the same old bull.

'One on, sir!'

'Thank you, Mr Peacock!'

It was Wandsworth all over again.

There were two screws in charge of receptions. One of them was sitting behind a desk that had a waist-high wooden balustrade in front of it. Open on the desk was the familiar huge ledger in which my 'property' would be duly recorded. The second screw, who looked to be in his early sixties with a thin, pencil-line moustache, was standing bolt upright at the side of the desk, staring straight ahead, with a swagger-stick tucked under his left arm. The screw behind the desk recited: 'Stand on the line in front of the rail and empty your pockets. Do you have any valuables? How much cash do you have in your possession? What religion are you?'

More than a bit pissed off and preoccupied with recent happenings, I didn't hear or understand one of the questions. I leaned forward to ask the screw to repeat it, resting my hand on the balustrade. Like a striking cobra, the screw at the side of the desk whipped his swagger-stick from under his arm and rapped it three times on the balustrade, making me jump.

'Get your hand off there, boy!'

I gave him my best 'drop dead' look. This goon had somehow made sergeant, which entitled him to his little stick. The screw behind the desk continued his monologue: 'Now take off your clothes and stand on the scales . . .'

Finally, Sergeant Goon led me through to the end of the main prison cell-block, where a locked iron gate led to an area containing ten more cells. A guard on the other side unlocked and opened the gate for me to enter.

'One on, sir!' snapped the sergeant.

I was shown to my new address: 'Cell 10. Death Row.'

The cells were tiny and dirty, with precious little space to move around. There was a bed with the traditional lumpy mattress, and a foul-smelling wooden commode in a corner. The door was a stout wooden frame, faced on the inside with heavy-gauge iron mesh fixed with staples. I could see across a narrow corridor to the cell immediately in front of me, occupied by a young burglar named Pedro Weekes. Pedro introduced himself and the other tenants of Death Row, whom I couldn't see, telling me their sentences and why they were segregated from the rest of the prison. Four of our number were 'waiting for de rope', while the others were considered to be 'security risks'.

Sometime later Pedro wrote a full list of the inmates and their crimes and passed it to me during an exercise period. I still have that list today. I asked my neighbour where the black door at the end of the corridor led to. He grinned.

'Oh, man! That door leads to Paradise Island! And you don't need a passport to get there, man! But the only problem with going to Paradise Island is, you never come back!' It was, of course, the 'topping shed'.

Many would argue that the man who should have been heading for the topping shed was one John Miller, but instead he was being tipped off by a man from the British High Commission to get as far away from Barbados as possible. Funny that!

Another man said to be holidaying in Barbados at the time

of my arrival, and at the exclusive Sandy Lane resort, was none other than Sir Hugh Fraser, whose family had at one time owned Harrods. He also chose not to stay around for the court case.

My time on Death Row gave me ample time to think about my kidnapping, yet it has only been in more recent years that enough pieces of the puzzle have come my way to form a picture. It suggests that the plot to kidnap me was known by some of the very highest in the land, including at least one member of the British Cabinet. Whether these gentlemen backed and supported my kidnapping because they believed they were righting a wrong or from other motives, I don't know. This is something for the media to discover, should they wish to.

Miller himself has said that the first kidnap attempt was paid for by a German business colleague based in London, one Baron Stephen Bentinck, nephew to a German steel millionaire, Baron Heine Thyssen, who put up the necessary £50,000. The *Sunday Times* Insight team would, however, have me believe that Miller's benefactor the first time around was one Steven (sic) Bentinck, the wealthy son of a Dutch ambassador.

The second, more expensive attempt Miller credits to Sir Hugh Fraser, a fellow Scot, who died on 2 May 1987. With Fraser's death I will probably never find out who else was behind or knew of my kidnapping, and if indeed Fraser was involved or had the official approval of his political friends. What is certain is that while Miller shopped the first attempt around the newspapers, something he lived to regret, for the second kidnapping he was more discreet, making far better use of his Scottish connections and those of the Scots Guards. I have also heard that Miller tried to use some entertainment industry contacts to round up the necessary cash.

Another name which keeps cropping up is that of Patrick Anderson, at the time heir to the International Carpets fortune. Anderson had visited Brazil on a couple of occasions and, I am told, even had a few problems with Old Bill at Heathrow Airport for trying to carry certain substances into England that he shouldn't. Anderson, it is said, played the role of the mysterious reporter, Patrick Richardson King, who was to meet me at the Roda Viva the night of my kidnapping. Miller would have us believe that 'King' got cold feet and hurried off to Miami. Others have told me that Anderson hotfooted it to England to try and sell the story to the press.

Whatever was going on behind the scenes, the other cons in Glendairy Prison showed me much sympathy and friendliness. Everyone was convinced that, despite what Miller may have planned, I was going to be sent back to Brazil. With a few exceptions the screws were friendly too, and agreed that I wouldn't have to return to England. One morning, when the shifts changed, a screw told me that he had heard on the radio that the Brazilian government had asked for me to be returned to Brazil. I couldn't believe it! I was sure the screw must have got it wrong, but later in the day, when Smithy paid me an official visit to discuss my appeal, he confirmed the good news.

I started to receive a lot of mail from friends and well-wishers from different parts of the world. Some were simple and to the point: 'Keep your chin up, Ronnie, our whole family is rooting for you to get back to Brazil!' And: 'Don't worry if the worst comes to the worst, Ronnie. You can now get good Afghanistan Black in Wandsworth!' Some of the letters were deeply touching and beautifully written. 'Liz' from Belfast sent me various letters and a huge black cat card 'for good luck' – plus a monetary donation when she read in a newspaper that I needed cash to pay my lawyers. To all those people who wrote, expressing their love and support, I most humbly and sincerely say thank you.

The lads on Death Row were not permitted to attend church services in the prison, so they conducted a religious service among themselves, with Mark Young, my next-door neighbour who was serving time for shooting a policeman, leading the prayers and choosing the hymns. Everybody joined in, singing lustily – even the screw on duty. Pedro Weekes sang nearly all the time, and not a day would go by without him singing his favourite piece, 'Diana'. One evening I heard him singing 'The Whole World in His Hands', putting in some words of his own: 'He got de great train robber in His hands . . .' I was hoping that I would be in His hands when the day arrived for my appeal to be heard.

In a dank but spacious dungeon beneath the court, I paced back and forth, contemplating my fate. It was exactly a month since I had landed in Barbados. What was it to be?

England and cold comfort? Or sunny Brazil? I would soon know.

A jailer came and unlocked my cell: 'Okay, Mr Biggs. You're on next!'

The courtroom was packed. The appeal was going to be heard by two judges from the High Court who had not yet taken their places on the bench. Smithy came over to the dock with a warm greeting and some words of comfort for me. He was confident that we would win. Mr Whittaker, bristling with self-importance, was standing to my left, no more than a yard away from the dock. He also looked confident.

'All stand!' The two black judges, looking somewhat incongruous in their white wigs, entered the court. When everyone was settled, the Clerk of the Court rose to say his piece and the hearing began. I was invited to sit down. Mr Smith got to his feet and ran smoothly through the story of my arrival in Barbados.

My appeal had been carefully prepared and was based on twelve different points. The judges listened attentively, interrupting from time to time with a question. As Smithy warmed to his work, outlining the points of the appeal, one of the judges stopped him. They were interested in hearing details of point number eight: the one about the document that the police had failed to deliver to the parliamentary official. Mr Smith was quick to provide the information, indicating that the witness was in court should he be needed.

After a short conversation with their heads together, the judges withdrew from the court to discuss the matter between themselves. There was a small hubbub when they left, everyone wondering what this signified. Smithy knew. He hurried over to the dock again.

'Now look, Ron,' he said with conviction, 'if those boys are out of court for more than ten minutes, you're going back to Brazil.'

The 'boys' were absent from the court for twenty-five minutes and when they returned I could see by their faces that Mr Smith was right. One of them addressed the court, speaking at length about the laws existing on the island and the necessity to observe those laws to the letter. It was quite clear that the procedure with regard to the document in question was imperative. That procedure had been neglected – and Mr Biggs was free to step down from the dock and leave the court.

The decision set off a commotion in the court, with people coming from all sides to congratulate me and shake my hand. I stood rooted to the spot in the dock, almost disbelieving the verdict, uncertain what to do next. A smiling David Levy appeared in front of me.

'Come on, Ron!' he exclaimed. 'Let's get out of here. You're a free man again.' Whittaker, who was standing within touching distance, didn't look at all happy. I offered him my hand in the time-honoured gesture of gentlemen.

'End of round two, Mr Whittaker!' I said. But the police chief declined to shake hands.

A crowd had gathered outside the court and people were milling around, patting me on the back and shaking my hand. Levy was trying to get me through the multitude to a taxi, wanting to take me to the Brazilian Embassy. Suddenly I found myself in the embrace of the fat lady with the missing teeth.

'I knew you would be freed!' she cried between rum-flavoured kisses. 'I knew because I've been praying for you day and night!' Tears of happiness were running down her brown cheeks – and mine!

At the Brazilian Embassy there was the same degree of euphoria, everybody pleased that I had finally been able to make the 'beeline' that had previously been denied to me. From the moment I arrived, the telephone did not stop ringing. Levy monitored the calls, anxious that I should not speak to any journalists. He had hopes that a major deal could be made with a newspaper and he did not want me to leak any part of the story of my release. In my elation, and with a beer in my hand, I was ready to tell everybody who was willing to listen – quite free of charge!

By late afternoon a televised telephone call to Mike was organized, but when the time came to speak to him I was so overwhelmed with emotion that I could hardly speak. I could hear Mike on the line saying excitedly, 'Dad! Is that you? Are you coming back? Dad! Are you coming back today?' but I only blubbered a few words to confirm that I really was going back to Brazil.

Levy had contacted a friend in Miami and arrangements were being made to charter a Lear jet to pick me up in Barbados and fly me on to Brazil. All we needed was $16,000, but during the afternoon we received two offers from television companies interested in covering my return to Brazil – ITN from London and TV Globo from Rio de Janeiro – and they were each happy to contribute $5000 towards the flight. Levy covered the remainder. A temporary passport, valid from 23 April to 2 May 1981, was prepared by the Brazilian Consulate to enable me to make the trip. I would be entering into Brazil legally this time and as a Brazilian!

My old friend Whittaker turned up at the embassy with my bits and pieces of 'property' which he had had picked up from the prison. He had regained his composure and went so far as to shake hands with me and congratulate me on my good luck.

The Lear jet arrived in Barbados stocked with champagne and caviare – this was not going to be an ordinary trip! Then, still unable to believe that it was all happening, I was driven to the airport with Levy in the car of a friendly Brazilian diplomat.

It was all a bit like *Casablanca* updated. It was dark, the tarmac was slick from recent rain and the sleek jet stood waiting. Come on, I thought, let's get out of here before someone issues an order to cancel the flight! I could well imagine Whittaker and a couple of his heavies turning up at the airfield with a warrant for my arrest. But we took our places in the plane and my fears dispersed as we sped down the runway and rose smoothly into the sky.

The sounds and the smell inside the plane brought back memories of the trip I had made tied up inside the canvas bag. But this time it was different. This time I wasn't seething with murderous rage. As I sat talking to the two reporters from the TV companies who were helping to finance the flight, I felt benevolent – even towards Miller and co!

In Glendairy Prison, lying on my lumpy mattress, I had fantasized more than once about the possibility of a miracle happening that would permit me to return to Brazil and Mike. And I had made a promise to myself that if that miracle ever happened, I would kiss the ground on my arrival! Short hours later, as I looked out of the window of the plane, I could see the

Brazilian coast below, red in the first light of dawn. The miracle that I had prayed for was happening! Minutes later, the Lear jet touched down at Belem Airport. It was the morning of 24 April 1981, forty days since I had been grabbed in Rio.

As soon as I stepped out of the plane I kept my promise, dropping to my knees like the Pope to kiss the ground. I wanted to embrace it! My trusty photographer friend, Armin, was waiting on the observation deck, camera in hand, but he had missed the shot.

'Do it again, Ron!' he bawled out. I was only too happy to oblige.

# 14. A Star Is Born: Mike Biggs

*Superfantastico!*
The Magic Balloon Gang

For most of the flight down to Rio from Belem I was pinned down in my seat by Brazilian journalists who were clamouring for details of the kidnapping. All I wanted to do was look out of the window and appreciate beautiful, bountiful Brazil as it passed below, but that was not to be!

David Levy, who had accompanied me from Barbados along with his lawyer, David Neufeld, was doing his very best to hold back the reporters, but he was not nearly as successful as Dr Brito had been on my flight from Brasilia to Rio in 1974. Levy, like Brito, had his reasons.

'Every word you tell them, Ronnie,' he warned, 'it's another grand off the value of your story!'

Later in the flight, once the journalists were satisfied that they had got their pound of flesh in advance of their colleagues awaiting my arrival in Rio, I was finally able to gaze out of the window and reflect upon the miracle that had allowed me to be on my way back to Rio – and with the blessing of the Brazilian government.

Cruzeiro flight 251 from Belem arrived a few minutes early at Rio's new international airport, touching down just before 10 a.m. A few minutes later, as I passed into the baggage claim area, I saw Mike on the other side of the sliding glass doors that separate the passengers from the people awaiting their arrival.

Mike was with John and Lia, waving his arms excitedly. They

237

were not alone. There was a huge crowd of journalists and photographers jostling around them. A kindly federal agent, seeing Mike's predicament, opened the glass door and pushed him through into the baggage area. Mike came running.

'Pai!'

As I picked him up and hugged him to me, he asked me through our tears, 'Dad, why do people cry when they're happy?'

As I had no luggage to speak of and had already legally entered Brazil on my arrival in Belem, I passed quickly through the airport formalities. Then, with Mike sitting on my shoulders, I went through the sliding doors and faced the army of newsmen. John and Lia were there, pushing through the crowd in an effort to get us to their car. Mike was shouting, 'Let my dad through!' while I tried to calm the impatient press corps. In all it took us some ten minutes to cross the arrival hall, a trip that on a normal day, with all the chaos you associate with airports, would take less than a minute.

As we scrambled into the Pickstons' Opala the press rushed to their cars to follow us into Copacabana. A similar scene of confusion greeted us at the entrance to the building where the Pickstons lived. Lia went in first, wielding her handbag, and laid open a path for us through the crowd of newsmen and curious onlookers. Finally we arrived at the apartment on the ninth floor and could start to celebrate my return to Rio with a nice cup of tea.

As I sipped at my tea and caught my breath, Mike sat on my lap and showed me my name 'tattooed' in big letters on his chest. You would have thought I had never been away.

My friends had done a wonderful job of looking after Mike while I was having my unscheduled holiday in Barbados. At first, when it was known that I had been kidnapped, John and Lia had tried to keep the news from Mike, but it was an impossible task given the media attention the incident had generated. Once Mike discovered the truth it must have been very difficult for the Pickstons to reassure him and keep his mind occupied. But John Stanley Pickston, who had not doubted for one moment that I would get back to Brazil, is a born funny man and, among other things, he can make kids stop crying with his false nose and moustache. Nor is he the British community's favourite pantomime dame for nothing, so during his time with Mike he taught him a number of song-and-dance routines he had brought to Brazil from England, which included one based on 'Knees Up Mother Brown'.

My thoughts of Mike and John were broken by the noise of the frustrated press corps who were now banging on the door, demanding an audience. Finally – much to Levy's despair – I agreed to hold a press conference in the play area on the first floor of the building. Once that was over, I wanted to enjoy my freedom and went with Mike and John to the beach. But the reporters were not about to lose interest in a story that had dominated the press over the last forty days and they followed us at close quarters, asking more questions and taking endless photographs. Finally, we decided to take refuge in the Copacabana Palace, the hotel where so long ago, as it now seemed, I had begun the drama with Miller and his men. The same kindly and attentive waiters were there, ready, as always, to make a fuss over 'their little prince', Mike.

A few days later I met up with Levy, who declared that I had 'thrown away' whatever chance we might have had of writing a story about my kidnapping. He was returning to England that same evening, as he now saw no reason to stay on in Rio. He had been staying at the Meridian, one of Rio's best and most expensive hotels, and there was one night remaining on the booking that he had made and paid for. He suggested that I make use of it.

Thinking that there might be some cash forthcoming from our recently published book, which had sold well, no doubt helped by the publicity the kidnapping had occasioned, I asked Levy if he could leave me with some money. He laughed without mirth and told me the bad news: the expenses I had incurred during my little adventure in Barbados were in excess of $50,000, which more than took care of my earnings. He was kind enough, however, to leave me with $200 and the keys to his room before catching a taxi to the airport.

I had already spoken to Ulla; now I called her again and asked her to meet me at the Meridian for a get-together. A week or so before Miller had grabbed me, Ulla and I had had a bit of a row and we were not exactly on speaking terms when I left the scene unexpectedly. Now seemed like a good time to forget our little squabble.

About a year before my kidnapping, Mike (aged nearly six) and I had moved into a rather luxurious apartment on the eighteenth floor of a building that overlooked the bay of Guanabara and the Sugar Loaf Mountain. It offered the same picture-postcard view that had first attracted me to Rio when I was hiding in Australia, but at a price.

When I got back from Barbados, I found myself facing school, electric light, gas and telephone bills, plus $1000 in rent for the nearly two months that I had been away. Things were tough and I had to borrow money from friends to make ends meet. Little did I know that certain things had happened with Mike while I was away which would provide the solution to our current financial crisis.

TV Globo, who had shown a great interest in my kidnapping from the beginning, had visited Mike at the Pickstons with a view to interviewing him for their Sunday evening prime-time show *Fantastico*, the same programme that his mother and I had appeared on seven years earlier when I had first been arrested. John Pickston prompted his protégé to go through his 'Knees Up Mother Brown' routine for the TV camera. Mike ended his performance with a heartfelt plea to the Brazilian authorities to do something about getting me back to Brazil. He knew that the Queen of England wanted me, he said, but he needed me more in Brazil to take care of him.

By a happy coincidence, the then Minister of Justice, Ibraham Abi-Ackel, was in the Globo studio waiting to be interviewed and saw Mike's section of the programme. When he appeared on the screen he was smiling and said words to the effect that an effort must be made to bring me back to Brazil. With the minister's words the great wheels of state and diplomacy were put in motion, all of which helped my speedy return.

Another gentleman who caught Mike's performance, and who was equally impressed, was a Spaniard by the name of Tomas Munoz. At the time, he was the president of CBS Records in Brazil.

The day Munoz knocked on my front door I was thinking

about moving to somewhere less expensive. But Munoz saw Mike as an 'extremely talented child'. If I had no objection, he said, he was interested in making a record with Mike and two other youngsters. He had come up with an idea to create a children's vocal group. Auditions were already taking place, but he knew he wanted Mike. We asked Mike what he thought of the idea and he agreed without hesitation!

I had nothing against Mike participating in a musical group, providing, I said, that it didn't interfere with his education. At the beginning, I suppose, I thought it might be fun for him, but not for a moment did I imagine it would develop into anything serious or financially rewarding.

Until Munoz's arrival on the scene, I had only ever heard Mike sing snatches of my best-seller 'No One is Innocent' and the first few notes of 'Oh, Susanna' when playing 'cowboys and Indians'. I mentioned this to Mr Munoz, but there seemed to be no problem; in fact he liked the idea of 'Oh, Susanna' as a piece for Mike to start rehearsing. The following day I went down to the CBS office in Praia do Flamengo and signed a contract.

When the group was formed it was given the name of A Turma do Balão Magico, or the Magic Balloon Gang. Besides Mike, two other extremely talented kids were chosen from the auditions: Simony, a six-year-old girl, and Toby, who was eight. With the release of their first long-playing record the group was an overnight success with the kids; the record's sales rocketed, a fat cheque was deposited in my bank account and the kids of the Balão Magico were presented with their first gold record!

Tracks from their first album were heard every day on the radio, even on programmes not aimed at the normal Balão Magico audience. It was not long before they were being invited to participate in variety and music shows on all the major Brazilian television networks.

CBS Records appointed a capable young Brazilian lady named Monica Neves to manage the group for them, and soon after the first record was released the kids began to travel around Brazil, doing live shows as well as making promotional visits to shopping centres and record shops. The terms of the contract with CBS allowed for one parent to accompany each child and, after I had been given permission by the federal police, I travelled with Mike on most of the journeys the group made.

At first the audiences at the live shows were small, but before long fans of Balão Magico were filling football stadiums from one end of Brazil to the other to see the talented trio. At Christmas time, the Globo network, which is the world's fourth largest, takes over the gigantic Maracana Stadium in Rio de Janeiro to stage a free show which is televised live to millions and millions of homes throughout Brazil. The show features acrobats, clowns and other traditional circus acts alongside show-business personalities and singers who entertain the crowd. The arrival of Father Christmas in a helicopter is the delirious finale.

As the audience is largely made up of children, the Balão Magico was a natural choice to take part in these shows as one of the main attractions. Each Christmas Mike, Toby and Simony sang and danced, without any show of nerves, in front of a live audience of close to 200,000 people.

The group's second album was an even bigger hit than the first. One of the songs was called 'Superfantastico' and on this track the kids were joined by one of Brazil's top recording artists, Djavan. This catchy tune became a great favourite with the public and it was used to wind up the group's shows, when they were invariably called back for an encore!

'Superfantastico' earned the Balão Magico a second gold record and their first platinum disc, as well as an even fatter cheque! The shows continued, with the kids giving as many as three performances over a weekend. Doting mothers would bring their children to the hotels where we were staying so that they could see the group up close and get autographs.

Simony was from a large family who had spent most of their lives in the circus. They were rough and ready folk and the girl's mother, Maria, was tough and avaricious. From the moment the Balão Magico was formed, she tried to get a larger cut of the proceeds from the record sales and the shows for her daughter. She argued that Simony was the most talented in the group and should receive half the total amount, with the two boys left to split the remaining half. Toby's mother, Dona Rosa, and I did not agree. Monica Neves, who was managing the group, also sided with us.

It was during one of our weekend tours that a row flared up between Monica and Maria over the issue of Simony's pay. It resulted in Maria threatening to take her daughter out of the group unless Monica was dismissed. Not to upset the apple-cart, or the goose that laid the golden egg, CBS Records sadly bowed to Maria's wishes and gave Monica the sack. Her place was taken by an impresario from São Paulo, a slick and devious fellow by the name of Paulo Ricardo.

Paulo Ricardo was on very close terms with Simony's mother and soon they were calling the shots and banking the shows – paying the expenses and splitting the profits down the middle.

Each parent in the group was, in theory, free to bank at least one show each month. But Dona Rosa and I waived the privilege, so Paulo Ricardo and Maria were raking it in.

Flying back to Rio after another weekend of shows, Ricardo dropped into the empty seat beside me and started buttering me up with a load of old cobblers about his interest in Mike's career. He felt like a brother towards me, he said. Then he came up with an offer that common sense should have made me turn down on the spot.

'Senhor Ronald,' he said. 'We've got three shows lined up for next weekend. One in Santa Catarina, one in Joinville and one in Blumenau. Now, I know that you've never banked a show before, but I would like you to bank these three shows with me. Do you fancy taking a gamble? You could take home at least twice the amount you usually do.'

There was one obvious snag in banking a show: in the event of the show being rained off or not taking place for whatever reason, all the expenses – including the $500 for each child for each show – fell upon the shoulders of the person doing the banking.

Even though I knew that there had to be some sinister motive behind the impresario's offer, I decided to have a little flutter. Not for the first time, nor probably the last, Ulla thought I was mad. The area where the shows were scheduled to take place was in the far south of Brazil and it was the rainy time of the year down there.

'You'll lose your shirt,' Ulla predicted.

It looked as if she was going to be right: it was a cold, grey and rainy Friday that greeted the Balão Magico as we flew into Santa Catarina the following weekend. It was raining when we landed and it was still raining when we got up the next morning – with the first show scheduled to take place at 11 a.m. Yet miraculously the weather cleared up and the sun appeared. The show was on!

I went to the stadium to look at my 'investment' and, in no time at all, the stadium dried out and the public began to come through the turnstiles. Thank heaven you can always rely on a Brazilian audience to leave everything until the last minute!

It turned out to be a good crowd and a good show, in fact it was *Superfantastico*! Maria and the myriad members of her family, who had commiserated with me when we arrived, were now grudgingly congratulating me on having 'backed a winner'. Maria tried to look pleased for me.

The next two shows, in Joinville and Blumenau, were also put on under ideal weather conditions before thousands of happy, cheering children – and I was in there cheering with them! Altogether – in addition to the lucrative aspect – it was a very pleasant weekend. In Blumenau, the German community had been celebrating their Oktoberfest – so my cup runneth over!

When the time came to settle, Paulo Ricardo was wearing a stiff smile. He asked me how much I thought there was to come to me for the three shows. With Mike's payment included I estimated that I was due to receive around $5500, but I accepted $1000 less without argument.

About this time a Japanese team from NTV came to Rio to make a documentary film with me called *Long Time No See, Ronnie*, a reference to what Slipper was supposed to have said when he met me in Rio. The film was to include Mike and 'my old adversary', who were both flown to Tokyo to participate in the production. Ulla was invited to go along as Mike's chaperone and, of course, jumped at the chance.

The Japanese producers were very anxious to have Mike's recording fame known to their viewers and a special record sleeve for the Balão Magico's latest album was produced for the Japanese market, with a portrait of Mike filling the back cover in place of a group shot. Meanwhile I was called upon to act out my own part in Rio, with Brazilian actresses playing the roles of Charmian and Raimunda.

The money was now flowing in from Mike's work with the Balão Magico, so I made an investment with a couple of friends. This resulted in a nightclub in Copacabana called Crepúsculo de Cubatão, which became one of the hot night spots in Rio, especially with the 'darks'. Crepúsculo eventually ran its course and became the Kitschnet, which had a similarly successful run before finally calling it a day in 1993. Towards the end, Kitschnet hosted a number of very successful male strip shows for the ladies and became Brazil's answer to the Chippendales.

The Balão Magico was now a household name and TV Globo gave the kids their own breakfast-time programme. The first of its kind in Brazil, it was the show which paved the way for Xuxa to become Latin America's most famous media celebrity. Her morning show for children on Globo has made her one of the world's highest paid entertainers.

The recordings for the Balão Magico's shows were made at the Globo studio in São Paulo, which meant that Mike had to fly down there four or five times a week. I would pick him up from school at midday, take him home for a quick shower and something to eat, then rush off to catch the two o'clock flight. The recording sessions often ran into late evening and we would return to Rio on the last plane, getting home after midnight. Not surprisingly, Mike was neglecting his homework and started getting poor marks at school. The programme was very popular, however, and thousands of fan letters poured into the studio each day.

At the height of Balão Magico's popularity, CBS Records decided to add another child to the group to keep the momentum going. He was a handsome and highly talented little coloured kid named Jairzinho. A little younger than Mike, Jairzinho seemed to me to be an asset to the group. His father, Jair Rodrigues, was and is a well-known samba vocalist and Jairzinho had certainly inherited his father's talent. My view, however, was not shared by Simony's mother or Paulo Ricardo. When CBS first announced that they were considering Jairzinho for the group, Maria called a meeting of interested parties to discuss the situation. We had fought hard to put our kids where they were, she argued, and she didn't think it was right that another kid should be allowed to walk in at the peak of their success. To make matters worse, Maria went on, Jairzinho was a neginho and it was unthinkable that our kids should share their hard-won fame with a black boy.

When I was invited to give my opinion, I argued in favour of Jairzinho joining the Balão Magico. A large part of the Brazilian population is made up of black, brown and beige people and I saw the addition of Jairzinho as a certain way to increase record sales and balance the group. But I stood alone: even Toby's mother, Dona Rosa, didn't think a fourth member was necessary. But, after many bitter and heated arguments, CBS, who paid the piper, won the day and little Jairzinho joined.

The kids, who had not taken part in the discussion, couldn't have cared less about another child entering the group: it gave them someone else to play with during the tedious flights to and from the shows. Mike palled up with Jairzinho immediately and they worked very well together on the television programme. Conversely, Mike had never really hit it off with Simony and the two of them frequently squabbled. Provoked, one day, tough-as-nails Simony called Mike 'the son of a thief'. Mike didn't hesitate with his reply: 'And you're the daughter of a bitch!' There's no business like show business, they say!

After John Miller and co. had tried to grab me the first time in April 1979, Ulla had suggested that Mike and I should move in with her and her children in Rio; she said I was a 'sitting duck' in Sepetiba and I tended to agree. She said the gang might try to get me again, so, obeying a law that Murphy would have been proud of, I sold off my bits and pieces in Sepetiba, paid the rent and moved to Santa Teresa, one of Rio's most historic, bohemian and beautiful neighbourhoods. Ulla's apartment, which her father had bought for her, was situated on the middle floor of a fine old house that had been converted into three apartments. The ground floor was occupied by an elderly tailor and his family, who were the only tenants in the building with access to a large but run-down and overgrown back garden. I used to look down with a certain amount of envy at the abandoned area beneath Ulla's bedroom and imagine what I could do with the place if it were mine. I reminded myself that it didn't cost anything to dream.

Sometime later, in early 1980, Ulla moved from Santa Teresa and let her apartment to a young Brazilian couple, while I moved out to Botafogo.

Then, in the February of 1984, I heard that the apartment beneath Ulla's was up for sale. I immediately took a taxi over to the house, where I found the owner of the apartment at home. The place was shabbier than I had thought and it was obviously going to take a lot of time and money to fix it up. But at $16,000 the price was very attractive. Without haggling, I gave the old tailor a cheque for half the amount by way of a deposit and arranged to pay the remainder within twenty-eight days. I bought the apartment in Mike's name, but I said nothing to him about the deal. I wanted to refurbish it and present it to him as a surprise. Within days of signing the contract, I arranged for a team of tradesmen and labourers to start work on the renovation.

It was exactly a year later that we moved in. The work wasn't finished but it was nearing completion and I, the ex-foreman, wanted to be around to supervise the final touches. The old tailor wouldn't have recognized the place. The worm-eaten flooring throughout the ground floor had been ripped out and replaced with white marble; all the old woodwork, cupboards and door frames had been burned and replaced with dark, polished hardwood; a twenty-two-by-thirteen-foot slate-lined swimming pool had been installed and Mike had his own suite, decorated with the colours of his favourite football team. We bought a beautiful Rottweiler puppy whom we named Blitz and a little later Lua, a miniature pinscher bitch, both of whom, like the apartment, are still with me today. As well as the dogs we also had a number of birds, including a magnificent blue and yellow macaw named Fred.

So finally, thanks to Mike – and, indirectly, to John Miller, without whose 'help' Mike's talent might never have been discovered – we had our own home and castle. Biggsy's bolt-hole in Brazil.

The popularity of the Balão Magico continued, with Jairzinho now being tagged 'the Michael Jackson of Brazil'. Three more albums were produced, one of which sold half a million copies and earned the group a double platinum disc. The group was called upon to advertise various products and contracted by one of Rio's best-known entrepreneurs, Chico Recarey, to put on a series of weekend shows at his 'emporiums of entertainment'. Every Saturday and Sunday afternoon saw the kids on stage singing their hits to capacity audiences of young fans.

After five action-packed years, the Magic Balloon Gang's gravy train started to slow down and finally came to an armchair stop. It had been a long and lucrative journey, now it was time for the kids to rest on their laurels and enjoy the sweet smell of their success as they planned what to do with the rest of their young lives.

Another person who chose to move on was Tomas Munoz. He had made CBS the most successful and profitable record company in Brazil and now he got the call to the corporation's offices in New York.

Nearly ten years on, Mike, now nineteen, has not had his taste for the spotlight dimmed and he is getting ready for another assault on the music industry. With a cupboard full of gold and platinum discs he certainly has something of a head start on his rivals.

# 15.  An Englishman Abroad –
## Old Friends Come Calling

After five hectic years of travelling around Brazil with the Balão Magico, it felt good to return to a somewhat more 'normal' life. Mike had missed a lot of school and had fallen asleep over his homework once too often. He had a lot of catching up to do. Although we were sitting on a fairly healthy bank balance it wasn't going to last forever, and with Brazil's high rate of inflation I thought I had better look at ways to protect our capital and make it grow.

Shortly before the Balão Magico folded, Raimunda had returned to Brazil pregnant and married to a Swiss bank clerk named Gerard. At first they went to live with Raimunda's parents in the north of Brazil then, when their child was born, a boy they named Andre, they came back to Rio. Gerard was supposedly a good cook and was interested in opening a restaurant in Rio – all he needed was the cash. Not wishing to look a gift horse in the mouth, I put up the money and Mike and I became fifty-fifty partners with Gerard and Raimunda in a small restaurant in a popular resort town close to Rio called Buzios.

Buzios had been put on the map in the 1960s when Brigitte Bardot chose it for her honeymoon. Since that time the once tiny fishing village had grown into a sophisticated weekend getaway for Rio's 'beautiful people', who arrived to take advantage of the peninsula's nineteen beaches during the day and its many bars and restaurants in the evening.

I hired a team of builders to give our place a face-lift and stocked the cellar with a good selection of wines. A barman and a waitress were engaged and Mr Big opened to the public with great expectations.

But the customers were few and far between and Gerard, as chef, found himself with little to do except tipple our best wine and 'fall' asleep behind the bar. The competition was just too strong and, like so many other would-be restaurateurs who have been lured to Buzios before and since, we went broke.

Fortunately, I was still considered good copy and was regularly sought out to give interviews for newspapers, magazines and television. Journalists came, it seemed at times, from all the corners of the globe but it was still mostly the boys and girls from Fleet Street who knew that 'Ronnie' could be relied upon for a good quote, whatever the topic.

I have also been invited over the years to take part in a number of advertising campaigns which have included coffee, locks and security systems. The attention these campaigns received earned me a sharp reminder from the federal police that I was still not permitted to work in Brazil.

Ironically, one of the most successful advertising campaigns to use my name I never received a penny for. It was a campaign for the British Leyland Mini which, according to the advert, 'Nips in and out faster than Ronald Biggs!'

Tour operators, who had begun to discover that in certain countries I was as much a symbol of Rio as Corcovado or Sugar Loaf, began to approach me with a view to entertaining groups of tourists who were interested in meeting me. 'The Biggs Experience' was the way one female journalist neatly described it. For fifty dollars tourists could visit me in my bolt-hole and enjoy my hospitality, eat, drink and splash around in the pool or sit fascinated while I held forth about the train robbery. What else? Photos were taken and autographs given. I often think I enjoyed these meetings as much as my guests, so I will continue to open up my house occasionally to visitors for the foreseeable future.

Many of my fans and admirers never get the chance or the opportunity to get to Rio and so write or send gifts instead. As my family and friends will tell you, I am not a great letter writer, so I apologize to those who did not get a personal reply.

Not all the mail is of a friendly nature and I have had

my share of hate mail over the years. Two letters, to be exact!

One of my first 'experiences' with visitors to Rio was a chance encounter in Copacabana. I was sitting at a seafront bar sipping a cold beer. It was quite early and there were only a few people about. The sea air was bracing and there was not a cloud on the horizon.

Four people were walking slowly towards me along the pavement, looking directly at me as they drew near. There were two men and two women. The younger woman came up to my table, smiling.

'Are you really 'im?' she asked.

'Yes,' I said, 'I think so.' Assuming she thought I was who I was.

'Ooh! Can I call my mum and dad and me boyfriend over? – I can't believe this! – Mum! Dad! It is Ronnie!'

The four were from Fulham; Mum and Dad, Brenda and Ted, all gor blimey Londoners. They was on a cruise, like, and their ship had docked in Rio, giving the passengers a few hours ashore. As they had left the docks on their way to explore Copacabana, Brenda had said, 'Wouldn't it be funny if we was to meet Ronnie Biggs!'

'And we've bloody well done it!' said her boyfriend.

Dad called for a round of beer and Brenda, still smiling, opened up with a string of questions. Ted butted in.

'She's a right fan of yours,' he told me. 'I reckon she's got more time for you than she'd ever have for me – straight! She'd take your socks as a souvenir if you'd give 'em to her.'

We drank our beers and chatted away. 'You must get fed up with people like us,' observed Dad. 'Perfect strangers, just coming up to you and wasting your time.'

I assured Dad to the contrary, telling him that I was always ready to meet my own people.

'One fing's for certain,' said Ted. 'When we get back to Fulham no one's ever going to believe us when we tell 'em that we met Ronnie Biggs!'

On my way home I saw a T-shirt in a shop window that had printed on the front the old tourist favourite: 'I know someone who went to Brazil and all I got was a lousy T-shirt.' It got me thinking and a couple of weeks later I took delivery of a thousand T-shirts similarly printed, but I changed the lettering to 'I know someone who went to Brazil and met Ronnie Biggs – honest!' They started selling like hot cakes, and they still do.

Since Jack Slipper's historic first trip to Brazil in 1974 I have been fortunate enough to meet many more equally illustrious figures, including lots of the musicians and other celebrities who have passed through Rio to give shows. One of these was Sting who, during our first encounter, was still with the appropriately named Police.

From the rockers to the punks, I have met them all and on many occasions have joined them on stage or in the studio. Don't expect *Ronnie Biggs' Greatest Hits*, but it is out there somewhere if you pulled all the tracks together. One recent visitor was reggae star Maxi Priest with whom – I discovered – I had a lot in common. Not only were we both Brixton boys, but we were also both carpenters at one time!

Another recent visitor was the record producer Gus Dudgeon and his wife Sheila. Any fan of Elton John will recognize Gus's name. Gus and Sheila first dropped by to meet me as they were sailing through Rio on the *QE2*. They promised to come back for the party to mark the thirtieth anniversary of the robbery and were as good as their word, falling in love with Rio in the process. Since his first visit, Gus has met Bruce Reynolds in London, so has learned more about the train robbery than most.

Lord Snowdon dropped by to take my photo on one occasion, while I was also proud to host one of my sporting heroes, Sir Stanley Matthews, arguably the greatest English winger of all time.

Another fascinating visitor was Albert Spagiarri, the brilliant thief who tunnelled under the main road to rob the Bank of Nice. Albert popped down to Rio for a chat in 1980. A very nice fellow but looking quite ridiculous in an obviously false moustache and Afro wig. Albert's crime, you may remember, was carried out without guns, without violence and without hatred, a message that he left written on the wall of the vault. He was caught, but soon managed to escape and made his way to South America, in the process becoming 'France's answer to Ronnie Biggs'.

When the initial cloak-and-dagger approach was made, there was no mention of who it was who wanted to meet me. I had to meet a French lady named Alice in Colombos, an old-fashioned tea-room in Copacabana.

Once more into the lion's den I went. Alice, who turned out to be a handsome lady in her mid thirties, came straight to the point.

'How much do you want to be paid to meet Albert Spagiarri?'

The name sounded as if he might be some mafioso, so I was cautious, especially after what had gone on the previous year.

'Who's Albert Spagiarri?' I asked.

Alice gave me the facts. *Paris Match* was in Brazil and they decided it would be a major scoop to film me and Albert together. I did not ask how *Paris Match* came to know that France's most wanted man was in Rio, but I hoped he had better luck with *Paris Match* than I had had with the *Daily Express*.

In less time than it had taken for me to decide to become one of the train robbers, I asked Alice for $5000 in cash to meet with Spagiarri, who was to pretend to interview me for French TV. 1980 had been a fairly lean year and I had accumulated more nagging debts. Alice got back to me the following day with the news I had been waiting to hear. *Paris Match* had agreed to my terms.

Albert and I were introduced to each other in an apartment near Colombos. We got on famously but for the fact that he couldn't speak a word of English and I had only the smattering of French guide-book phrases that I had picked up in Paris. Without the false moustache and large wig, Albert could probably have walked the streets of Copacabana quite unnoticed, but when we did go out everyone stared. My old mate Eric Flower would have loved him!

Our meeting was recorded for television, but the director swore to me that the encounter was exclusively for screening in France. I can't say that I was altogether surprised, however, when our little get-together was shown on *Fantastico* the following Sunday evening.

For the recording I had to pretend that I did not know who it was who was interviewing me.

'What would you do, Mr Biggs, if you came face to face with Albert Spagiarri?' Spagiarri asked.

'Who is Albert Spagiarri?' I replied.

'He, Mr Biggs, is the most famous runaway in the world.'

'Sorry, pal,' I said with a grin. 'You're looking at the world's most famous runaway.' Spagiarri was in no position to argue.

There were some rather more pertinent questions awaiting me when I went to sign in at the federal police headquarters the following week. Interpol would have liked to sit in on our little chat, I was led to believe, and I was warned that I was skating on very thin ice.

By 1986 I was hoping that my hustling days were well and truly over as I was introduced to Polish film director Lech Majewski. Majewski had read all about me and decided that he was the person to make the film of my life. He had only a couple of quite ordinary films to his credit, including one called *Flight of the Spruce Goose*, which was about as commercially successful as the Howard Hughes airliner of the same name.

Lech visualized *Prisoner of Rio* as a masterpiece in the making. Finance had been arranged by a Swiss-based sales-distribution company, Multi Media, but, like most of the deals I find myself involved in, the movie was to be made on a budget that was far too low for its pretensions.

Initially, Lech said that his intention was to make a true film of my life, a good film, a film that he and I would both be happy with and proud of. The problem was that it would take at least half-a-dozen full-length films to tell the whole 'Biggs story'.

As we were in Rio, Lech saw my kidnapping as a good base for the film he had in mind and I was invited to join him and his American girlfriend, Julia Frankel, in writing the screenplay. We began work immediately. Every day I would go to the hotel where Lech and Julia were staying to work on the project. We seemed to be making good progress when, after nearly two weeks of work on the 'true story', Lech changed his mind and announced that we were going to turn to fiction and write yet another kidnap plot, this time to be carried out by an outraged Scotland Yard inspector, 'Jock' MacFarland, who was obsessed with the idea of getting 'that bastard' out of Brazil. Up until that moment I had given the work my best shot, but all my interest died when I heard Lech's decision. The stuff Lech and Julia wrote was wishy-washy at best and sometimes downright corny. A number of times I clashed with the hard-headed Pole and in the end I let him get on with it, although I still ended up with a screenwriting credit.

Paul Freeman was chosen to play Biggs, walking into a kidnap set-up for the third time, and Steven Berkoff was to take the role of the avenging Glasgow-born Inspector MacFarland. Other actors involved included Peter Firth and the Brazilians José Wilker, Florinda Bolkan and Zezé Motta.

Production proper finally got underway in July 1987, and I had a cameo role as a guest at my own party. During the following months of bickering and backbiting *Prisoner of Rio* struggled through to the end, going way over budget in the process.

Everybody hated Lech, especially Berkoff, but Lech took this in his stride; it was customary for everyone to dislike the director, he said. I discovered a certain affinity with Steven and it turned out that we shared a common experience: we had both been to Stamford House Remand Home and we both remembered the perverted old director of that disgraceful establishment, Johnny O'Hare. Steve lamented the fact that he had not thought of making a film with me. He said he would have written the screenplay, directed the film and played the leading role, instead of getting involved with 'this megalomaniac Majewski'.

'I myself fail to understand why people can change a perfectly good yarn for some hokum,' Berkoff told *Time Out* on his return to London. 'But that is the nature of people who film the people who live . . . If someone like Biggs expresses doubts about some elements of the script, then a producer who fails to listen does so at his own peril. After all, it comes from the horse's mouth. He was there.'

I was there, Steve, so hopefully you will have found this book to be the 'perfectly good yarn' you were looking for. The truth with no frills.

*Prisoner of Rio* was finally unveiled for the first time to its expectant buyers at the Cannes Film Festival in May 1988. Now if ever there is an event that is fuelled by hype, it is the Cannes Film Festival. Hundreds of new films are launched there each year and if your film doesn't have a gimmick or a hook it can get lost in the crowd. The Cannes Film Festival also claims to be the world's last annual media event, with more than 3000 journalists crushing into the French Riviera town for the ten days of festivities.

A publicity scam was concocted for *Prisoner of Rio* for the benefit of the world's press. 'Mr Biggs will be putting in a personal appearance at the festival,' the producers announced. Speculation and rumour suggested that they had me hidden away on one of the luxury yachts that were anchored off the beach. When the pressmen – and the cops – gathered to take advantage of what could be the biggest single attraction of the 1988 festival they were not to be disappointed. Mr Biggs was certainly in Cannes – only it was Mr Michael Biggs. Surprise, surprise!

While the press on the whole took the scam well, the same could not be said for the film itself, which got a critical hammering. By coincidence or mismanagement, it was released in Britain at around the same time as a film about Buster Edwards. *Buster* starred everyone's favourite rock star, Phil Collins, alongside the equally popular Julie Walters; predictably, *Prisoner of Rio* did not receive the kudos that Lech Majewski had forecast.

Neither *Buster* nor *Prisoner of Rio* is exactly a masterpiece, but you will probably find them at your local video store where I hope they are firmly catalogued under 'fiction'.

My share of the proceeds from *Prisoner of Rio* came to a paltry $13,000, far short of the vast sums that had been mentioned at the beginning of the negotiations. But it was enough to keep the wolf from the door for a year or so.

I have met hundreds of tourists over the years. A lot of them have become my friends and make return trips to Rio to maintain our friendship. Irish Americans Dennis and Maura Clare, for instance, are a kind-hearted couple from New York, who have been visiting us since Mike was a year old. Richard Keaney, another Paddy, came to Rio for the first time in 1987. His friends 'back home' had told him that he couldn't return without some pictures of him and me together. So one Saturday morning Richard – a wacky Gene Wilder look-alike – found his way to our home in Santa Teresa. He turned up carrying an airline bag which contained a bottle of whisky and a cheap camera. Drinks were poured and Richard shot off the roll of film that was in his camera. It was evening when he left. Early the next morning he telephoned with a tale of woe; he had been held up by a brace of street kids and they had taken off with his watch, his cash and his camera – with the 'precious' film inside it. He had bought another camera, he told me – but would I let him return to take another set of photographs? I agreed and arranged a friend for life. Richard has been back to Rio every year since, always arriving with a ten-pound slab of Cheddar cheese and other gifts.

Richard was in Rio when I received a most illustrious guest: my friend and hero, bantam Paul Seabourne.

At the time, 1990, I was engaged in making a documentary film with an Australian bloke named Bob Starkey. He was going to cover a party I was giving to mark my twenty-five years on the run, and he had asked me who I thought should 'star' in his production. Without hesitation I suggested Paul – I was having the celebration thanks entirely to him. Bob agreed and made contact with Paul in London. Miraculously he wasn't inside.

Paul was quite ready for a trip to Rio and a first-class flight was arranged. Bob wanted to get our first meeting in twenty-four years on film, so he set up his camera at the airport where the passengers disembark. First-class travel had provided Paul with a fine selection of alcoholic beverages to choose from and my old pal arrived very obviously drink-lagged. But it was just fantastic to see the little bugger again.

Our re-encounter was shot by a drinks stand where we were to toast each other with double whiskies. This scene was repeated several times, as were the doubles. We laughed and joked and took the piss out of each other's old looks. Wet though he was, his wit was as dry as ever. I didn't tell him, but the long years that he had spent in the nick showed. A number of his front teeth were missing and he walked with a stoop. But it was the same old Paul and it was great to have him in Rio.

Back at the 'Biggs mansion', I introduced Paul to Richard,

who had crashed out on a settee the previous evening. A bottle of vodka was produced and my two guests were soon chatting away, both smoking like chimneys. Richard, who knew who Paul was and why he was in Rio, was 'honoured to meet the man who got Ronnie out of prison'. He was loving every minute in Paul's company. During the afternoon they both passed out.

Seeing that Paul was *hors de combat*, Bob proposed that we should forget filming for the day and get off to a seven o'clock start the next morning. With this in mind I went to bed early, leaving the guests to sleep it off.

No one seems to know what hour it was when Paul woke up and found that he and Richard had smoked all their fags, but it was certainly after midnight. Driven by the craving that only cigarette smokers will understand, he went off to look for a tobacconist or perhaps a slot machine as he would have back home in London. It was late and dark: only a fool would be abroad in Rio on a night like this. Thinking that he only had to 'pop up the road', he had gone out wearing a pair of thin-soled airline slippers. Santa Teresa is not the easiest area to find your way around in, but Paul followed the tramlines which he presumed would lead him back to the house. He kept walking and finally came to an area where he found bars and nightclubs that were open. With £500 in his pocket and not a word of Portuguese, Paul had wandered into Lapa, a very tough neighbourhood where transvestites swing their handbags and muggings are commonplace.

We were on the point of organizing a search party when Paul turned up in a taxi just after seven o'clock. The taxi-driver, who claimed that he had been driving my house guest around for the last four hours in the hope that he would recognize the road, was demanding $300 from the *gringo louco* (mad gringo). Needless to say, despite his age, Paul, who had followed the wrong tramlines, wanted to sort the bloke out.

We got on 'location', Paradise Island, by two that afternoon and Paul promptly fell face down in the sand. Bob loved the footage that he was getting of the two old jailbirds 'havin' a fuckin' ball'. This was the stuff he wanted: 'warts an' all'!

By the evening Paul had made a remarkable recovery and looked quite reasonable. We were off to do some more filming.

This time, the two old lags across a dinner table in a swanky waterfront restaurant, with the Sugar Loaf looming in the background. The strains of 'You and the Night and the Music' reached us. We were rolling!

Bob, who was playing the role of interviewer, asked me if I was 'suffering' in Brazil. This was in reference to a remark that Jack Slipper had made on one of our various satellite encounters. Asked if he thought I deserved to be pardoned or not, Mr Slipper replied that he thought I should continue to 'suffer' in Brazil. Keeping a straight face, I was giving Bob a list of the ways I suffered. Not allowed to work. Not permitted to marry. Not allowed in bars or nightclubs. Have to sign in twice a week at the police station . . .

'Why don't you say something about your "mansion" in Santa Teresa with the heated swimming pool?' Paul asked helpfully. 'And while you're about it you should mention Rosa, the maid, and the house-boy you've got working for you . . .'

Interfering old fool. I was glad to see the back of him. But something tells me that I haven't seen the last of the old bugger!

While Paul was in Rio I was approached by the then cult BBC-TV programme *Saturday Night Clive* to see if I would be willing to do a satellite link-up with the show's host, Aussie Clive James, to talk about crime on television and television in general. Much to their surprise, I think, I agreed to do the show and was ready to cross humorous swords with Mr James, but either he or the BBC got cold feet and I was told my services would not be required after all.

My dear friend Bruce Reynolds was another very welcome and distinguished guest in our 'sumptuous' apartment overlooking Rio's industrial zone. Bruce came to Brazil for a short spell with a tough-looking customer named Tony Thake, the boss of a transport business. The last time I had seen Bruce was on that fateful day way back in August 1963 when I had moved into the 'big time'. Although we had spoken on the phone before he came over, it was still an enormous pleasure to meet him again. Bruce, who had served fifteen years out of a twenty-five-year sentence for his part in planning and executing the train robbery, was also marked by the long period of incarceration, which had left him emaciated and looking much older than he should have. Nevertheless, we had a great get-together and a lot of laughs. Tony, a gentleman if not a scholar, filmed our reunion and the fun and games, in the hope of finding someone interested in buying the unusual footage. Tony had financed the trip to Brazil for both of them as Bruce was living on the dole at that time, and probably still is as he has chosen to stay out of the public eye.

A day or so after Bruce arrived in Rio, we were joined by his son, Nick, who is every bit as likable and irreverent as his old man. Their stay in Rio was all too short, but I'm sure we'll all meet again in the not-too-distant future.

Visitors have come from far and wide and while I would expect to be known in Britain and Australia, I also find I have a stream of visitors from Scandinavia, South Africa, Canada, Japan and Germany. I even find that I have a growing following in the US, where a recent visitor, Steve Koschal, has discovered that there is quite a market for Ronnie Biggs autographs. Steve is an autograph expert and I think even he has been surprised by the interest collectors have shown in my scrawl.

Steve is a near neighbour in Florida of my nephew Terry, who is also a regular visitor to Rio. Terry has taken after his Uncle Ron and likes to dabble in the kitchen, only he does it on a professional scale with his own catering company. Whenever he comes to town all hell breaks loose in the kitchen as he, Rosa and I all fight for space on the stove.

Besides Charmian and the boys, Terry and his brothers, Jack and Chris, plus Terry's own son, Steve, are my closest relatives. Terry's father was my older brother, Jack, who died on the eve of the Great Train Robbery.

A visitor to these shores whom I had never thought I would see again was ex-sleuth Jack Slipper.

Hearing that I was about to stage a party to commemorate the thirtieth anniversary of the train robbery, the *Sunday Express* telephoned me to see if I would be willing to meet Slipper in Rio. There had been rumours that I was planning to invite him to the party. The BBC had also shown a lot of interest in the bash and were talking about turning up in Rio with as many of the train gang as wished to come along and talk about old times.

Anxious not to miss out on a story of an encounter between the ex-cop and myself, the *Sunday Express* was ready to 'do the dirty' on the rest of Fleet Street and the BBC.

I was not expecting Slipper to turn up under any circumstances, so I was quite surprised when Oonagh Blackman, the *Sunday Express* reporter, phoned to say that he had agreed to come to the mountain, although not to the party. Well, one thing was for certain: neither one of us was going to do it for love. My fee was £1000. I don't know what Jack's payment was, but I do know that his first-class airfare would have shown very little change from 5000 quid.

Our meeting, in June 1993, was much ado about nothing and the *Sunday Express* had nothing specific in mind when they planned it. They were hoping that something 'newsworthy' might come from Slipper and me being brought face to face after all these years.

We met in a quiet corner of the pool area at the back of the Inter-Continental Hotel in São Conrado. The same hotel where I had gone to meet Bobby Moore and Kenny Lynch in 1979.

'I'm not going to say the obvious,' said Slipper as we shook hands.

Seeing Oonagh Blackman standing close by waiting to hear our first gems of conversation I said, 'You don't have to say anything. But what you do say will be taken down and will result in the *Sunday Express* selling a lot of newspapers!'

We left the hotel and went for a stroll along the beach chit-chatting while Stuart Mason, the newspaper's photographer, snapped away with a variety of cameras. I told Slipper I was surprised that he had accepted the *Sunday Express'* invitation to meet me, knowing that his gesture was sure to meet with disapproval in certain quarters. But he was no longer a policeman and he was able to come and go as he saw fit. He was just anxious to keep his visit as secret as possible so that it didn't turn into a 'circus'. He had even made his flight reservations under an assumed name.

He asked after Mike and Ulla, whom he had met in Tokyo. I politely asked after his wife, knowing she had suffered for a number of years from arthritis. Nobody would have guessed – or believed – that the two white-haired old gents ambling along the beach in the winter sunshine were the ex-guv'nor of the Sweeney and Britain's most wanted man.

It had been thirsty work and Jack and I were in need of a drink. Jack suggested that we should go to a bar where we would be unrecognized, so I took them to a shopping mall a couple of hundred yards from their hotel where there is a comfortable bar-restaurant called Guimas. A female acquaintance, Beatriz, whom I had not seen for several years, was working at the bar as a waitress and immediately came to our table to greet me. Moments later an American musician friend, Bill Horn, walked through the door: 'Hi, Ron, who are your friends?'

So far Slipper and I had not had a chance to exchange a word. As Bill moved away from our table Slipper commented, 'I'm glad that I didn't suggest going to a place where you're well known!'

Over drinks, with Oonagh ever at the ready with her pen and note-pad poised, the two one-time adversaries opened up the conversation that the *Sunday Express* team were waiting for: 'The Last Secret of the Great Train Robbery'.

We found ourselves talking about 'the man who had coshed the train driver'. Slipper assured me that the Yard knew the identity of this person, who was never taken into custody.

'It was the big fellow,' said Slipper with conviction. 'If I gave you the initial of his first name, would you give me the initial of his second name?'

'Not likely!' I replied. 'You can say whatever initials you like, but I'm not about to say yea or nay to anything.' And that was 'the last secret' which must have set the *Sunday Express* back about £20,000 to find out!

The next morning, when I was due to meet Slipper in Copacabana, I took Johnny Pickston along. For some years John had been playing 'golf' on Copacabana beach, hitting a tennis ball from one litter bin to the next. He had become quite a dab hand at it and, knowing of Jack Slipper's passion for golf, was anxious to challenge the ex-policeman. On 'holiday' in Rio, how could he refuse?

It was a fun day, with beers on the beach. Later the photographer suggested that Jack and I should stand with our arms around each other's shoulders in front of the Trocadero Hotel where he had 'nicked' me nearly twenty years earlier. But that, said Slipper, was going a bit too far.

For me, the highlight of his visit came when we all sat down to dinner in a Japanese restaurant in Ipanema called *Madame Butterfly*.

Besides Slipper, the *Sunday Express* couple and myself, Mike and Johnny Pickston were in the jolly company. We ordered drinks and a 'jumbo' sized dish of mixed *sushi* and *sashami*. The food was beautifully served in a large flat boat and was placed in the centre of the table. We all fell to with our chopsticks.

Man of the world Jack Slipper had no difficulty manipulating the little sticks of wood, but the lights were low and Jack wasn't wearing his glasses, so he couldn't see the tiny pieces of Japanese culinary art too well. He reached out with his chopsticks, deftly picked up a walnut-sized piece of *wasabi* – the fiery green paste made from horseradish – and, as we watched in horror, popped it into his mouth. As the *wasabi* hit his sinuses, Slipper leapt up from the table, looking for somewhere to spit and reaching for his glass of beer at the same time to put the fire out.

Thanks for the dinner, Jack, it was a nice one!

John Pickston offered to take the group to the airport when it was time for them to return to England, and as I had nothing on I went along for the ride. Over a drink or two at the airport Jack and I talked about the 'flak' he was certain to receive when he got back to England. But Jack's an old campaigner, well accustomed to the shit that's thrown in the press. When there's a few quid to be earned he'd be a fool not to go for it. And the readers love it, so why not?

As he was leaving we shook hands firmly.

'All the best, Ronnie.'

'You too, Jack. See you soon.'

It turned out to be sooner than we had expected, as just over a month later, but this time over a satellite hook-up, we again came face to face. The travelling tec was in Hamburg to have a chinwag with his favourite fugitive. But this time I had to say the obvious: 'Jack, we're going to have to stop meeting like this . . .'

# 16. Thirty Years On – Summing Up

My story stands at the moment as it began – hard up.

For the want of a few quid, I had plunged headlong into an enterprise that was to lead me into almost thirty years of a life 'on the run'. Had I heeded the advice of the old fortune-teller in Hastings things might have turned out very different. I might have spent the rest of my life freezing my nuts off on a bleak building site somewhere in Britain. So, if you ask me if I have any regrets about being one of the train robbers, I will answer 'No!' without hesitation. I will go further: I am proud to have been one of them. Equally happy to be described as the tea-boy or the Brain. I was there and that is all that matters. One of the only surviving witnesses to what was undoubtedly 'the Crime of the Century'. I am also proud of the fact that my 'track record', such as it was, enabled me to be invited to work with such eminent fellow thieves and good company.

A controversy raged at the time over the sentences the train gang were given. Some thought the punishment was too harsh and there were those who thought the thirty-year sentences fitted the crime. I am one. Armed with coshes, we had attacked the Royal Mail, injured a defenceless man and made off with more than two million quid belonging to the banks. Don't believe the story that the money was on its way to be destroyed. Much of it was in mint condition. It was obvious we were going to go down for a long time.

In retrospect, I don't think the coshing of the train driver had any bearing on the sentences that were handed down. Had he not been injured, I believe we would have been given thirty-year terms anyway. Robbing the Royal Mail was a crime against the Crown, of course, and came close to being an act of treason. We all knew what we were getting into and we all knew we'd get 'big bird' if we were nicked.

For my part, I was prepared to do my time, keep my nose clean and try not to break the rules. Although parole did not exist in the British penal system in 1964, it was evident that a parole scheme would soon be introduced and I believed that it would be possible to get out after ten years or so. Not a pleasant prospect to think of 'treading out' that length of time, but I was ready to get on with it, for the time being anyway. Had the then governor of Wandsworth Prison given more serious thought to my plea to be treated like any other con when I was being harassed into a probable nervous breakdown, I might well have served out my time as a model prisoner and been released along with the other members of the gang in 1975.

But I didn't. I ran away, and I'm glad I did. And I would do it all again without the slightest hesitation.

'But, Ronnie, you *must* regret the fact that you can't go back to England,' the British tourists and the press insist.

'You're wrong,' I tell them. 'I could go back tomorrow if I wanted to.' But, of course, I don't want to. At least, not if it means going to jail. To hell with that!

So many visiting Brits tell me that I wouldn't recognize the old place now, and it certainly isn't what it was when I last saw it nearly thirty years ago. They tell me that I'm 'far better off' where I am, even with Brazil's various problems.

Although I have said that I have no regrets about my involvement in the train robbery, that isn't strictly true. It is regrettable that Mr Mills was injured and terrified out of his wits. During Jack Slipper's recent visit to Brazil we spoke about the train driver and his injuries and Mr Slipper voiced the opinion that the coshing of Jack Mills amounted to 'unnecessary violence'. I agreed with him, but I pointed out that the driver was only struck once and not 'beaten repeatedly, with blows from an iron bar and left broken and bleeding beside the railway track', as I had read in a copy of the *Daily Express* at the time of my capture in 1974. Even in 1993, the *Sunday Express* still saw fit to describe how Jack Mills was 'cut down by a blinding whirl of iron bars'.

It goes without saying that I will always regret losing my wife and children when I left them in Australia and went to Brazil. Perhaps that is when I should have given myself up. Perhaps not. Of course I love them as much as ever, as they love me, and although I'm a lazy letter writer we do communicate, especially when we sit around and think of 'old times' and how good they were. Perhaps my new fax machine, a sixty-fourth birthday present from my nephew Terry, will make communications easier.

Charmian and the boys have been back to Brazil several times since our tearful parting in 1974 and, hopefully, they will all be coming to Brazil this year to celebrate my sixty-fifth birthday and the thirty-first anniversary of the Great Train Robbery. If not, there is always 1995 and the thirtieth anniversary of my 'flight to freedom' from Wandsworth. Another bash that shouldn't be missed.

Farley and Chris are now grown men and have nothing but respect for 'the old fart'. Charmian did a magnificent job of bringing them up. She also found time to study and won herself a BA degree with honours in history and English literature.

From time to time there is speculation in the press about my position in Brazil. A year or so ago I saw a newspaper report to the effect that as Mike was coming up for eighteen years of age, there was a strong possibility that the Brazilian authorities were on the point of giving me the bum's rush out of their country. I have heard nothing official to that effect. Perhaps my situation will change when Mike turns twenty-one in August 1995 and is recognized as an adult. I hope not.

The thought that I might be returned to prison one day does not worry me unduly. It's a bridge I'll cross if and when I have to. Pretty soon I'll be entering into the last scene of all and, if I'm to become a dribbling nuisance, one of Her Majesty's hostelries might be just the place to spend my twilight years. Furthermore, I would be able to catch up on my reading and old friends from the past. Perhaps have Paul Seabourne and Ronnie Leslie pay me a visit. I hear they are still in the removal business, stout lads that they are.

As you have read, John Miller – or McKillop – is a very dangerous man. As a result of his confessed mischief, I came close to suffocating in a canvas bag and drowning in shark-infested waters. He was also guilty of traumatizing my six-year-old son. Kidnapping is a very grave crime; a despicable crime, punishable by death in some enlightened parts of the world. Tragically, kidnapping has been rife in Brazil and almost every day the television news shows heartbroken parents pleading for the return of their loved ones, just as Mike pleaded for me.

Many people have asked why charges were never brought against Miller and his gang. I ask the same question, but nobody ever seems to want to give me a straight answer. Describing his adventures in Barbados in a book he had supposedly written, Miller tells how 'Our Man' from the High Commission arrived at his hotel and told him, quote: 'Mr Miller, Her Majesty's Government would strenuously advise you to leave Barbados.' Unquote.

Representatives of the Brazilian government were on their way to the island, he was informed, and wanted to return with me to Brazil. They were also bearing a request to the Barbadian government for Mr Miller's extradition to Brazil on a charge of kidnapping. He and the rest of the rabble should have been detained, but they were allowed to flee from the island unhindered. Perhaps the late Sir Hugh Fraser had a hand in it – or one of Sergeant Miller's old officers, or someone even higher in British government circles.

There's a postscript to the Miller conspiracies. Soon after I arrived back in Brazil from Barbados, an official enquiry was held with regard to my kidnapping. I had to make a statement which was taken down by a federal policeman on a typewriter. Dr Bizzo, the *delegado*, was conducting the enquiry. Describing my arrival on the *Nowcani II*, I remembered the piece of paper that Miller had held up, the one with the circular emblem at the top, which Miller had said had 'made doors open like magic'. The *delegado* stopped me. It was not necessary to enter into details, he said, and the reference to the document did not appear in my statement which, of course, I signed. Later, together with Armin and John Pickston and the pilot of the Lear jet that had taken me to Belem, I appeared before a court where charges of kidnap were read out against Miller and his accomplices.

Frederick Smith QC, Ezra Alleyne and Alan Shepherd. I cannot thank these three learned gentlemen enough for their magnificent work in getting me back to Brazil from Barbados. Without doubt the three finest lawyers I have ever met – and I've met plenty! I remember them with true affection and admiration. I also remember that certain fees due to them were never paid and I hope that they will contact me and say that they have overlooked the matter. I hope that these gentlemen have continued to apply their legal skill and it would be interesting to know if 'Perry Mason' has lost a case yet.

Perhaps this would be a good point to convey my thanks to all the other good and 'bad' people in Barbados who gave me their support and friendship when I was there, especially the gang on Death Row. I love you all! And please let me hear from someone, telling me that hanging has been abolished in Barbados. Except for kidnappers, of course.

There are some people who, after thirty years, still ask me if I have any money left from the train robbery. Some laugh indulgently when I tell them that my whack was gone after only three years. But it is true. Over a third of the money went in my escape from Wandsworth to Australia; other large sums were ripped off by my minders, while I was also probably too generous for my own good in the early days when I gave large cash hand-outs to family and friends. So don't go looking for buried treasure, because you won't find any. If I still had my pot of gold why, by the end of 1992, was I back hustling my T-shirts?

Despite a radio spot during the Earth Summit, 1992 was a tough year financially. The tourists had thinned out and the pickings were meagre. Johnny Pickston and I were 'working' together. He was the funny man who would get the punters interested, so four nights a week he and I would sit in the bar of the Leme Palace Hotel playing countless games of cribbage, waiting for the horde of tourists that never came. Then our luck changed; one night the bar suddenly filled up with a crowd of people who were participating in the British Steel Challenge, a round-the-world yacht race.

While I was signing autographs, accepting numerous drinks, posing for photographs and answering questions, John was exposing the merchandise. You lucky people!

Most of them were pleasant, friendly folk looking for a little adventure in their lives. One was an ex-prison officer who spoke fondly of 'Gordon' (Goody), whom he had got to know well over the years. Another fellow, a carpenter from Bath who was a crew member on *Heath Insured*, introduced himself as Bill Vincent and lost no time in telling me that he had a murky past and had 'done a bit of porridge'. He was rather drunk when I met him and he stayed that way for the best part of the time that the crews were in Rio. He quickly became a regular at the Leme Palace bar and we became quite pally. I got the impression that Bill was an unhappy man and, subsequently, on the last leg of the 28,000-mile race he 'executed a perfect dive' from *Heath Insured* and swam away from the yacht, never to be seen again.

On 15 November 1992 I went to see the boats sail out of Rio on their 8800-mile leg to Australia, and noticed that a lot of the sailors were wearing their recently acquired 'Ronnie Biggs' T-shirts. A few people, writers and newsmen who had been covering the yacht race, were still in Rio and I received a phone call from one of them who was interested in taking some of my shirts back to the UK with him. I threw a dozen into a bag and met my 'customer' in a bar close to his hotel in Copacabana. He was with several other people who turned out to be buyers as well and within a few minutes I had autographed and sold my twelve shirts.

While I was 'working' I was answering their questions, the 'evergreens' as I call them. One of the group was an enthusiastic Scot, who listened in silence as I related the time-worn facts. Finally he asked, 'Have you ever thought of writing your story?'

'It's funny that you should say that,' I told him, 'because I've been thinking of it for some time.'

'If you need any help in London,' he said, handing me his business card, 'get in touch.'

I had become fond of writing as a kid. Something of a dreamer, my favourite subject at Santley Street School was

'Composition', and I was the only kid in the class who ever asked for extra paper to write my little stories, frequently being called a 'crawler' by the less literary minded.

My first serious attempt at writing occurred when I was in the Royal Air Force. After spending thirteen weeks on a training course to become electricians, the trainees were provided with writing material and invited to evaluate the three months of instruction. Among the things I wrote was a suggestion that the length of the course could be reduced by at least a third if the dirty jokes and 'bullshit' sessions were eliminated. Much time was also lost lining up and marching to and from the workshops etc. Satisfied with my work and naïvely believing that my exposé was something of merit, I handed in my paper to the flight sergeant who was conducting the survey.

'Who's A/C 2 Biggs?' asked the flight sergeant, looking up from his examination of our written work with knitted eyebrows.

I raised my hand and replied brightly, 'I am, Flight Sergeant!'

He held up my paper.

'Do you realize that you could be courtmartialled for this?' he bawled. 'This is against the good order and discipline of the RAF!'

Some years before the encounter at the British Steel Challenge gave me the idea of writing a book, I had met and become friends with a fellow Englishman and almost equally longtime Rio resident, Christopher Pickard. Chris is a writer and journalist known in Rio as the author of a best-selling guidebook to the city and as the opinionated columnist of *Rio Life*, an English-language magazine which is distributed among Rio's English-speaking community. Chris also makes everyone very jealous by going off to write a gossip column at the Cannes Film Festival for *Moving Pictures*.

Chris and I had met from time to time over the years and some time ago we began kicking ideas around with a view to producing a light-hearted guidebook in my name, tentatively entitled *Ronnie's Rio*. Chris made a number of enquiries regarding the feasibility of our project, but always came back with the same answer: there was far more interest in the story of my life.

With a little help from a Macintosh, I had a first chapter, the story of my escape from Wandsworth, shaped up in no time and a few weeks later, when Chris had business to take care of in London, he took the first chapter to London which was enough to interest publishers. The final result of my labours and computer proficiency is what you have before you!

Quentin Crisp once wrote that there are three reasons for becoming a writer: 'The first is that you need the money; the second, that you have something to say that you think the world should know; the third is that you can't think what to do with the long winter evenings.' I wholeheartedly agree with Mr Crisp on all three points.

Another very good reason to write *Odd Man Out* was that over the years there have been many misleading reports and gross exaggerations about me in the press, and it was time to put the record straight. It's worth a laugh when I read that I'm supposed to have laid 500 more chicks than Bill Wyman, but it's no joke to see myself headlined as an assassin.

When members of the Royal Family visit Rio, certain newspapers are sure to report that I am doing my best to get an audience with whoever it might be to plead for a pardon, or some similar crap. When Princess Di was over here a while back, the pack of newsmen who follow the royals paid me a visit. They had organized a whip-round among themselves and offered me £500 to pose in a Princess Di T-shirt and to say a few words about the dear lady's visit: 'Smile, Ronnie!'

During the session, a couple of reporters drew me aside with an offer they thought I couldn't refuse. They knew Princess Di's itinerary for the following day and at a certain hour she would be in downtown Rio, bestowing smiles upon the barefoot street urchins. For a further 500 quid, one of the conspirators said, all we want you to do is reach through the crowd and lay your hand on Lady Di's arm . . . And say, I suggested, 'We've got to stop meeting like this'?

I suppose I shouldn't be too hard on the press, after all, it is the press who brought me the cock-eyed fame I enjoy today.

When Eric Flower and I went over the wall from Wandsworth, the papers warned that we were probably armed and ready to shoot. The public were advised not to 'have a go'. Gradually the image changed as it became obvious that I was not the vicious desperado I was painted as, and eventually I found myself on first-name terms with Fleet Street. When a crime of any magnitude occurs, the press invariably telephone me for my comments. When a driver of a security company drove off with a million pounds not long ago, the press got in touch immediately.

'What would you do, Ronnie,' asked one reporter, 'if this fellow was to turn up on your doorstep? What would be your advice to him?'

'To let me take care of his cash!' I said, and the reporter hung up, delighted with my reply.

The newspapers have often carried stories to the effect that I long to see the green, green grass of home, homesick for jellied eels and Bird's custard powder etc. Dreaming of a pardon that will enable me to return to spend my last years in England. But you can forget it! I don't expect to be pardoned and to be perfectly honest I don't want to be. Stop being Ronnie Biggs? You must be joking!

So all that is left now is to tidy up the loose ends of my story.

I am often asked about 'the four who got away', but as I've never had any contact from any of them there's little I can or will say on that score. Old Peter, who was sixty-three at the time of the robbery, has probably passed on. It's quite amazing that the police never discovered his identity. I heard from Slipper that the police had 'made inquiries' among railwaymen at Redhill but the old man was never suspected, so I hope he got to enjoy his whack. What happened to the other three is anyone's guess; I just hope their good luck continues! As for the rest of the gang, I have lost contact over the years, only keeping up with Bruce Reynolds whom, of course, I knew before the robbery.

Charmian still lives in Melbourne with the younger of our two sons, Farley, and holds a responsible position in the public relations department of a major company. She has never remarried, but I believe she had a number of 'flings' that didn't work out; she once declared that she had 'an unhappy knack of picking wrong 'uns'.

My eldest son, Chris, is currently working in Tokyo with a possibility of wedding bells with a young Australian girl. Let's see which of the boys makes a grandfather of me first.

Mike and Jessie Haynes have split up and found themselves new mates. I've lost contact with them and I would dearly love to hear from them. Likewise Eric Flower and his wife, Carol, and all my other friends and acquaintances that I have mentioned throughout the book. My address is simply 'Ronald Biggs – Rio de Janeiro', but if you want to make certain the letter gets to me, you may like to add PO Box (Caixa Postal) 234, RJ – 20001-970.

Raimunda has settled in Zurich, Switzerland, where she lives happily with her little boy, Andre, and a Swiss fellow who's only half her age, seemingly satisfied with the arrangement! She works for an airline company, so she is able to come to Brazil at least once a year and I'm glad to say that we are still very close.

From a sign that says 'Sex Room' hanging on the door of his bedroom, one gets the impression that Mike does other things between his homework and his singing practice. He's the leader of a small group of young musicians who are trying to break into the adult world of music with their band Bandauepa, specializing in Brazilian music. Mike has developed into a handsome young man, a fine mixture of Brazilian Indian and South London, who speaks English with a distinct Cockney accent. He's a great kid and just on his looks alone he's a world-beater. We're a great team and, as he wrote when he was quite young, 'There's nothing better than father and son.'

Ulla and I are still together, but we continue to live apart – a form of 'marriage' I would recommend without hesitation. The arrangement certainly seems to work well for us as we both like to be free to pursue our individual interests and hobbies. Ulla's into art and loves to paint, while I spend hours pottering around the potting shed.

The future is as uncertain as my past and my position is as precarious as ever. Technically I still may not work and I still face possible deportation. If I could have a wish granted it would be for the Brazilian authorities finally to grant me my permanent visa, and accept that for nearly twenty-five years I have lived in their country as a law-abiding citizen and a Carioca at heart!

But tomorrow is another day and as I still can't work and have no old-age pension as such to look forward to, I have another group of visitors arriving for a barbecue lunch and 'The Biggs Experience'. It's a rare rainy day in Rio today, but tomorrow I expect it will be sunny again!

There were times when I was writing this book that I thought the two most important words in my life were 'The End'. Yet now the time has come to say goodbye, I realize that this is not the end, but only a new beginning.

# Appendix 1

# Key Dates

| | | |
|---|---|---|
| 1929 | 8 August | Ronald Arthur Biggs born in Lambeth, London |
| 1940 | | Because of World War II, evacuated to Devon and Cornwall |
| 1942 | | Returns to London |
| 1943 | May | Biggs' mother dies aged 53 |
| 1945 | January | First court appearance, aged 15 |
| | June | Second court appearance |
| | November | Third court appearance |
| 1947 | May | Signs up for Royal Air Force |
| 1949 | 17 February | First prison sentence – six months for robbery |
| | February | Dishonourable discharge from RAF |
| | July | Sentenced to three months in Wormwood Scrubs |
| | | Meets Bruce Reynolds in Wormwood Scrubs |
| | November | Sentenced to Borstal |
| 1950 | March | First appearance at Old Bailey |
| | April | Meets Eric Flower in Wormwood Scrubs |
| | | Second spell in HMP Lewes for Young Prisoners |
| 1953 | 30 March | Four-year sentence for robbery |
| 1955 | December | Released from HMP Dartmoor |
| 1957 | October | Meets Charmian Powell, the future Mrs Biggs |
| 1958 | 2 April | Sentenced to two and a half years |
| | | Charmian and Michael Haynes receive suspended sentences |
| 1959 | 1 December | Released from HMP Wandsworth |
| 1960 | 20 February | Marries Charmian Powell |
| | 17 May | Charmian Biggs' 21st birthday |
| | 23 July | Nicholas Grant born |
| 1963 | 24 March | Christopher Dean born |
| | 29 July | Leatherslade Farm purchased by gang |
| | 6 August | Gang arrives at Leatherslade Farm |
| | 8 August | THE GREAT TRAIN ROBBERY |
| | 13 August | Leatherslade Farm discovered by the police |
| | 14 August | First arrests – Roger Cordrey and Bill Boal |
| | 22 August | Charlie Wilson arrested |
| | 24 August | Police visit Biggs for first time |
| | 4 September | Arrested by police |
| 1964 | 20 January | Opening of Great Train Robbery trial |
| | 6 February | Retrial of Biggs ordered |
| | 26 March | Trial ends. Guilty verdict on entire gang |
| | 8 April | Opening of Biggs' retrial |
| | 14 April | End of second trial. Guilty verdict on Biggs |

|      | 15 April | Sentenced to 30 years |
|------|----------|------------------------|
|      | July | Appeals heard in London |
|      |  | Transferred to HMP Wandsworth |
|      | 12 August | Charlie Wilson escapes from Winson Green |
| 1965 | 8 July | ESCAPES FROM WANDSWORTH |
|      | October | Escapes to France |
|      | 29 December | Leaves Paris for Sydney |
|      | 30 December | Arrives in Sydney |
| 1966 | February | John Weater released from prison |
|      | April | Carol Flower arrives in Australia |
|      | 10 April | *Sunday Express* publishes photos of 'wanted' men |
|      | 12 April | Jimmy White arrested |
|      | 14 June | Charmian, Nick and Chris land in Australia |
|      | 26 June | Bill Boal dies in prison |
|      | 19 September | Buster Edwards gives himself up |
| 1967 | 21 April | Farley Paul born in Australia |
| 1968 | 25 January | Charlie Wilson arrested in Canada |
|      | 8 November | Bruce Reynolds arrested in England |
| 1969 | March | Frances Reynolds' story published in *Sunday Mirror* |
|      | 16 October | Biggs' photo broadcast on Australian television |
|      | 17 October | POLICE RAID THE BIGGS' HOUSE IN MELBOURNE |
|      | 24 October | Eric Flower arrested in Sydney |
| 1970 | February | Train driver, Jack Mills, dies of lymphatic leukaemia |
|      | 5 February | Boards SS *Ellinis* in Melbourne |
|      | 23 February | SS *Ellinis* docks in Panama |
|      | 11 March | LANDS IN RIO DE JANEIRO |
|      | April | Detective Chief Superintendent Tommy Butler dies |
|      | September | Side trip to Buenos Aires to renew visa |
| 1971 | 2 January | Eldest son, Nicholas, dies in car crash in Australia |
|      | February | News of Nicholas' death reaches Rio |
|      | February | First Carnival in Rio |
|      | March | Side trip to Bolivia to renew visa |
|      | April | First apartment in Rio de Janeiro |
|      | April | Roger Cordrey first of gang to be released from prison |
|      | July | Meets Raimunda for first time at Bola Preta club |
|      | September | Visa in passport no longer valid in Brazil |
| 1972 |  | Charmian asks Biggs to return to Australia |
|      |  | Mike Haynes asks for his passport back |
| 1973 | February | Manages to send the passport to Australia |
|      | July | Haynes family returns to UK |
|      | November | Talks with Benckendorff about giving himself up |
|      | December | Benckendorff travels to London and meets with Colin Mackenzie |
| 1974 | January | First contact with *Daily Express*' Colin Mackenzie |
|      | 30 January | Mackenzie arrives in Rio |
|      | 1 February | ARRESTED IN RIO BY JACK SLIPPER |
|      | 4 February | Detective Chief Inspector Jack Slipper returns to London without Biggs |
|      | 7 February | Transferred from Rio to prison in Brasilia |

| | | |
|---|---|---|
| | 10 February | Charmian arrives in Brasilia |
| | 16 February | 'Holds' press conference with Charmian |
| | March | Fernand Legros deported by Brazil to France |
| | April | Family Court confirms paternity of Raimunda's expected child |
| | 6 May | Released from custody |
| | 16 May | Charmian, Chris and Farley arrive in Brazil |
| | June | Charmian, Chris and Farley return to Australia |
| | 16 August | Michael Fernand Nascimento de Castro Biggs born |
| 1975 | | Colin Mackenzie publishes *The Most Wanted Man* |
| | January | Raimunda and Mike travel to England |
| | January | Moves family to Sepetiba |
| | February | Mike christened in France. Legros acts as godfather |
| | April | Buster Edwards and Jimmy White released |
| | August | Buster Edwards sent back to prison for six months |
| | August | Roy James first of the '30 years' to be released |
| | September | Raimunda returns to Europe for second visit |
| | November | Jim Hussey released |
| | November | Press discover Biggs in Sepetiba |
| | December | Gordon Goody released |
| 1976 | February | Tommy Wisbey released |
| | June | Bobby Welch released |
| | July | Gary van Dyk visits Rio to explain 'German' hoax to Biggs |
| 1977 | February | Piers Paul Read visits Rio to talk with Biggs |
| | 15–17 April | HMS *Danae* incident |
| 1978 | February | Sex Pistols visit Brazil |
| | March | Raimunda returns from Europe |
| | | Piers Paul Read's *The Train Robbers* published in UK |
| 1979 | April | First kidnap attempt by John Miller |
| | | Moves from Sepetiba back to Santa Teresa in Rio |
| 1980 | | Albert Spagiarri visits Biggs in Rio |
| 1981 | February | Moves from Santa Teresa to Botafogo |
| | 16 March | KIDNAPPED IN RIO |
| | 23 March | Arrives in Bridgetown, Barbados, with kidnappers |
| | 24 April | Returns to Rio from Barbados 40 days after kidnapping |
| | | Release of first A Turma do Balão Magico album |
| | December | First Christmas show at Maracana Stadium |
| 1982 | | On tour with Balão Magico |
| | | Balão Magico given own show by TV Globo |
| | December | Second Christmas show at Maracana Stadium |
| 1983 | October | Release of second Balão Magico album |
| | | On tour with Balão Magico |
| | December | Third Christmas show at Maracana Stadium |
| 1984 | February | Buys apartment for Mike in Santa Teresa |
| | | Filming of *Long Time No See Ronnie* for Japanese TV |
| | | Opening of Crepúsculo de Cubatão nightclub |
| | | Invests in restaurant in Buzios |
| | December | Fourth Christmas show at Maracana Stadium |

| | | |
|---|---|---|
| 1985 | January | Moves with Mike into their own Santa Teresa apartment |
| 1986 | | Balão Magico disbands |
| | | Meets Polish film director Lech Majewski |
| | | Starts work on screenplay for *Prisoner of Rio* with Majewski |
| 1987 | July | Cameras roll on *Prisoner of Rio* |
| 1988 | May | *Prisoner of Rio* screened at Cannes Film Festival |
| | | Mike Biggs attends Cannes Film Festival |
| 1990 | July | Paul Seabourne visits Biggs in Rio |
| 1991 | | Bruce and Nicholas Reynolds visit Rio |
| 1992 | 16 August | Mike Biggs' 18th birthday |
| | December | Agrees to write his memoirs |
| 1993 | March | Becomes computer literate |
| | | Starts work on *Odd Man Out* |
| | June | Jack Slipper visits Biggs in Rio for *Sunday Express* |
| | 8 August | 30TH ANNIVERSARY OF THE GREAT TRAIN ROBBERY |
| | | Biggs' 64th birthday |
| 1994 | January | ODD MAN OUT PUBLISHED IN LONDON BY BLOOMSBURY |

# Appendix 2

# Ron's Frequent Flyer Miles

| | |
|---|---|
| London–Paris | 210 miles |
| Paris–Sydney | 10,540 miles |
| Sydney–Adelaide | 860 miles |
| Adelaide–Sydney | 860 miles |
| Sydney–Adelaide | 860 miles |
| Adelaide–Darwin | 1970 miles |
| Darwin–Adelaide | 1970 miles |
| Adelaide–Melbourne | 420 miles |
| Melbourne–Adelaide | 420 miles |
| Adelaide–Melbourne | 420 miles |
| Melbourne–Adelaide | 420 miles |
| Adelaide–Melbourne | 420 miles |
| Melbourne–Panama | 9040 miles |
| Panama–Caracas (Venezuela) | 860 miles |
| Caracas–Rio de Janeiro | 2810 miles |
| Rio de Janeiro–Buenos Aires | 1600 miles |
| Buenos Aires–Rio de Janeiro | 1600 miles |
| Rio de Janeiro–Puerto Suarez (Bolivia) | 1250 miles |
| Puerto Suarez–Rio de Janeiro | 1250 miles |
| Rio de Janeiro–Bridgetown | 2900 miles |
| Bridgetown–Rio de Janeiro | 2900 miles |

*Approximate total (to date): 43,580 miles (70,120 km)*

*The above does not include the many thousands of miles that Ronald Biggs covered in Brazil when he accompanied his son Mike on the nationwide tours of A Turma de Balão Magico.*